HARMONIC MATERIALS
IN TONAL MUSIC

HARMONIC MATERIALS IN TONAL MUSIC

A PROGRAMED COURSE

Part II   Second Edition

Paul O. Harder

Dean of Arts and Humanities
CALIFORNIA STATE COLLEGE, STANISLAUS

Allyn and Bacon, Inc.
Boston · London · Sydney · Toronto

Library of Congress Catalog Card Number: 73-90243

ISBN: 0-205-04423-9
Fourth printing . . . February, 1976

Printed in the United States of America.

PREFACE

This book is the second of a two-part study of tonal harmony. The material covered includes seventh, ninth, eleventh, and thirteenth chords, various types of altered chords, and modulation. In the present edition, the programed approach is retained; but the format is improved, and numerous refinements and clarifications have been made to induce better comprehension and more rapid learning. Part I (second edition) contains an appendix on piano styles which may be used by those who wish to supplement this text with creative writing. A glossary of altered chords should prove helpful. Also, supplementary assignments have been supplied for each chapter. These may be used, at the discretion of the instructor, for reinforcement or testing purposes.

This course emphasizes the basic elements of harmony which have retained their validity throughout the period from about 1600 to 1900. Music from this period is still very much a part of our musical life. Not only does a large part of the current repertoire consist of eighteenth- and nineteenth-century music, but tonal harmony is the basis of practically all commercial music. All composers, no matter what style they generally may prefer, turn to tonal harmony when such material is appropriate to their expressive purpose. This book is not devoted to the study of any one composer's works, nor is it limited to four-part writing; various applications of harmonic principles are shown in musical examples drawn from a variety of periods and compositional types.

Since most of the music we hear and perform is based on tonal harmony, it is essential that serious students become familiar with this system. For the composer, competence in writing requires thorough understanding of techniques practiced by composers of previous generations. For the performer, the ability to convey delicate nuances and subtleties of phrasing often stems from a cultivated sensitivity to harmonic processes.

Experience has shown the programed approach to be adaptable to many learning situations. It can be used not only by a single student working independently, but also by students in very large classes. Still more important is the flexibility that programed material brings to the instructor. The core of knowledge contained in this book may be expanded by emphasis upon creative writing, analysis, or the study of music literature. Because students evaluate their own exercises, the instructor is free to prepare more vital and creative supplementary learning experiences.

The development of this course was supported by the Educational Development Program at Michigan State University. The author is grateful to Dr. John Dietrich, Assistant Provost, and Dr. Robert Davis, Director of the Educational Development Program for their assistance; also to Drs. Jere Hutcheson, Clifford Pfeil, and Gary White, who helped develop practical classroom methods. Particular tribute, though, must be paid to the many students who cooperated in proving out the approaches incorporated in this book. Many of their suggestions, which could only come from intimate contact through actual experience, have had a direct influence on the ultimate form of the material.

Paul Harder

CONTENTS

HOW TO USE THIS BOOK

This book features the use of programed instruction to convey conceptual information and provide drills to develop techniques for handling harmonic materials. In programed instruction, information is presented in small, carefully sequenced parcels which combine in cumulative fashion to give students mastery of the subject. The parcels into which the material is divided are called *frames*. Most frames require a written response, which may be a word or two, or consist of the solution of a musical problem. Since correct answers are provided by the book itself, this type of material is self-correcting; thus students may work entirely alone and proceed at their own pace. When used in class, supplementary examples and lessons may be supplied by the instructor as he sees fit.

The principal part of each frame is located on the right-hand side of the page. The answers, which appear on the left-hand side, should be covered with a slip of paper or a ruler (merely the hand will do). After the response is written, the appropriate answer is uncovered so the response may be checked immediately. Since each step in this process is small few mistakes are made. Because of this, learning is reinforced and misconceptions have little chance to become part of the student's thinking.

TO THE STUDENT

Do not begin to use this book unless you have mastered the material contained in Part 1 of this study, or its equivalent.

With regard to the use of programed material, there are many cases in which your answer need not be exactly the same as that supplied by the text. Thoughts may often be expressed differently, or items of information listed in different order, yet still be correct. Use common sense to decide whether or not you comprehend a particular item. But if you make several real mistakes in a row you probably have failed to grasp an important point. Seek out the missed information by turning back a few pages. If errors persist obtain assistance from your instructor.

Many musical examples are given in the text to acquaint you with the ways various composers use harmonic devices. You should play these examples at the piano so that they are actually *heard*. It is not sufficient to approach this study on an intellectual level alone; you must have command of the harmonic vocabulary as an aural phenomenon as well. The purpose of conceptualizing musical processes is to render more understandable the response elicited by auditory stimuli. Remember, music is an aural art; it is apprehended better by the ear than the eye.

1 Introduction to Seventh Chords: The Dominant Seventh

The harmonic materials presented in Part 1 of this study were limited to triads. Most dissonance was incidental to the harmony—the result of nonharmonic tones. Seventh chords, on the other hand, introduce dissonance as an integral part of the harmony. Seventh chords consist of four tones; thus they are more complex than triads. Whereas triads are limited to four types (major, minor, diminished, and augmented), there are seven types of seventh chords. Seventh chords are used not only for their tonal variety, but also for the tension supplied by their dissonance. Urgency of resolution is a feature of seventh chords, and this feature contributes to the sense of harmonic motivation so much a part of more advanced harmonic idioms.

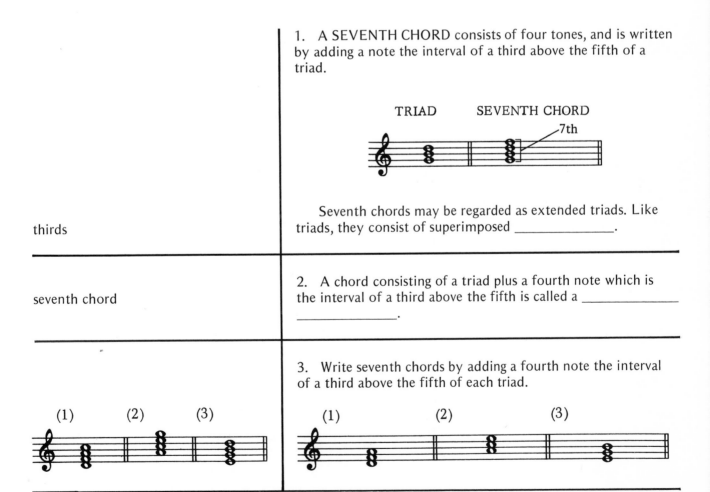

1. A SEVENTH CHORD consists of four tones, and is written by adding a note the interval of a third above the fifth of a triad.

TRIAD   SEVENTH CHORD

Seventh chords may be regarded as extended triads. Like triads, they consist of superimposed _____.

thirds

2. A chord consisting of a triad plus a fourth note which is the interval of a third above the fifth is called a _____ _____.

seventh chord

3. Write seventh chords by adding a fourth note the interval of a third above the fifth of each triad.

(1)   (2)   (3)

(1)   (2)   (3)

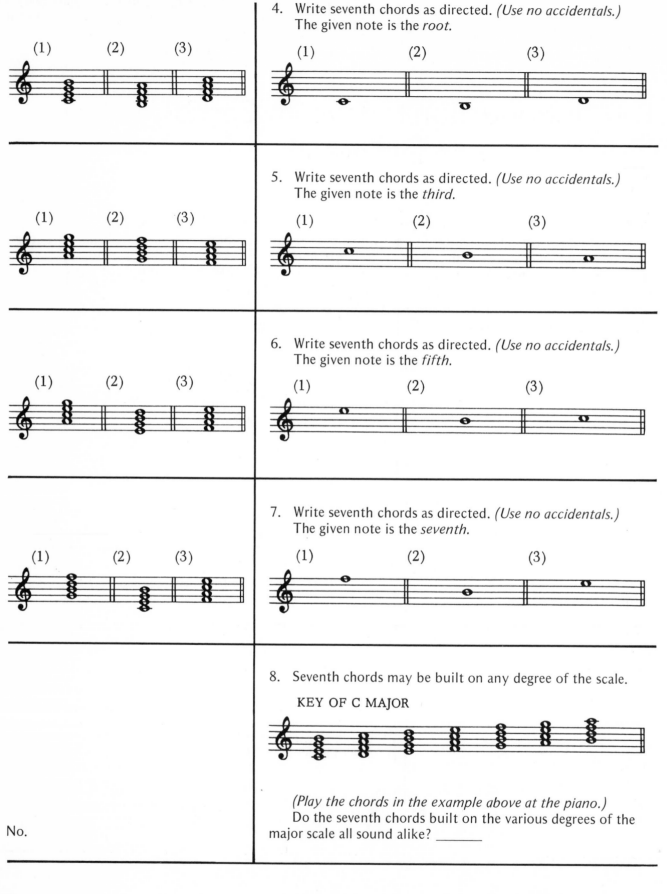

4. Write seventh chords as directed. *(Use no accidentals.)*
   The given note is the *root*.

   (1)   (2)   (3)

5. Write seventh chords as directed. *(Use no accidentals.)*
   The given note is the *third*.

   (1)   (2)   (3)

6. Write seventh chords as directed. *(Use no accidentals.)*
   The given note is the *fifth*.

   (1)   (2)   (3)

7. Write seventh chords as directed. *(Use no accidentals.)*
   The given note is the *seventh*.

   (1)   (2)   (3)

8. Seventh chords may be built on any degree of the scale.

   KEY OF C MAJOR

   (Play the chords in the example above at the piano.)
   Do the seventh chords built on the various degrees of the
   major scale all sound alike? _____

No.

9. The quality of a seventh chord is identified through two of its features: the type of triad, and the quality of the interval between the root and the seventh.

Analyze the seventh chord below as directed.

(1) Type of triad: _____
(2) Quality of 7th: _____

(1) Major
(2) Minor

---

10. The chord shown in the preceding frame is called a MAJOR-MINOR seventh chord. The first part of this term (major) refers to the type of triad; the second part (minor) refers to the quality of the interval between the root and the

_____.

seventh

---

11. Analyze the seventh chord below as directed.

(1) Type of Triad: _____
(2) Quality of 7th: _____

(1) Diminished
(2) Minor

---

12. The chord shown in the preceding frame is called a _____-_____ seventh chord.

diminished-minor

---

13. Analyze the seventh chord below as directed.

(1) Type of triad: _____
(2) Quality of 7th: _____

(1) Minor
(2) Minor

minor-minor

14. The chord shown in the preceding frame may be called a MINOR-MINOR seventh chord. It is customary, however, to eliminate one part of the term when the quality of the interval between the root and the seventh is identical with the type of triad. Thus, the term *minor seventh chord* means the same as _____-_____ seventh chord.

---

diminished

15. A seventh chord which consists of a diminished triad plus the interval of a diminished seventh above the root is called a _____ seventh chord.

---

16. Indicate the name of each chord.

(1) Major-minor
(2) Major
(3) Minor

(1) _____ seventh chord
(2) _____ seventh chord
(3) _____ seventh chord

---

diminished

17. If you called the second chord in the preceding frame a major-major seventh chord, or the third chord a minor-minor seventh chord, you were not wrong, as this nomenclature is sometimes used. It is simpler, however, to avoid unnecessary repetition of terms.

   The term *diminished seventh chord* indicates a chord consisting of a diminished triad plus the interval of a _____ seventh above the root.

---

18. Indicate the name of each chord.

(1) Diminished-minor
(2) Minor-major
(3) Minor

(1) _____ seventh chord
(2) _____ seventh chord
(3) _____ seventh chord

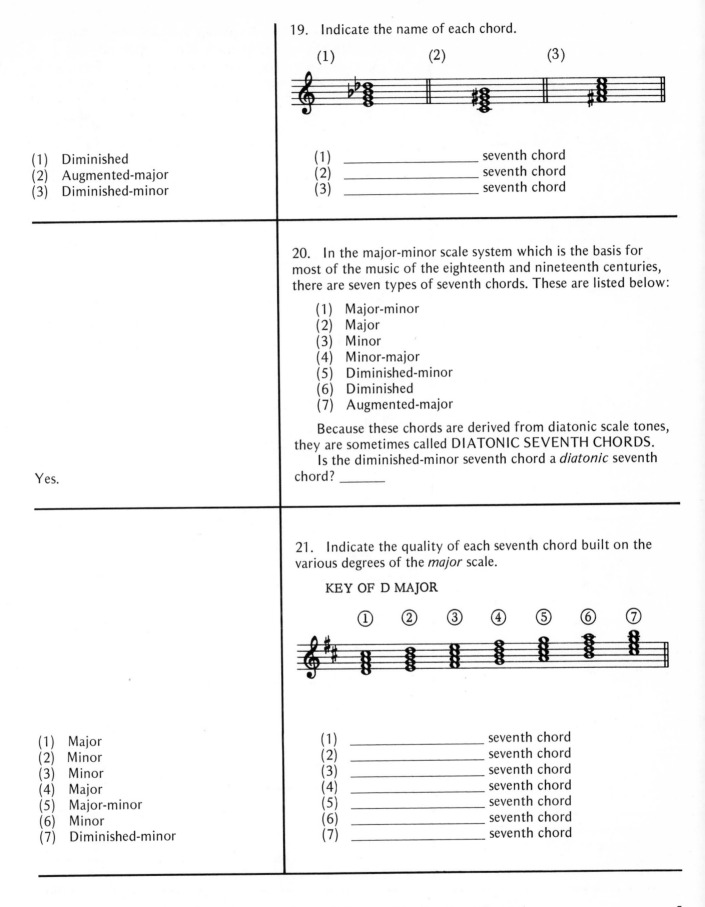

19. Indicate the name of each chord.

(1)   (2)   (3)

(1) Diminished
(2) Augmented-major
(3) Diminished-minor

(1) _____ seventh chord
(2) _____ seventh chord
(3) _____ seventh chord

20. In the major-minor scale system which is the basis for most of the music of the eighteenth and nineteenth centuries, there are seven types of seventh chords. These are listed below:

(1) Major-minor
(2) Major
(3) Minor
(4) Minor-major
(5) Diminished-minor
(6) Diminished
(7) Augmented-major

Because these chords are derived from diatonic scale tones, they are sometimes called DIATONIC SEVENTH CHORDS.

Is the diminished-minor seventh chord a *diatonic* seventh chord? _____

Yes.

21. Indicate the quality of each seventh chord built on the various degrees of the *major* scale.

KEY OF D MAJOR

①   ②   ③   ④   ⑤   ⑥   ⑦

(1) Major
(2) Minor
(3) Minor
(4) Major
(5) Major-minor
(6) Minor
(7) Diminished-minor

(1) _____ seventh chord
(2) _____ seventh chord
(3) _____ seventh chord
(4) _____ seventh chord
(5) _____ seventh chord
(6) _____ seventh chord
(7) _____ seventh chord

22. Indicate the quality of each seventh chord built on the various degrees of the *harmonic minor* scale.

KEY OF D HARMONIC MINOR

(1) Minor-major
(2) Diminished-minor
(3) Augmented-major
(4) Minor
(5) Major-minor
(6) Major
(7) Diminished

(1) _____ seventh chord
(2) _____ seventh chord
(3) _____ seventh chord
(4) _____ seventh chord
(5) _____ seventh chord
(6) _____ seventh chord
(7) _____ seventh chord

first

23.   Before proceeding, you should learn the quality of the seventh chord on the various degrees of major and minor scales. You should know, for example, that the major-minor seventh chord occurs as a diatonic seventh chord only on the fifth scale degree in either major or (harmonic) minor. Also, play the chords in the preceding two frames at the piano to become familiar with their sounds.
   The minor-major seventh chord occurs as a diatonic chord only in harmonic minor on the _____ scale degree.

2nd, 3rd, (and) 6th
(Any order.)

24.   In the *major* scale, the minor seventh chord appears on the _____, _____, and _____ degrees.

7th   2nd

25.   The diminished-minor seventh chord appears on the _____ degree of the *major* scale, and on the _____ degree of the *harmonic minor* scale.

No.

26.   Does the diminished seventh chord occur as a diatonic chord in the major scale? _____

27.   Except for the diminished seventh chord (discussed later), the Roman numeral used to indicate a seventh chord is the

same as for a triad on the same root plus the number seven (7) placed at the upper right-hand corner.

D: I⁷   ii⁷   iii⁷   IV⁷   V⁷   vi⁷   vii°⁷

Notice that the quality of the triad is shown by the form of the Roman numeral. The quality of the seventh, however, is not identified. It is assumed that the seventh is a tone of the diatonic scale unless an alteration is shown.

Spell the chord indicated by the Roman numeral.

A♭: ii⁷ _____

B♭ D♭ F A♭

---

28. Spell the chords indicated by the Roman numerals:

(1) D: V⁷ _____
(2) B♭: vi⁷ _____
(3) E: vii°⁷ _____

(1) AC♯EG
(2) GB♭DF
(3) D♯F♯AC♯

---

29. Write the appropriate chord symbol for each chord. *(Indicate quality carefully.)*

(1)   (2)   (3)

F: ___   A: ___   E♭: ___

(1) iii⁷
(2) vii°⁷
(3) I⁷

---

30. The example below shows the chord symbols used to indicate the diatonic seventh chords in D harmonic minor:

d: i⁷̸   ii°⁷   III⁺⁷   iv⁷   V⁷   VI⁷   viiᵈ⁷

Two of the chord symbols above need to be explained. These are i⁷̸ and viiᵈ⁷. In the first case the figure 7̸ indicates that the seventh of the chord is raised a half-step. The slash drawn through the seven distinguishes between this chord (DFAC♯) and the tonic seventh chord in natural minor which would consist of the following notes: ___ ___ ___ ___.

DFAC

31. The quality of the triad is shown by the form of the Roman numeral, thus the symbol V^7 is sufficient to indicate the dominant seventh chord in the preceding frame. But when the seventh is an altered tone it is necessary to show the alteration by the actual accidental used (or by a slash if the note is raised a half-step).

The chord symbol varies slightly according to the accidental (unless the slash is used).

What is the quality of each chord above? _____-_____ seventh chord.

Minor-major

---

32. Write the appropriate chord symbol for each chord.

(1) i⁷
(2) i⁷ or i♯⁷
(3) i⁷ or i♭⁷

---

33. Chord (1) in the preceding frame is a minor seventh chord. The fact that no accidental is used in the chord symbol shows that the _____ minor scale is used.

natural
(or pure)

---

34. Notes of the natural minor scale are considered "diatonic" and require no special figure in the chord symbol. Alterations (usually the raised sixth or seventh degrees) are shown either by the form of the Roman numeral or by a sign indicating the alteration of the seventh.

A note raised in pitch a half-step always calls for a sharp in the chord symbol. (True/False) _____

False.
(If you answered incorrectly, review Frames 30-33).

35. The second chord symbol in Frame 30 which needs explanation is that used to indicate the leading tone seventh chord (vii^{d7}). Diminished seventh chords appear frequently and perform a variety of harmonic functions. In this book, for the sake of simplicity, diminished seventh chords are represented by replacing the circle which stands for a diminished triad with a small d. Although the figure d is not a traditional figured bass symbol, it is an apt reference to the quality of the diminished seventh chord.

Spell the chord indicated by the symbol.

F♯ACE♭   g: vii^{d7} _____

---

36. Spell the chords indicated by the symbols.

(1) B(♮)DFA♭

(2) E♯G♯BD

(3) A(♮)CE♭G♭

(1) c: vii^{d7} _____

(2) f♯: vii^{d7} _____

(3) b♭: vii^{d7} _____

---

37. Note the difference between the two chords below:

Identify the quality of each chord.

(1) Diminished-minor

(2) Diminished

(1) _____ seventh chord

(2) _____ seventh chord

---

38. The example in the preceding frame shows that the circle is retained in the case of a diminished-minor seventh chord. The small d is used only for _____ seventh chords.

diminished

---

39. Write the proper symbol for each chord. *(Be sure to check the quality before writing.)*

(1) ii^{o7}

(2) vii^{d7}

(3) vii^{o7}

---

40. Continue as in the preceding frame.

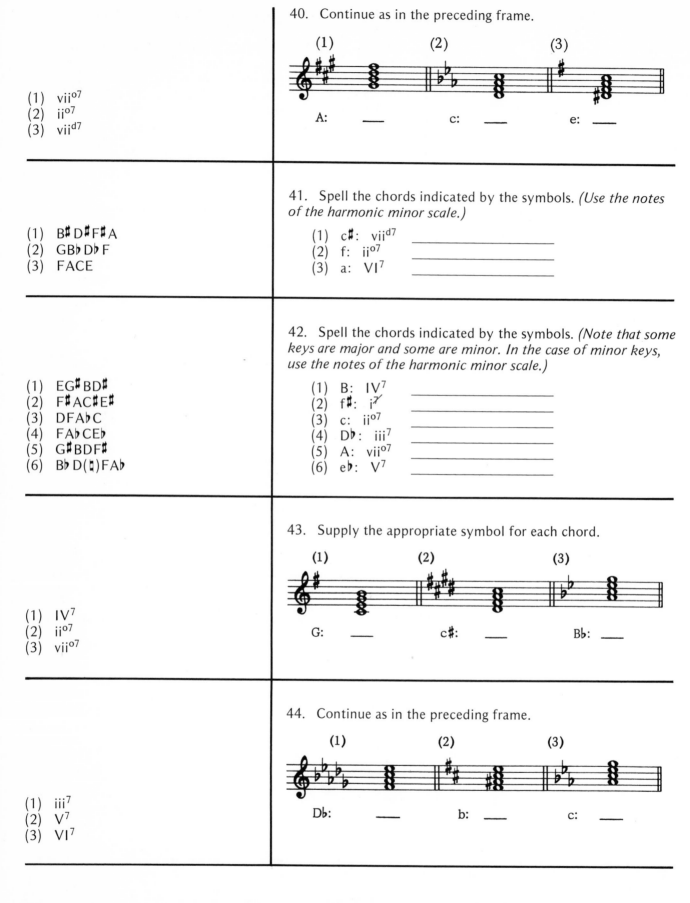

(1) vii°⁷
(2) ii°⁷
(3) vii^{d7}

A: ____   c: ____   e: ____

41. Spell the chords indicated by the symbols. *(Use the notes of the harmonic minor scale.)*

(1) c♯: vii^{d7} _____

(2) f: ii°⁷ _____

(3) a: VI⁷ _____

(1) B♯ D♯ F♯ A
(2) G B♭ D♭ F
(3) F A C E

42. Spell the chords indicated by the symbols. *(Note that some keys are major and some are minor. In the case of minor keys, use the notes of the harmonic minor scale.)*

(1) B: IV⁷ _____

(2) f♯: i^{♮7} _____

(3) c: ii°⁷ _____

(4) D♭: iii⁷ _____

(5) A: vii°⁷ _____

(6) e♭: V⁷ _____

(1) E G♯ B D♯
(2) F♯ A C♯ E♯
(3) D F A♭ C
(4) F A♭ C E♭
(5) G♯ B D F♯
(6) B♭ D(♮) F A♭

43. Supply the appropriate symbol for each chord.

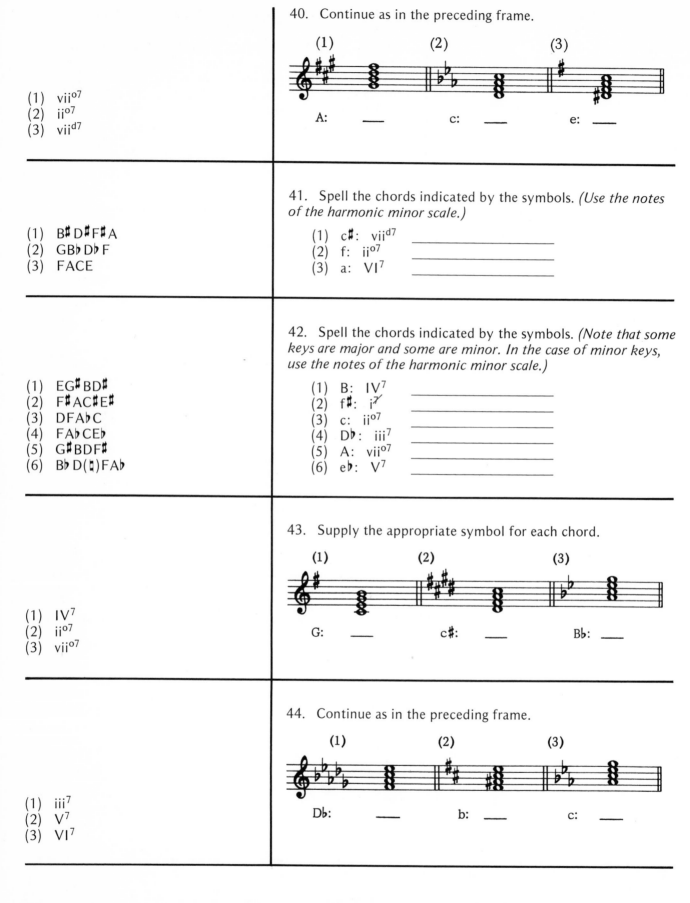

G: ____   c♯: ____   B♭: ____

(1) IV⁷
(2) ii°⁷
(3) vii°⁷

44. Continue as in the preceding frame.

D♭: ____   b: ____   c: ____

(1) iii⁷
(2) V⁷
(3) VI⁷

45. Continue as in the preceding frame.

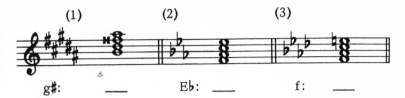

(1) III+7
(2) ii7
(3) i7 or i♮7

46. Continue as in the preceding frame.

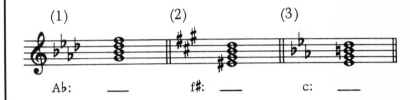

(1) vii°7
(2) viid7
(3) III+7

47. The alternate sixth and seventh degrees of the melodic minor scale (ascending and descending forms) produce a large number of seventh chords.

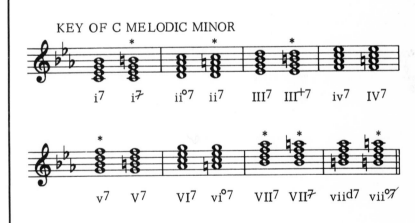

KEY OF C MELODIC MINOR

i7   i7   ii°7   ii7   III7   III+7   iv7   IV7

v7   V7   VI7   vi°7   VII7   VII7   viid7   vii°7

Although all of these chords are available to the composer, several of them are seldom used. These have been marked with asterisks in the above example.

Which scale has the most tonal variety (a) harmonic minor, (b) melodic minor, or (c) major? _____

(b) melodic minor.

48. Seventh chord qualities and their corresponding chord symbols in major and minor keys are partially summarized on the following page:

Quality	Major	Minor
Mm^7	V^7	V^7
M^7	I^7, IV^7	VI^7
m^7	ii^7, iii^7, vi^7	iv^7
mM^7	—	i^7
dm^7	vii^{o7}	ii^{o7}
d^7	—	vii^{d7}
AM^7	—	III$^+$

(No response.)

49. Seventh chords, like triads, are used in various inversions. The figured bass symbols used to indicate seventh chords in *root* position are shown below:

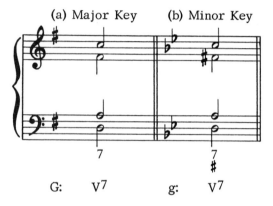

The figured bass symbol for a seventh chord in root position is simply the number seven (7) unless either the third or fifth of the chord is altered, in which case the alteration is shown by the appropriate symbol. The figured bass symbol 7 indicates a seventh chord in _____ position.

root

50. The figured bass symbol used to indicate seventh chords in *first inversion* is shown below:

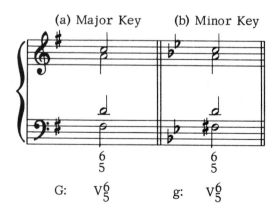

3rd

Notice that the numbers 6 and 5 are incorporated into the chord symbol. Thus the chord symbol itself shows the inversion of the chord.

The figured bass symbol $\frac{6}{5}$ beneath a bass note indicates a seventh chord in first inversion. Therefore, the note in the bass is the (root/3rd/5th/7th) _____ of the chord.

51. The chords below are in *second inversion*.

(a) Major Key   (b) Minor Key

$$\begin{array}{cc} \frac{4}{3} & \frac{6}{4}\\ & 3 \end{array}$$

G: $V\frac{4}{3}$ g: $V\frac{4}{3}$

The symbol $\frac{4}{3}$ suffices to indicate a seventh chord in second inversion unless the sixth above the bass is altered as in (b) above. The root of the seventh chord in second inversion is located a (interval) _____ below the bass note.

5th

52. The chords below are in *third inversion*.

(a) Major Key   (b) Minor Key

$$\begin{array}{cc} \frac{4}{2}\text{ (or 2)} & \frac{4}{2} \end{array}$$

G: $V\frac{4}{2}$ g: $V\frac{4}{2}$

Usually the symbol $\frac{4}{2}$ is used to indicate a seventh chord in third inversion, but sometimes this is reduced to merely 2. The figured bass symbol can not be abbreviated in (b) because the figure 4 is needed to show the alteration of F to F-sharp. When the symbol $\frac{4}{2}$ (or 2) appears beneath a bass note, that note is the (root/3rd/5th/7th) _____ of the chord.

7th

Introduction to Seventh Chords: The Dominant Seventh   *13*

53. The previous few frames have shown that figured bass symbols are combined with Roman numerals to show the various inversions of seventh chords.

Root position: I^7, ii^7, etc.

First inversion: I^6_5, ii^6_5, etc.

Second inversion: I^4_3, ii^4_3, etc.

Third inversion: I^4_2, ii^4_2, etc.

These symbols are used consistently throughout this study except when it is of no importance to identify specific inversions.

The figure $^4_3$ signifies that the (root/3rd/5th/7th) _____ of a chord is in the bass.

5th

---

54. Check (√) the correct option:

1. Chord symbols show not only the scale degrees on which chords are built, but also the inversions.
2. The symbol V^6_5 indicates that the third of the dominant seventh chord is in the bass.

True statements:
(1) _____ (2) _____ Both _____ Neither _____

Both √

---

55. Supply the chord symbol for each chord.

(1)   (2)   (3)

Bb: ___   d: ___   Ab: ___

(1) V^4_2
(2) V^4_3
(3) V^6_5

---

56. Continue as in the preceding frame.

(1)   (2)   (3)

e: ___   Eb: ___   g: ___

(1) ii^{o6}_5
(2) I^4_2
(3) V^4_3

57. Indicate the bass note for each chord.

Bass Note

(1) A♭: V^6_5 _____

(2) c: V^4_2 _____

(3) E: vii^{o4}_3 _____

Answers (left column):
(1) G
(2) F
(3) A

58. Slightly more complicated symbols are required to show the inversions of diminished seventh chords.

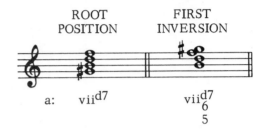

ROOT POSITION   FIRST INVERSION

a: vii^{d7} $vii^{d7}_{\substack{6\\5}}$

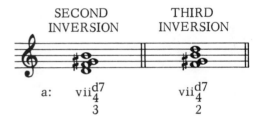

SECOND INVERSION   THIRD INVERSION

a: $vii^{d7}_{\substack{4\\3}}$ $vii^{d7}_{\substack{4\\2}}$

Indicate the bass note for each chord.

Bass Note

(1) f: $vii^{d7}_{\substack{4\\2}}$ _____

(2) b: $vii^{d7}_{\substack{6\\5}}$ _____

(3) c♯: $vii^{d7}_{\substack{4\\3}}$ _____

Answers (left column):
(1) D♭
(2) C♯
(3) F♯

59. Supply the chord symbol for each chord.

(1)   (2)   (3)

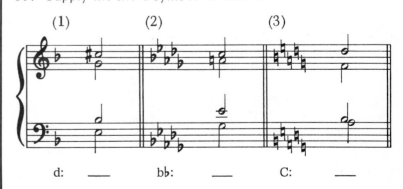

d: ___   b♭: ___   C: ___

Answers (left column):
(1) $vii^{d7}_{\substack{6\\5}}$
(2) $vii^{d7}_{\substack{4\\2}}$
(3) vii^{o4}_2

60. Chord (3) in the preceding frame is a diminished-minor seventh chord, not a diminished seventh chord. The symbol for the former (vii°$^4_2$) is somewhat simpler than the latter (vii$^{d7}_4$)

because the circle refers to the quality of the triad, whereas the figure d refers specifically to the quality of the seventh. Thus the number 7 is needed to show which interval is diminished.
    Write the appropriate chord symbol for each chord.

(1) vii°$^6_5$

(2) vii$^{d7}_5$$_6$

61. All four tones of a seventh chord are usually present in simple four-part writing. This means that no doubling is necessary; each of the four voices takes one of the chord tones. Observe this practice in the frames which follow.
    Complete the chords as indicated by the figured bass. *(Use close structure.)*

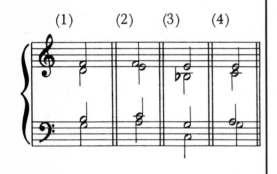

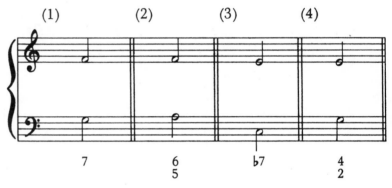

62. Complete the chords as indicated by the figured bass. *(Use open structure.)*

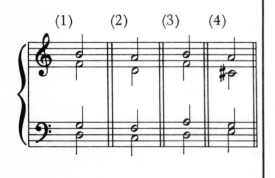

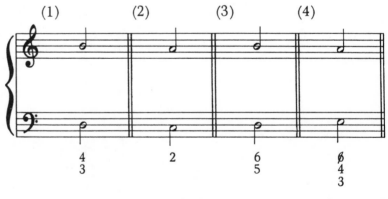

63. Complete the chords as indicated by the figured bass. *(Use open structure.)*

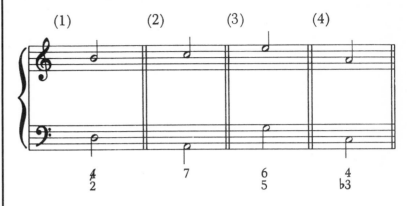

(1)   (2)   (3)   (4)

$\begin{array}{cccc} & & & \\ {}^{4}_{2} & 7 & {}^{6}_{5} & {}^{4}_{\flat 3} \end{array}$

64. Write the proper figured bass symbol beneath each chord.

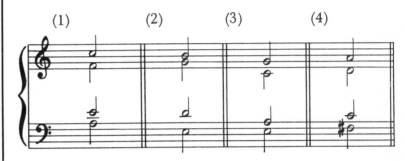

(1)   (2)   (3)   (4)

(1) $^6_5$

(2) 7

(3) $^4_3$

(4) $^6_5$

65. Continue as in the preceding frame. *(Don't forget to indicate altered notes.)*

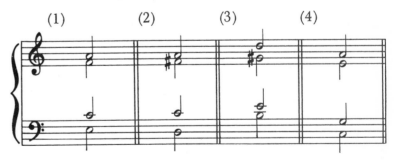

(1)   (2)   (3)   (4)

(1) $^4_2$ or 2

(2) $^7_3$ or $^7_\sharp$

(3) $^6_4_3$

(4) $^6_5$

66. The V^7 chord is known as the DOMINANT SEVENTH CHORD. This chord is by far the most prevalent of all seventh chords. For this reason, its use will be examined in detail.

Like the dominant triad, the dominant seventh chord usually progresses to the tonic or submediant triads.

Supply the Roman numeral analysis for the last four chords.

Brahms, *Ein deutsches Requiem*, Op. 45, I

Ziemlich langsam und mit Ausdruck

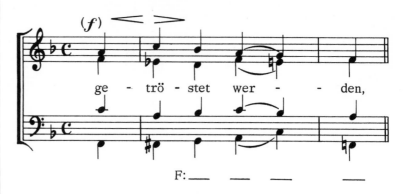

ge - trö - stet wer - - den,

F: ___ ___ ___ ___

ii - I⁶ - V⁷ - I

---

67. The dominant seventh chord is a major-minor seventh chord. It consists of a major triad plus a minor seventh above the root. This type of chord has two dissonant elements: the seventh, and the tritone* which occurs between the third and seventh. It is the resolution of these dissonant elements which governs the part writing.
     Refer again to the example in the preceding frame. Which two notes comprise the tritone in the dominant seventh chord? _____ and _____ .

---

*The term tritone means three (whole) tones. It is the same as the augmented fourth, or diminished fifth.

B♭ (and) E

---

68. The tritone and its resolution (from the example in Frame 66) are shown below:

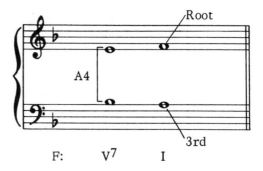

Notice that each of the notes of the tritone (B♭ and E) moves by a half-step to the note of resolution. Could the voices find a place in the same chord (F major) with equal smoothness by moving in the opposite direction? _____

No.

---

69. The inversion of the example in Frame 68 produces the interval of a diminished fifth.

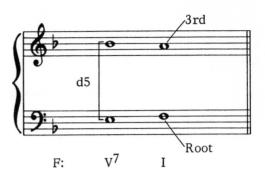

F: V⁷   I

Whereas the tones which constitute the interval of an augmented fourth resolve *outward* to the root and third of the tonic triad, the tones of a diminished fifth resolve _____ .

inward

---

70. The tendency for the tones of the augmented fourth to resolve outward and those of the diminished fifth to resolve inward is the result of the melodic attraction of active tones to inactive ones.

The inactive tones of the major scale are the tones of the tonic triad. The remaining tones are active, and are attracted to the inactive ones primarily in the direction of the arrows.

KEY OF F MAJOR

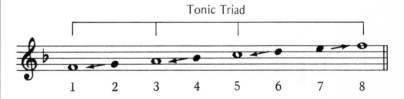

In each case active tones move to the *nearest* member of the tonic triad. The second scale degree is a whole-step removed from both the first and third; but, since the attraction of the keynote (F) is stronger than the third (A), the downward tendency predominates.

Which two of the active scale degrees are only a half-step removed from the notes to which they are attracted? _____ and _____ .

4 (and) 7

---

71. Because of their close proximity to tones of the tonic triad, the fourth and seventh are the most active degrees of the major scale. This melodic activity is intensified when they are combined to form a tritone. For this reason, the effective resolution of the dominant seventh chord depends upon resolving the fourth and seventh scale degrees in accordance with their natural tendency.

(1)   (2)

Resolve each tritone to notes of the tonic triad in the smoothest possible manner.

(1) D Major   (2) Eb Major

72. The overriding importance of resolving the tritone according to the melodic activity of its constituent tones often leads to irregular doubling in the chord which follows.

Mozart, *Symphony No. 41*, K. 551

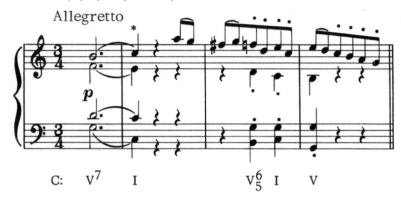

Describe the irregular doubling in the chord at the asterisk.

_____

_____

There are three roots, one third, but no 5th.

73. Another dominant seventh chord occurs in the third measure of the example in the preceding frame. In this case the tritone occurs between the soprano and bass voices. Does this tritone resolve normally? _____

Yes.
(The note D in the soprano is an embellishment.)

74. Write the second chord in each case. *(Be sure to resolve the tritone normally even though irregularities of doubling may occur.*

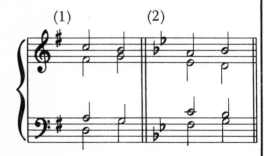
(1)   (2)

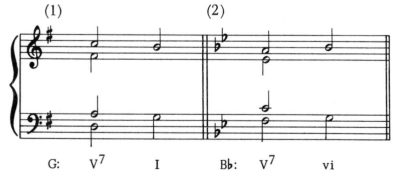
(1)   (2)

G: V⁷   I   Bb: V⁷   vi

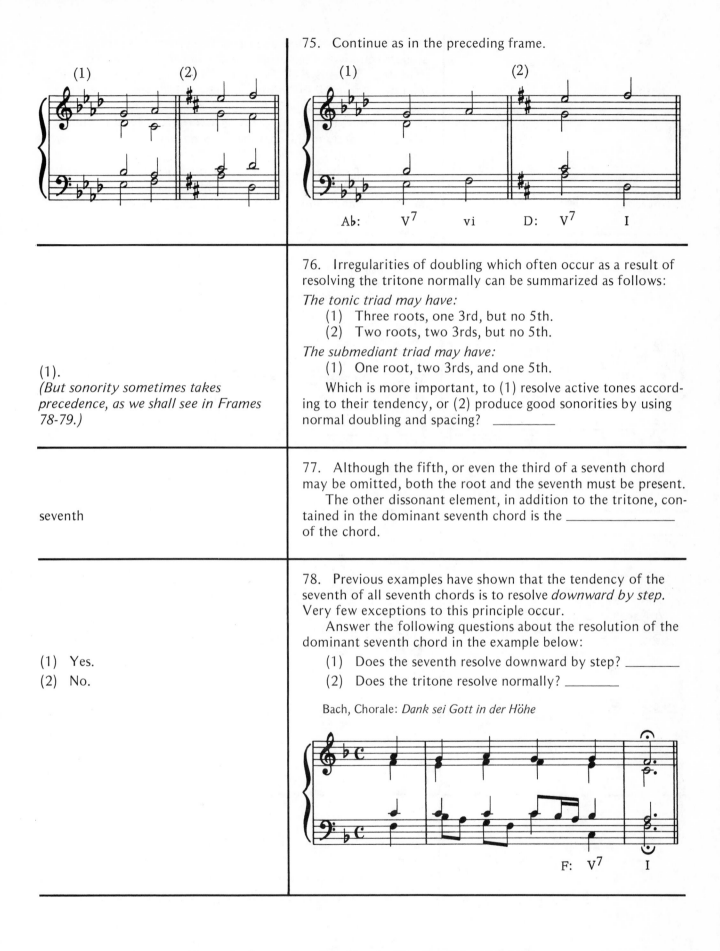

75. Continue as in the preceding frame.

Ab: V⁷ vi   D: V⁷ I

---

(1).
(But sonority sometimes takes precedence, as we shall see in Frames 78-79.)

76. Irregularities of doubling which often occur as a result of resolving the tritone normally can be summarized as follows:

The tonic triad may have:
    (1) Three roots, one 3rd, but no 5th.
    (2) Two roots, two 3rds, but no 5th.

The submediant triad may have:
    (1) One root, two 3rds, and one 5th.

    Which is more important, to (1) resolve active tones according to their tendency, or (2) produce good sonorities by using normal doubling and spacing? _____

---

seventh

77. Although the fifth, or even the third of a seventh chord may be omitted, both the root and the seventh must be present.

    The other dissonant element, in addition to the tritone, contained in the dominant seventh chord is the _____ of the chord.

---

(1) Yes.
(2) No.

78. Previous examples have shown that the tendency of the seventh of all seventh chords is to resolve *downward by step*. Very few exceptions to this principle occur.

    Answer the following questions about the resolution of the dominant seventh chord in the example below:

    (1) Does the seventh resolve downward by step? _____
    (2) Does the tritone resolve normally? _____

Bach, Chorale: *Dank sei Gott in der Höhe*

F: V⁷ I

Introduction to Seventh Chords: The Dominant Seventh

21

79. The example in the preceding frame shows that, due to the desire to end with the stronger sonority provided by a complete triad, the tritone (Bb - E) is not resolved normally. Specifically, the leading tone (E in the alto voice) drops down to the fifth of the tonic triad instead of obeying its melodic tendency to ascend to the keynote (F). This occurs frequently in the inner voices, but rarely in the soprano, where the weak melodic effect is more evident.

downward

Although the tritone in this case does not resolve normally, the seventh (Bb in the tenor voice) moves according to its natural tendency which is _____ by step.

80. Complete the second chord in each case so that a *complete* triad with regular doubling (two roots, one third, and one fifth) results. *(Be sure to resolve the seventh downward by step.)*

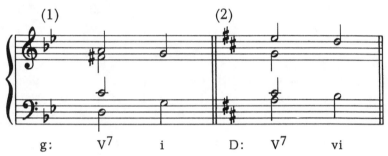

g: V⁷   i   D: V⁷   vi

81. Continue as in the preceding frame. *(Use no irregular doubling.)*

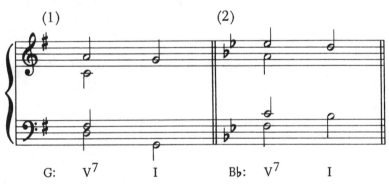

G: V⁷   I   Bb: V⁷   I

82. When the dominant seventh chord is in first inversion the seventh scale degree is in the bass. Because of its prominent position, the natural tendency of the leading tone to move upward to the keynote is intensified. *This tendency should rarely be violated.*

Mozart, *Fantasia in C Minor*, K. 475

D: V$^6_5$ I   V

No.

Is there any irregularity in the resolution of the dominant seventh chord in the above example? _____

83. Write the second chord in each case in such a way that no irregularity of doubling or resolution of active tones results.

(1)   (2)

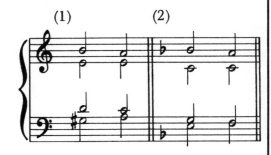

(1)   (2)

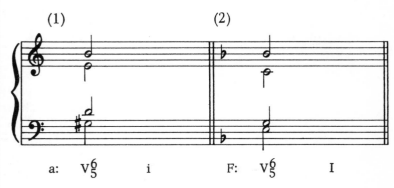

a: V$^6_5$ i   F: V$^6_5$ I

84. Analyze with Roman numerals the phrase below. *(Don't be misled by nonharmonic tones.)*

Bach, Chorale: *Jesu, Deine tiefen Wunden*

Bb: ____ ____ ____ ____ ____ ____

Bb: vi   V   I^6 V$^6_5$ I V I

No.	

85. The chord at the asterisk in the preceding frame is a dominant seventh chord. Aside from the 9-8 suspension in the tenor (in the following chord), are there any irregularities of doubling or resolution? _____

86. A dominant seventh chord in second inversion is shown below:

Schumann, *Papillons,* Op. 2

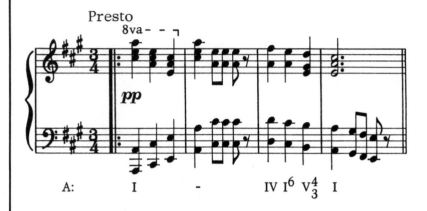

Like triads, seventh chords in second inversion are relatively weak sonorities. The one in the example above is used as a "passing chord" to connect the tonic in first inversion with the same chord in root position.

Which note is in the lowest voice when a seventh chord is in second inversion? (Root/3rd/5th/7th) _____

87. Supply the Roman numeral analysis for the phrase below:

Haydn, *Quartet,* Op. 76, No. 4

Eb: ___ ___ ___ ___

5th.

Eb: I   V$\frac{4}{3}$ I   V   I

88. Complete the part writing in such a way that no irregularities of doubling occur.

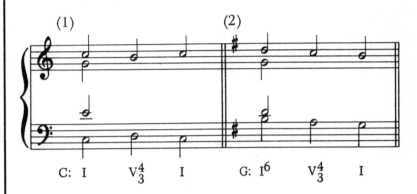

89. Supply the Roman numeral analysis for the phrase below:

Bach, Chorale: *Gott lebet noch*

F: ___ ___ ___ ___ ___

F: vi IV I⁶ V$\frac{4}{3}$I V

90. The third inversion has the seventh in the bass.

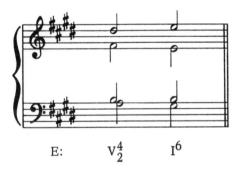

E: V$\frac{4}{2}$ I⁶

By being in the bass voice, the natural tendency of the seventh to resolve downward (by step) is emphasized. The dominant seventh chord in third inversion almost always resolves (as above) to the tonic triad in _____ inversion.

first

(1)　　　　(2)

91. Write the second chord in such a way that no irregularities of doubling occur.

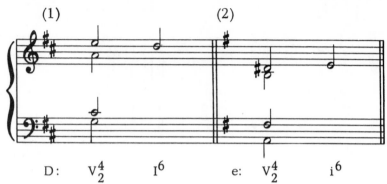

(1)　　　　(2)

D:　V$_2^4$　　I^6　　e:　V$_2^4$　　i^6

92. Supply the Roman numeral analysis for the fragment below:

Beethoven, *Sonata*, Op. 13

Ab:　I　V$_2^4$　I^6　V^6　I

Ab: ___ ___ ___ ___ ___

93. In all of the examples shown thus far the seventh resolves downward by step. Exceptional resolutions of the seventh are extremely rare. Two examples are shown below:

(a)　　　　(b)

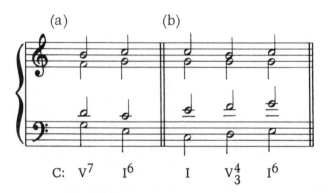

C:　V^7　I^6　　I　V$_3^4$　I^6

Notice that in both cases the bass voice takes the note to which the seventh would normally have resolved (the third of the tonic triad).

Learn this principle: *If the bass takes the note of resolution, the seventh may rise to the nearest chord tone.*

What is the *normal* resolution of the seventh?

Downward by step.

94.   The tendency for the seventh of a seventh chord to resolve downward by step is seldom ignored. The *approach* to the seventh, on the other hand, is made in a variety of ways. Actually, it may be approached in any way that produces an effective melodic contour taking into account its tendency to resolve downward.

Greater freedom may be exercised in the approach to the seventh than in its resolution.   (True/False) _____

True.

95.   Whereas the seventh may be approached in any way that results in a good melodic line and satisfactory partwriting, several patterns are encountered more frequently than others. These are by preparation, by step, and by leap (from below).

(a) Preparation   (b) Step   (c) Leap

G: ii   V^7 I   I   V^7 I   V   V$^6_5$ I

The seventh in each of the above examples may be likened to a nonharmonic tone. In (a), for example, the pattern of approach and resolution suggests a suspension. The pattern in (b) is like that of a passing tone, while the pattern in (c) suggests a(n) _____ .

appoggiatura

96.   Like (b) in the preceding frame, the example on the following page shows a seventh approached and left by step. What nonharmonic tone is suggested by this pattern? The _____ _____ .

neighboring tone

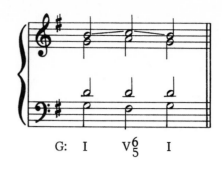

G: I   V$^6_5$ I

SUMMARY.

The dominant seventh chord is used more frequently than any other. The addition of the seventh to the dominant triad does not change its function. In fact, the introduction of a dissonant element (the seventh) serves to increase the activity of the dominant triad and makes more imperative its usual resolution to the tonic or submediant triads.

Two dissonant elements are contained in the dominant seventh chord: the seventh, and the interval of a tritone between the third and seventh. The proper resolution of the tritone, which is dictated by the melodic tendencies of the various scale degrees (the seventh tends to resolve upward while the fourth degree tends to resolve downward), is one of the factors which affects the part writing of passages containing dominant seventh chords. The second factor is the desirability of obeying the tendency of the chord seventh to resolve downward by step.

Greater freedom is exercised in the approach to the seventh than in its resolution. Nevertheless, the majority of sevenths occur in patterns which suggest nonharmonic tones. The approach by preparation is like the suspension; the approach by step is like the passing tone or the neighboring tone; and the approach by leap is like the appoggiatura.

Dominant seventh chords are used in root position and in all inversions. When the more active tones (the seventh and third) are placed in the bass or soprano, their melodic tendencies are more apparent. You must take care in such cases that these tendencies are not violated.

2   Nondominant Seventh Chords

Seventh chords occur on all degrees of the diatonic scale. Compared with the dominant seventh chord, however, the remainder are of low frequency. This is due to the fact that, in most music, dominant harmony possesses structural importance next to that of the tonic. Thus, dominant chords occur relatively frequently in comparison to other chords. Also, harmonic variety depends upon the interplay of sonorities possessing various degrees of activity. Excessive use of similar sonorities—seventh chords, for example—leads to bland effects. Harmonic vitality is achieved by exploiting a wide variety of chords, including the ever useful triads.

No. *(Seventh chords are more active.)*	97. Except for the tonic, seventh chords have the same harmonic function as their corresponding triads. Do seventh chords and triads possess the same degree of activity? _____
nonharmonic	98. The desire for melodic and rhythmic activity causes many chord sevenths to appear as nonharmonic tones rather than chord tones. This is particularly true of nondominant harmony.* It is often difficult to decide whether or not a particular dissonant tone is actually a member of the chord or merely the result of melodic (nonharmonic) activity. Such decisions are made by assessing the importance of the dissonance as a harmonic effect, and duration is often the deciding factor. To be an integral part of the chord a seventh must not be heard as a _____ tone. _____ *The term *secondary seventh chords* is used by some writers to refer to all seventh chords other than the dominant seventh.
(There may be some difference of opinion, but most analysts will classify this note as a passing tone.)	99. Would you classify the note circled in the example on the following page as a nonharmonic tone, or as part of a seventh chord? _____

Mendelssohn, *Andante con Variazioni*, Op. 82

Andante assai espressivo

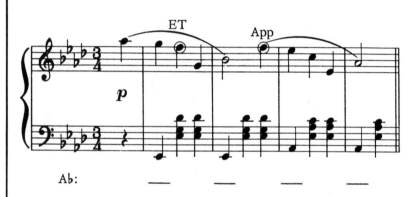

100. In the preceding frame, the circled note (A-flat) occupies merely the last half of the beat, and occurs in a pattern characteristic of the passing tone. This note is, of course, the chord seventh, and may be analyzed as such if you wish; but, in any case, its function is more melodic than harmonic.

Supply the Roman numeral analysis for the example below. *(Analyze one chord per measure.)*

Schubert, *Waltz*, Op. 9a, No. 13

A♭: V⁷ - V⁷ - I - I

A♭: ___ ___ ___ ___

Harmonic.

101. Does the seventh of the dominant seventh chord in the preceding frame (first and second measures) have a harmonic or melodic function? _____

102. Check (√) the correct option:

1. The harmonic function of the seventh varies according to its duration and melodic status.
2. Many seventh chords can be "explained away" as the result of nonharmonic tones.

True statements:

(1) _____   (2) _____   Both _____   Neither _____

Both √

103. Check (√) the correct option:

1. All seventh chords are the result of nonharmonic usage.
2. The seventh of a seventh chord must be an integral part of the chord.

True statements:

(2) √

(1) _____ (2) _____ Both _____ Neither _____

104. The SUPERTONIC SEVENTH CHORD occurs frequently as part of a cadence formula.

Mozart, *Quartet*, K. 465

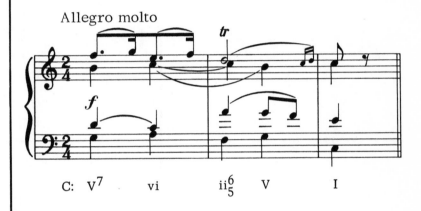

C: V^7 vi ii^6_5 V   I

first

The supertonic seventh chord in the above example is in _____ inversion.

105. The same cadence formula as that in the preceding frame is shown in a minor key below:

Beethoven, *Sonata*, Op. 2, No. 1

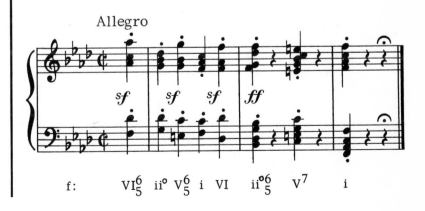

f: VI^6_5 $ii°$ V^6_5 i   VI $ii°^6_5$ V^7 i

diminished-minor

The supertonic seventh chord in a major key is a minor seventh chord. In a minor key the supertonic seventh chord is a _____ seventh chord.

106. The supertonic seventh chord in root position occurs more frequently in major than in minor. Supply the Roman numeral analysis for the example below:

Bach, Chorale: *Herr Christ, der ein'ge Gott's-Sohn*

Bb: ___ ___ ___ ___ ___

Bb: vi   ii^7 V   I^6 V   I

107. The supertonic seventh chord in root position is used much less frequently in a minor key because of the diminished fifth which occurs above the bass. The ii^{o7} in root position in the example below is part of a sequential pattern.

Chopin, *Prelude*, Op. 28, No. 22

g: ___ ___ ___ ___

g: i^6 VI   ii^{o7} V^7

108. The supertonic seventh chord is rarely used in second inversion. Third inversion, however, is more common. An example is shown at the asterisk on the following page:

Bach, Chorale: *Was willst du dich, o meine Seele*

d: i   ii°$^4_2$ V^6 i iv^6 ii°$^6_5$ ii° V   VI

The seventh of the supertonic seventh chord in the example above occurs in a pattern which resembles the (nonharmonic tone) _____ .

suspension

---

109. The MEDIANT SEVENTH CHORD is rarely used. It occurs more frequently in major than in minor, and often is part of a harmonic sequence. It usually resolves to the submediant.

Bach, Chorale: *O Ewigkeit, du Donnerwort*

F: I   vi ii^6 iii^7 vi^7 vii°^{6} I^6 V

What irregularity of doubling occurs in the mediant seventh chord (at the asterisk) above?

_____
_____

There are two 3rds and the 5th is omitted.

---

110. Supply the Roman numeral analysis for the example on the following page:

C: iii⁷   vi⁷   ii⁷   V⁷

An augmented second in the tenor voice.

Chopin, *Etude,* Op. 10, No. 1

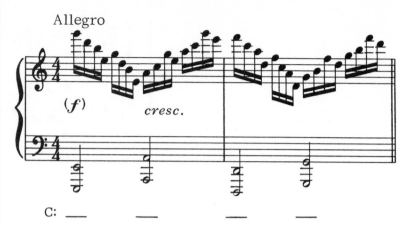

C: ___   ___   ___   ___

111. The mediant seventh chord in minor is extremely rare. Because of the alternate seventh degrees of the melodic minor scale there are two forms.

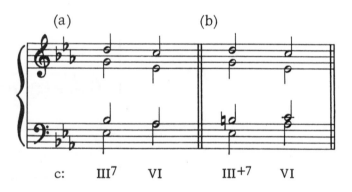

c: III⁷   VI   III⁺⁷   VI

The resolution of each chord is to the submediant triad, but in (b) the leading tone (B-natural) necessitates a doubled third in the second chord. What part writing error would result if the submediant triad had been written as in (a)? _____

_____

_____

112. Most seventh chords resolve to a chord whose root is a fifth below, but the SUBDOMINANT SEVENTH CHORD does not usually resolve in this way, except when part of a harmonic sequence. This is due to the weak sonority of the leading tone triad. A common resolution is to the dominant triad or seventh chord. Supply the Roman numeral analysis for the example on the following page:

F: vi   IV⁷ V⁷ I

Bach, Chorale: *Vater unser im Himmelreich*

F: ___ ___ ___ ___

---

113. Another common resolution of the subdominant seventh chord is to the supertonic triad or seventh chord.

Bach, *Well-Tempered Clavier,* Vol. 1, Prelude I

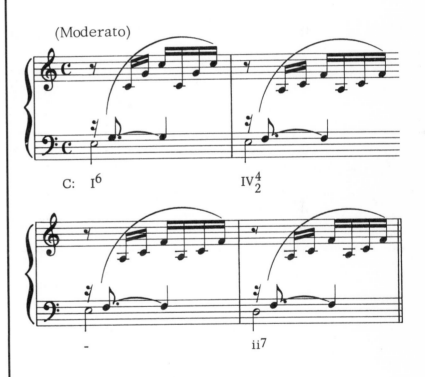

(Moderato)

C: I⁶   IV⁴₂

-              ii⁷

In this example, the subdominant seventh chord is in _____ inversion.

third

---

114. In minor, there are two forms of the subdominant seventh chord, both of which usually resolve to the dominant triad or seventh chord.

Nondominant Seventh Chords   35

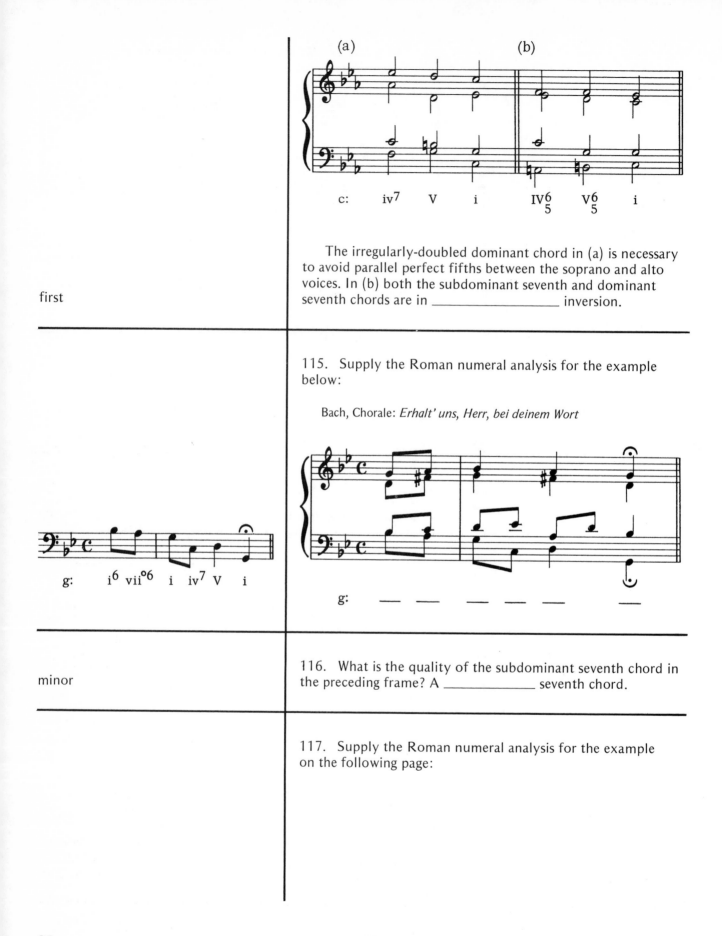

(a)   (b)

c: iv⁷   V   i   IV⁶₅   V⁶₅   i

The irregularly-doubled dominant chord in (a) is necessary to avoid parallel perfect fifths between the soprano and alto voices. In (b) both the subdominant seventh and dominant seventh chords are in _____ inversion.

first

115.   Supply the Roman numeral analysis for the example below:

Bach, Chorale: *Erhalt' uns, Herr, bei deinem Wort*

g: i⁶ vii°⁶   i   iv⁷   V   i

g: __ __ __ __ __ __ __

minor

116.   What is the quality of the subdominant seventh chord in the preceding frame? A _____ seventh chord.

117.   Supply the Roman numeral analysis for the example on the following page:

Chapter 2

d: III i IV$^6_5$ V$^6_5$ i V

d: ___ ___ ___ ___ ___ ___

False.
(It is a major-minor seventh chord.)

118. The chord at the asterisk in the preceding frame is a minor seventh chord. (True/False) _____

---

dominant

119. In a minor key the subdominant seventh chord may be either a minor seventh chord or a major-minor seventh chord, depending upon which of the alternate sixth scale degrees is used. Each of these types of subdominant seventh chords commonly progresses to the _____ triad or seventh chord.

---

minor

120. The SUBMEDIANT SEVENTH CHORD occurs most frequently in root position. It may resolve to the subdominant, supertonic, dominant, or leading tone triads or seventh chords.

(a) (b)

C: vi^7 ii^7 vi^7 V^6

What is the quality of the submediant seventh chord in a major key? A _____ seventh chord.

(No response.)

121. The seventh of the submediant seventh chord in (b) of the preceding frame is retained in the alto to become a part of the following chord. This is called a PASSIVE RESOLUTION. In spite of the smooth voice leading passive resolutions occur rarely. This is because the tension of the dissonant seventh is best resolved by normal resolution which is downward by step.

122. Supply the Roman numeral analysis for the example below:

Bach, Chorale: *Schmücke dich, o liebe Seele*

F: _____ _____ _____ _____ _____ _____

F: iii   vi⁷ vii°⁶ I⁶   IV   I⁶

---

123. In a minor key the submediant seventh chord has two forms.

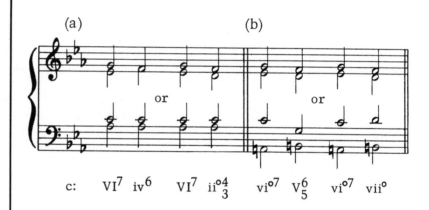

(a)   (b)

c: VI⁷ iv⁶   VI⁷ ii°⁴₃   vi°⁷ V⁶₅   vi°⁷ vii°

Identify the quality of the two types of submediant seventh chords used in a minor key (as shown above).

(a) _____ seventh chord

(b) _____ seventh chord

(a) Major

(b) Diminished-minor

---

124. Complete the harmonic analysis for the example on the following page:

Puccini, *La Bohème*, Act IV

Andante calmo

pp

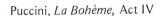

per-chè vol - li con te so-la re - sta - re

Andante calmo

c: i⁴₂ VI⁷- ii°⁴₃- i⁶₄ -

c: i⁴₂   —   —   —   —

a: i   V   i⁶ V vi°⁷vii° i   V

125. Supply the Roman numeral analysis for the example below:

Bach, Chorale: *Warum betrübst du dich, mein Herz*

a: __   __   __   __

126. The LEADING TONE SEVENTH CHORD performs the same function as the dominant seventh chord. It is used in root position, first and second inversions, but rarely in third inversion.

(a) Major Key   (b) Minor Key

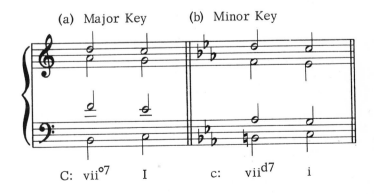

C: vii°⁷   I   c: vii^{d7}   i

Nondominant Seventh Chords

diminished-minor

What is the quality of the leading tone seventh chord in major? A _____ seventh chord.

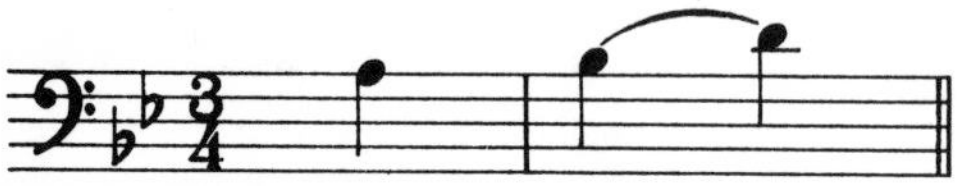

127.   The leading tone seventh chord is used less frequently in major than in minor. Supply the Roman numeral analysis for the first two chords in the example below:

Mozart, *Quartet*, K. 458

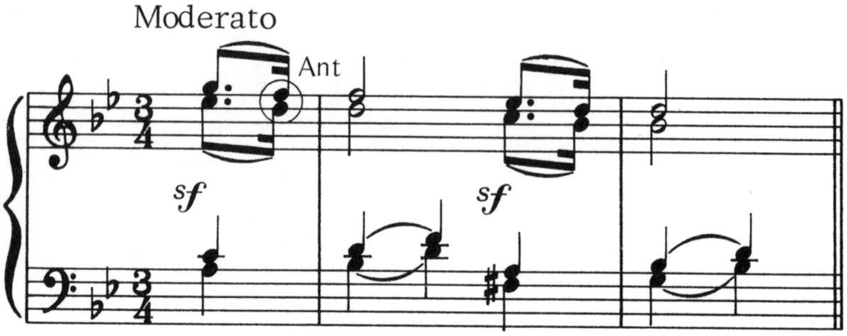

Bb: vii°⁷   I   -

Bb: ___   ___   vii^d7/vi   vi

128.   In a minor key the leading tone seventh chord is a diminished seventh chord.

Beethoven, *Sonata*, Op. 13

c: vii^d7₄₃   -   i

second

The leading tone seventh chord above is in _____ inversion.

129.   Supply the Roman numeral analysis for the example on the following page:

Bach, Chorale: *Herzliebster Jesu, was hast du verbrochen*

b: V   IV⁶V⁶₅   i - viiᵈ⁷i   V

b:

130. The leading tone seventh chord is often used to produce a cadence effect which is somewhat less positive than that of the dominant seventh chord.

Mozart, *Sonata*, K. 333

Allegretto grazioso

g: viiᵈ⁷₆₅   i⁶   viiᵈ⁷₆₅   i⁶

The leading tone seventh chord almost always progresses to the _____ triad.

tonic

131. The TONIC SEVENTH CHORD progresses to the subdominant triad, or occasionally to the supertonic triad or seventh chord.

(a) Major Key   (b) Minor Key

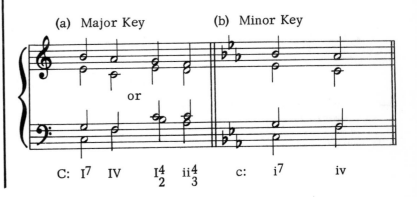

or

C: I⁷   IV   I⁴₂   ii⁴₃   c: i⁷   iv

In minor, the lowered seventh scale degree is used in order to descend smoothly to the third of the subdominant triad.

Identify the quality of the tonic seventh chord in major and minor keys (as shown above).

(a) Major

(b) Minor

(a) _____ seventh chord

(b) _____ seventh chord

---

132. Supply the Roman numeral analysis for the example below:

Bach, Chorale: *Puer natus in Bethlehem*

C: ___   ___   ___   ___

C: V_2^4 I^6 I^7 IV   I

---

133. The example below shows the tonic seventh chord in minor.

Brahms, *Intermezzo*, Op. 117, No. 2

Andante non troppo . . .

p

b♭: i^6 i^7 iv^7

Yes.

Does the seventh of the tonic seventh chord in the example above resolve normally? _____

134.   Seventh chords often appear in sequence patterns. The harmonic activity generated by a chain of active chords gives such passages a strong sense of forward motion.

Mozart, *Sonata*, K. 332

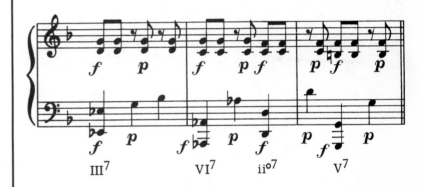

Do any of the sevenths resolve irregularly in the example above? _____

No.

C: I⁶ $\quad$ – $\quad$ ii⁷ $\quad$ V

I⁷ $\quad$ IV $\quad$ vii°⁷ $\quad$ iii

vi⁷ $\quad$ ii $\quad$ V⁷ $\quad$ vi

ii$^6_5$ $\quad$ V⁷ $\quad\quad$ I

135. Complete the Roman numerals for the example below:

Kuhlau, *Sonatina,* Op. 88, No. 3

Allegro burlesco

C: $\quad$ I⁶ $\quad$ – $\quad$ ___ ___ ___ ___

___ $\quad$ ___ $\quad$ ___ $\quad$ ___

136. In general, a seventh chord can be used at any place where the corresponding triad can be used.

Rewrite the alto and tenor voices in such a way that by changing *one note* the supertonic triad becomes a seventh chord.

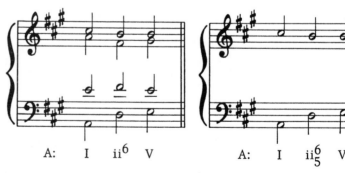

A: $\quad$ I $\quad$ ii⁶ $\quad$ V $\qquad\qquad$ A: $\quad$ I $\quad$ ii$^6_5$ $\quad$ V

137. Rewrite the alto and tenor voices in such a way that by changing *three notes* the submediant, supertonic, and dominant triads become seventh chords.

Bb: I vi ii V I

Bb: I vi⁷ ii⁷ V⁷ I

138. Rewrite the alto, tenor, and bass voices in such a way that by changing *two notes* the subdominant and dominant triads become seventh chords.

e: i iv V i⁶

e: i iv⁷ V$\frac{4}{2}$ i⁶

139. When harmonizing a melody each note can now be considered the root, third, fifth, or *seventh* of a chord. In the key of C major, for example, the first scale degree may be harmonized by any one of four chords.

C: I vi IV ii⁷

Indicate with Roman numerals the four chords which may be used to harmonize the *fourth* scale degree in a major key.

IV, ii, vii°, V⁷

140. When harmonizing a melody, the necessity of resolving the seventh downward by step must be considered. For a particular note to be harmonized as the seventh of a seventh chord, *the note which follows must be a second lower to allow for proper resolution.*

6.

Which note(s) in the melody below could be harmonized as the seventh of a seventh chord? ____

KEY OF E-FLAT MAJOR

① ② ③ ④ ⑤ ⑥ ⑦

2, 6.

141. Which note(s) in the melody below could be harmonized as the seventh of a seventh chord? _____

KEY OF B MINOR

① ② ③ ④ ⑤ ⑥ ⑦ ⑧ ⑨

---

142. Variety in sonorities is an important factor in writing expressive harmony. Over-use of seventh chords quickly destroys their effectiveness. They should be saved for crucial points in the phrase where their particular color and activity will contribute best to the overall musical effect.

Which is the most frequently-used diatonic seventh chord?

_____

The dominant seventh chord.

SUMMARY.

A seventh chord may be built on any degree of the scale. The harmonic function of a seventh chord is the same as the corresponding triad except for the tonic. In this case the addition of a seventh causes the inactive tonic triad to become active.

The seventh of a seventh chord introduces essential (harmonic) dissonance into music in contrast to the unessential dissonance of a nonharmonic tone. Since the seventh is the active element it should not be doubled. Also, the tension of this tone is resolved most satisfactorily if it proceeds *downward by step*. The seventh should rarely be resolved otherwise.

3   Altered Nonharmonic Tones and Secondary Dominants

For greater color and variety than is available from the tonal material of diatonic scales, composers sometimes use tones which are not included in the prevailing tonality. These are chromatic alterations of diatonic tones and are called "altered" or "foreign" tones. Such tones occur either as altered nonharmonic tones or as members of altered chords. In this chapter we shall begin to study the various ways altered tones are used.

143.   Tones which are foreign to the prevailing tonality often appear as ALTERED NONHARMONIC TONES. In the example below, the circled notes are *not* included in the G major scale.

Beethoven, *Trio*, for two oboes and english horn, Op. 87

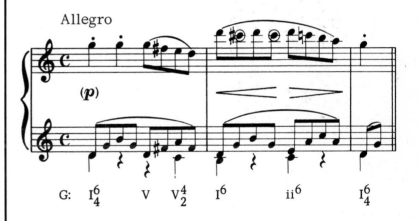

The type of nonharmonic tone illustrated by the circled notes is the _____ _____.

neighboring tone

144.   Altered nonharmonic tones are used to supply tonal color and variety. They are also used to bring attention to particular harmonies. A tone which is foreign to the tonality naturally attracts attention to itself and to the chord with which it is associated. In the example on the following page, the altered tones (D-sharps) occur with the tonic triad in second inversion.

Beethoven, *Sonata,* Op. 31, No. 2

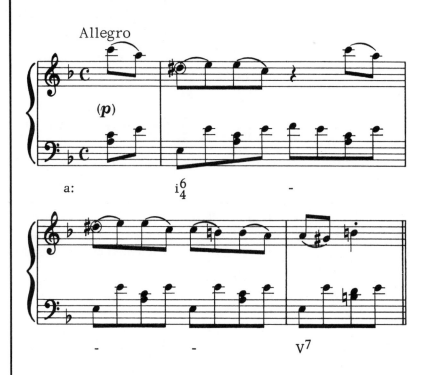

fourth

The altered tones in this case are the raised _____ scale degree.

---

seventh

145.   The altered passing tone in the bass (at the asterisk) in the example below is the lowered _____ scale degree.

Bach, Chorale: *Schaut, ihr Sünder*

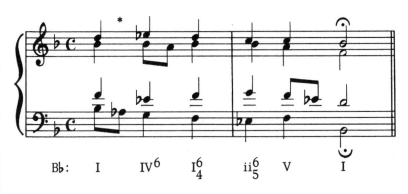

---

146.   The two most frequent alterations of diatonic scale degrees in major are shown in the previous two frames. These are the *raised fourth* and the *lowered seventh* degrees. Each of these provides a gesture toward an important structural triad as shown on the following page.

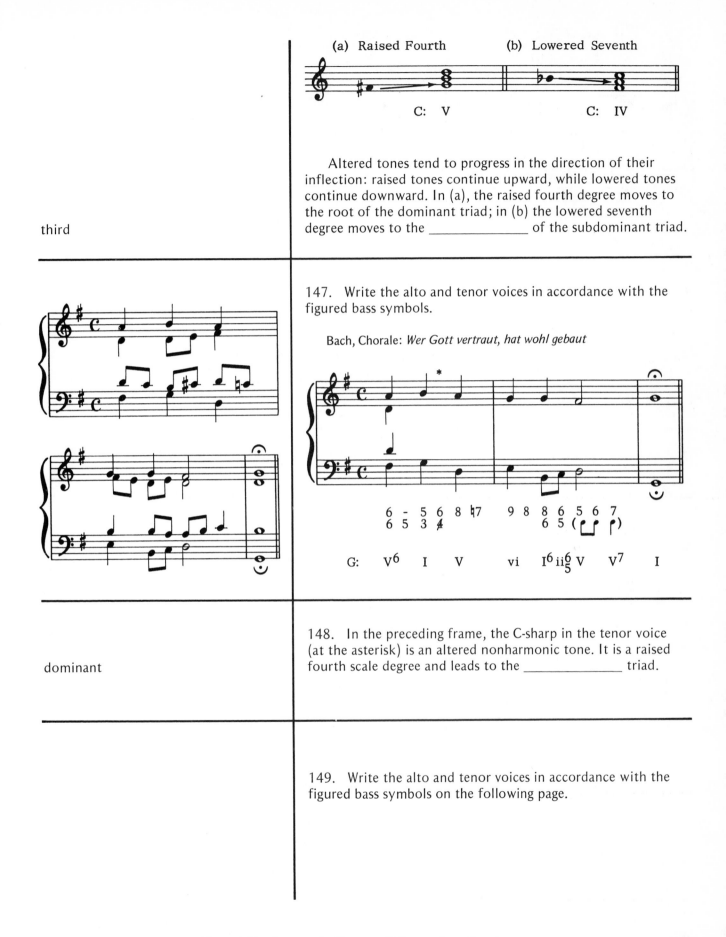

(a) Raised Fourth   (b) Lowered Seventh

C: V   C: IV

Altered tones tend to progress in the direction of their inflection: raised tones continue upward, while lowered tones continue downward. In (a), the raised fourth degree moves to the root of the dominant triad; in (b) the lowered seventh degree moves to the _____ of the subdominant triad.

third

147. Write the alto and tenor voices in accordance with the figured bass symbols.

Bach, Chorale: *Wer Gott vertraut, hat wohl gebaut*

6 - 5 6 8 ♮7   9 8 8 6 5 6 7
6 5 3 4   6 5 (♩ ♩)

G: V⁶   I   V   vi   I⁶ ii⁶₅ V   V⁷   I

dominant

148. In the preceding frame, the C-sharp in the tenor voice (at the asterisk) is an altered nonharmonic tone. It is a raised fourth scale degree and leads to the _____ triad.

149. Write the alto and tenor voices in accordance with the figured bass symbols on the following page.

Bach, Chorale: *Ach Gott und Herr, wie gross und schwer*

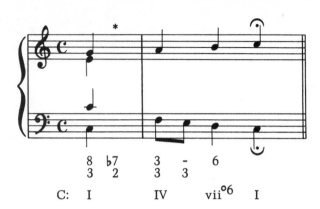

$$\begin{array}{cccc} 8 & \flat 7 & 3 & - & 6 \\ 3 & 2 & 3 & 3 \end{array}$$

C: I   IV   vii°⁶   I

---

lowered

150.   In the preceding frame, the B-flat in the tenor (at the asterisk) is an altered nonharmonic tone which provides a gesture toward the subdominant triad. It is a _____ seventh scale degree.

---

151.   Altered nonharmonic tones other than the raised fourth or lowered seventh scale degrees are comparatively rare. The more likely alterations of the various scale degrees in major are shown below. *(The white notes indicate the tone to which each usually progresses.)*

KEY OF C MAJOR

True.

Altered tones tend to continue in the same direction as their inflection. (True/False) _____

152.   The more likely alterations of the various scale degrees in minor are shown below. (The white notes indicate the tone to which each usually progresses.)

KEY OF C MINOR

1st   2nd   3rd   4th

Fewer tones are considered altered in minor than in major because of the wealth of tonal variety provided by the alternate sixth and seventh degrees of the melodic minor scale.

The altered tone which occurs most frequently *in both major and minor* is the raised fourth scale degree. The *lowered* seventh scale degree is encountered frequently in major. Is this also an altered tone in minor? _____

No.
(The lowered seventh is a diatonic tone in melodic minor.)

---

153.   Both of the tones indicated by asterisks in the example below are *chromatic* passing tones.

Chopin, *Mazurka*, Op. 33, No. 3

C: I   V⁷   I

Do both of these altered tones resolve in the direction of their inflection? _____

Yes.

154. Chromatic alterations sometimes cause two or more passing tones to occur in succession.

Liszt, *Du bist wie eine Blume*

The two passing tones (B and B-sharp) fill in the melodic interval of a _____ between A and C-sharp.

third

155. Chromatic alterations sometimes cause simultaneous false relations.*

Chopin, *Valse*, Op. 64, No. 1

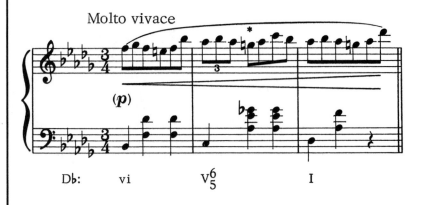

The G-natural at the asterisk clashes with the chord seventh G-flat in the left hand. What type of nonharmonic tone is demonstrated here? _____

Neighboring tone.

*See Frame 602.

156.   Double neighboring tones are shown below.*

Brahms, *Waltz*, Op. 39, No. 14

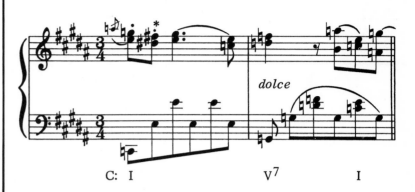

C: I   V⁷   I

2nd (and)
4th

The notes at the asterisk are the raised _____ and _____ scale degrees.

_____

*For another example of double altered nonharmonic tones see Frame 203.

157.   Melodic activity generated by nonharmonic tones is increased by chromatic alteration. Altered tones tend to continue in the direction they are inflected. The two most common alterations are the raised fourth and the lowered seventh scale degrees. The raised fourth degree usually continues up to the fifth, thus providing a tonal gesture towards the dominant. The lowered fifth degree resolves to the sixth, which often is set as the third of the subdominant chord.
   In addition to motivation, altered tones provide color. They do not necessarily weaken the influence of the tonal center, but a chromatic melodic style often is associated with an abundance of altered chords.

(No response.)

158.   In addition to their nonharmonic function, tones which are foreign to the prevailing tonality often are absorbed into the harmony to produce ALTERED CHORDS. Such chords perform a role similar to that of altered nonharmonic tones: they produce more colorful harmony, and, in some cases, help stress the structural function of the diatonic chords to which they resolve.
   A chord which contains a tone foreign to the prevailing tonality is called a(n) _____ chord.

altered

chromatic	159. Altered chords appear frequently in the works of eighteenth-century composers. The evolving chromatic harmonic idiom of the nineteenth century, however, caused them to occur with ever-increasing abundance during this period. The profuse use of altered chords is associated with a _____ harmonic idiom.
7.	160. Much nineteenth-century music contains what seems to be a bewildering array of altered chords. Study of altered chords is simplified, however, by the fact that most fall into but four classes: SECONDARY DOMINANTS, BORROWED CHORDS, CHROMATIC MEDIANTS, and AUGMENTED SIXTH CHORDS. Further, most altered chords belong to the first of these groups (secondary dominants). Because of this, we shall begin our study of altered chords with secondary dominants. Which chord in the example below is an *altered chord*? ____ Bach, Chorale: *Ach Gott, wie manches Herzeleid* 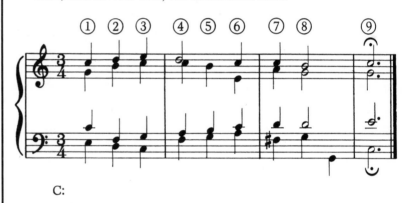
C	161. Chord number seven in the example of the preceding frame contains a note (F-sharp) which is foreign to the key of C major. Therefore, it is an altered chord. This chord (DF♯AC) relates to the one which follows as a dominant seventh to a tonic. *It is as if for a brief moment the key of G major had been established.*  But if you will play this phrase at the piano, it will be clear that the key of G major is NOT established. The altered chord does no more than provide a dominant-like reinforcement of the dominant triad (GBD) in the key of ____ major.

	162. The reinforcement of a diatonic triad in the manner shown in Frame 160 accomplishes several things: the dominant triad is elevated in status, additional color is introduced by the alteration, and greater harmonic motion is produced by changing the nondominant supertonic seventh chord (DFAC) to the more active dominant seventh chord-type (DF♯AC).
major-minor	The nondominant supertonic seventh chord (DFAC) is a minor seventh chord. What is the quality of the chord in its altered form (DF♯AC)? A _____ seventh chord.
	163. The term *tonicization* refers to the concept of emphasizing a particular diatonic chord by embellishing it with an altered chord which bears a dominant relation to it. This concept is used by some theorists to account for much more extended nontonic tonal orientations than merely a single chord. There is a close relation between secondary dominants and modulation, as will be shown later.
tonicization	Altered chords of the secondary dominant type are a simple manifestation of the principle of _____.
	164. The actual analysis of the example in Frame 160 remains to be shown. Since we have determined that all of the chords in this example are in the key of C major, a symbol must be used for the altered chord (DF♯AC) which not only makes this clear, but also expresses the *function* of the chord.
	Bach, Chorale: *Ach Gott, wie manches Herzeleid*
	C: I⁶ vii°⁶ I ii⁶₅ V vi V⁶₅/V V - I
dominant	The oral expression of the symbol V^6_5/V is either "dominant six-five of the dominant," or, more simply, "five six-five of five." This chord is the dominant seventh of the _____ in the key of C major.

165. The altered chord (at the asterisk) in the preceding frame is called a SECONDARY DOMINANT. It results in a tonicization of the dominant (GBD) in C major. This chord can be used in any inversion, but root position and first inversion occur more frequently.

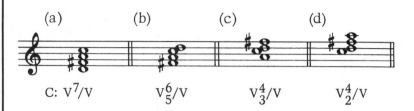

(a)   (b)   (c)   (d)

C: V^7/V V^6_5/V V^4_3/V V^4_2/V

In (d), the seventh is in the lowest voice. Thus, the following chord would likely be the dominant in _____ inversion.

first.

---

166. Supply the Roman numeral analysis.

Bach, Chorale: *Herzliebster Jesu, was hast du verbrochen*

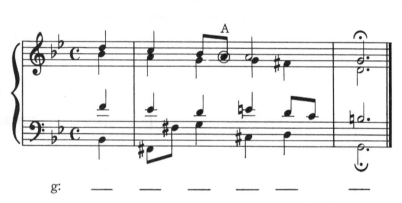

g: _____ _____ _____ _____ _____ _____

g: III vii^{d7} i V^6_5/V V   I

---

167. Only one type of secondary dominant has been shown thus far: the major-minor seventh chord (dominant seventh) whose root is a perfect fifth above the root of the chord to which it relates. Actually, there are several types of chords which perform a "dominant" function similar to the dominant seventh chord. These are shown below with the appropriate symbol for each:

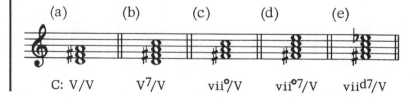

(a)   (b)   (c)   (d)   (e)

C: V/V V^7/V vii^o/V vii^{o7}/V vii^{d7}/V

GBD.

Spell the chord to which each of the secondary dominants in the preceding example normally resolves. _____

---

168. The diminished seventh chord (e) in the preceding frame is used to embellish either major or minor triads, whereas the diminished-minor seventh chord (d) relates to major triads only.
(Compare the effect of the two examples below by playing them at the piano.)

(a) Undesirable   (b) Desirable

a: vii°⁷/iv   iv   a: vii^d7/iv   iv

The effect in (a) is unpleasant due to the tritone which occurs between the two chords. Diminished-minor seventh chords should progress to _____ triads.

major

---

169. A tritone is not produced by relating a diminished-minor seventh chord to a *major* triad.

P4

G: ___   ___

G: vii°⁷/V–V

Supply the chord symbol for each chord.

---

170. Supply the chord symbol for each chord. *(Take care to show the precise quality of each chord.)*

(1)   (2)   (3)

Bb: ___   e: ___   Ab: ___

(1) Bb: vii°/V
(2) e: V⁷/V
(3) Ab: vii°⁷/V

171. Continue as in the preceding frame.

(1)   (2)   (3)

D: ____   g: ____   A: ____

(1) D: vii^d7^/V → (1) D: vii^{d7}/V
(2) g: vii^d7^/V
(3) A: V/V

---

(1) D: vii^{d7}/V

(2) g: vii^{d7}/V

(3) A: V/V

---

172. Some of the oral expressions you may use for the symbols which represent secondary dominants are shown below:

V/V   "five of five"

V^7/V   "five seven of five"

vii^{o7}/V "seven seven of five"

vii^{d7}/V "seven diminished seven of five"

Write an oral expression (similar to those above) for the symbol vii$^{o6}_{5}$/ii. _____

Seven six-five of two.

---

173. Most of the secondary dominants shown in previous frames relate to the dominant chord (V). Actually, any major or minor triad (except, of course, the tonic) may be attended by secondary dominants. *(Diminished and augmented triads are excluded because they are incapable of performing a tonic function.)*

From the diatonic triads of the E major scale select those which may be attended by secondary dominants. *(List by Roman numeral.)* _____

E: I   ii   iii   IV   V   vi   vii°

ii, iii, IV, V, and vi

---

174. The melodic minor scale produces a large number of diatonic triads. The example below shows most of the triads which are available in the key of E minor. Select those chords which may be attended by secondary dominants. *(List by Roman numeral.)* _____

e: i   ii°   III   III$^+$ iv

III, iv, V, VI, and VII

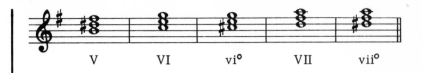

| V | VI | vi° | VII | vii° |

False.
(Secondary dominants can relate only to major or minor triads.)

175. Any diatonic triad in either a major or minor key may be attended by a secondary dominant. (True/False) _____

(No response.)

176. There are two types of secondary dominants: (1) chords which bear a *dominant* relation to the following chord; (2) chords which bear a *leading tone* relation to the following chord. Both types perform the same harmonic function, but root relations are different.

Dominant relation

V/x   }
V^7/x }   root is a *perfect fifth above* root of tonicized chord

Leading tone relation

vii°/x   }
vii°^{7}/x }   root is a *half-step below* root of tonicized chord
vii^{d7}/x }

(1)   (2)   (3)

177. Write the chords indicated by the Roman numerals.

(1)   (2)   (3)

F: V^7/ii   g: V^7/VI   D: vii°/iii

(1)   (2)   (3)

178. Continue as in the preceding frame.

(1)   (2)   (3)

E♭: V^7/IV   E: vii^{d7}/vi   d: V^7/V

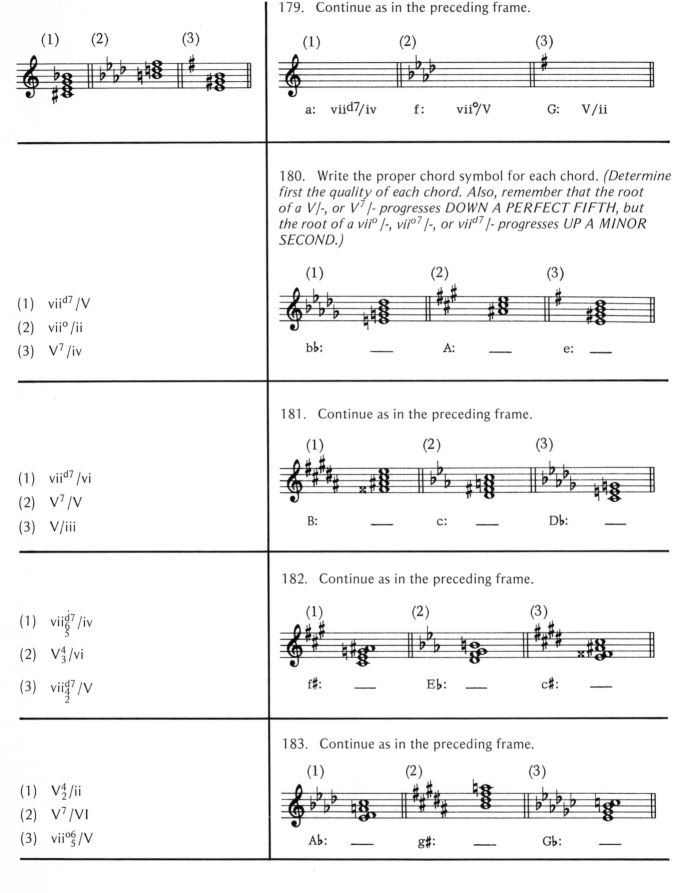

179. Continue as in the preceding frame.

(1)   (2)   (3)

a: vii^{d7}/iv   f: vii°/V   G: V/ii

---

(1) vii^{d7}/V

(2) vii°/ii

(3) V^7/iv

180. Write the proper chord symbol for each chord. *(Determine first the quality of each chord. Also, remember that the root of a V/-, or V^7/- progresses DOWN A PERFECT FIFTH, but the root of a vii° /-, vii^{o7} /-, or vii^{d7} /- progresses UP A MINOR SECOND.)*

(1)   (2)   (3)

b♭: ___   A: ___   e: ___

---

(1) vii^{d7}/vi

(2) V^7/V

(3) V/iii

181. Continue as in the preceding frame.

(1)   (2)   (3)

B: ___   c: ___   D♭: ___

---

(1) vii$^{d7}_{6\atop5}$/iv

(2) V$^4_3$/vi

(3) vii$^{d7}_{4\atop2}$/V

182. Continue as in the preceding frame.

(1)   (2)   (3)

f♯: ___   E♭: ___   c♯: ___

---

(1) V$^4_2$/ii

(2) V^7/VI

(3) vii$^{o6}_5$/V

183. Continue as in the preceding frame.

(1)   (2)   (3)

A♭: ___   g♯: ___   G♭: ___

Chapter 3

184. It is not always necessary to use symbols as complicated as those in the preceding two frames. Often the purpose of an analysis is served equally well by not indicating the precise inversion. In such cases you may simplify symbols by representing chords as if they all were in root position.

(No response.)

---

185. Write the *four* secondary dominants which likely would precede the supertonic triad in the key of A major. Supply, also, the proper Roman numeral for each.

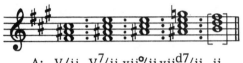

A: V/ii V⁷/ii vii°/ii vii d7/ii ii

(See next frame.)

The chord to which each progresses.

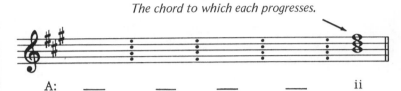

A: ___ ___ ___ ___ ii

---

186. The vii°⁷/ii was omitted from the possible secondary dominants in the preceding frame because the resolution of a diminished-minor seventh chord to a minor triad produces an undesirable effect. *(See Frame 168.)*

(No response.)

---

187. Write the *five* secondary dominants which may precede the dominant triad in the key of D-flat major. Supply, also, the proper Roman numeral for each.

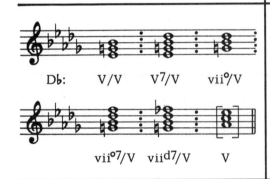

Db: V/V V⁷/V vii°/V

vii°⁷/V vii d7/V V

The chord to which each progresses.

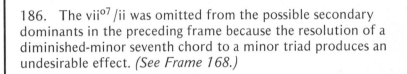

Db: ___ ___ ___ ___ ___ V

---

188. Complete the Roman numeral analysis for the example below. *(The circled notes are nonharmonic tones.)*

A: I   V⁷/ii

ii   ii⁴₃   V⁹

Chopin, *Prelude*, Op. 28, No. 7

Andantino

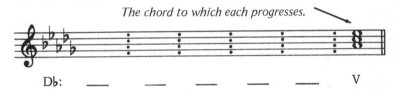

(p)

A: ___ ___ ___ ___ V⁹

---

189. Supply the Roman numeral analysis for the example below:

Beethoven, *Sonata*, Op. 28

Allegro vivace

D:

190. Complete the Roman numeral analysis for the example below:

Schubert, *Symphony No. 8*, in B minor

Andante con moto

E: ___   ___ I^6_4 ___ ___

191. Supply the Roman numeral analysis for the example below:

Schumann, *Album for the Young*, Op. 68, No. 31

Sehr kräftig

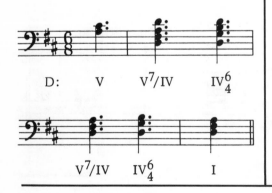

D: ___   ___   ___   ___

192. Complete the alto and tenor voices and analyze with Roman numerals.

Bach, Chorale: *Wenn ich in Angst und Not*

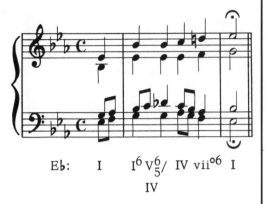

$$\begin{matrix} 5 & - & 6 & - & 6 & 3 & - & 6 \\ 3 & 3 & 3 & 4 & \flat 5 & 3 & 3 & \end{matrix}$$

E♭: ___ ___ ___ ___ ___ ___

E♭: I   I⁶ V⁶₅/ IV vii°⁶ I
          IV

193. Supply the Roman numeral analysis for the example below:

Schubert, *Erlkönig*, Op. 1

Schnell

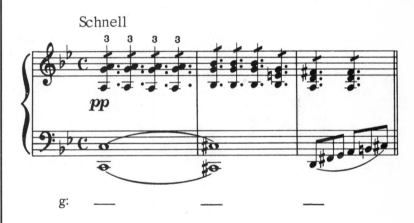

pp

g: ___ ___ ___

g: ii°⁶₅ vii^d7/V V

194. Complete the alto and tenor voices and analyze with Roman numerals on the following page.

F: I   ii⁶ viidd7/V

V   V   (7) I

Bach, Chorale: *Befiehl du deine Wege*

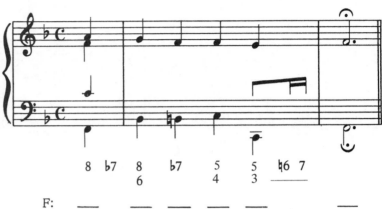

    8 b7 8 b7 5 5 ♮6 7
          6   4 3

F: —— —— —— —— —— ——

---

altered

195. The E-flat in the alto voice of the example in the preceding frame does not prevent the phrase from being entirely in the key of F-major. This device is called an _____ nonharmonic tone.

---

196. Supply the Roman numeral analysis for the example below:

Beethoven, *Piano Concerto No. 4*, Op. 58

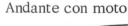

G: V/vi V$\frac{4}{2}$/vi vi⁶ V$\frac{6}{5}$/ii

ii   V   I

Andante con moto

molto *cantabile*

G: —— —— —— —— ——

197. Supply the Roman numeral analysis for the example below:

Mozart, *Fantasia in C Minor*, K. 475

Andantino

Bb: ___ ___ ___ ___

---

deceptive

198. The example in the preceding frame shows a typical use of the vii^{d7}/vi chord. When used in this way, it provides additional color and impetus to the _____ cadence.

199. Since the leading tone triad is diminished, it is not capable of performing a tonic function. Secondary dominants, therefore, may not be used in connection with it. The triad on the *lowered* seventh degree of the melodic minor scale, however, is a major triad and sometimes is embellished by a secondary dominant.

Supply the Roman numeral analysis for the example below:

Bach, *Toccata in D Minor*, for organ

Vivace

d: ___ ___

d: V$^4_2$ i^6

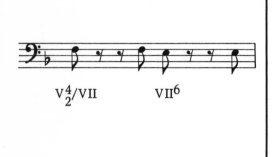

$\mathrm{V}\frac{4}{2}/\mathrm{VII}$ VII^6

$\mathrm{III}\frac{4}{2}$ VI^6 vii^{d7}

200. Supply the Roman numeral analysis for the example below. *(The circled notes are nonharmonic tones.)*

Beethoven, *Sonata*, Op. 53

Allegro con brio

C: I $\mathrm{vii}^{d7}/\mathrm{vi}$ vi V^7/vi IV

C: ___   ___   ___   ___

201. The example in the preceding frame shows that secondary dominants do not always resolve as expected. The V^7/vi does not progress to the submediant (vi), but to the subdominant (IV). This is comparable to the resolution of the V^7 to VI instead of to the tonic as occurs in the deceptive cadence.

Resolve the secondary dominant two ways as indicated by the Roman numerals. *(Avoid writing an augmented second in one of the voices.)*

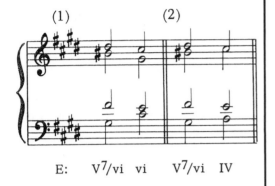

E: V^7/vi vi V^7/vi IV

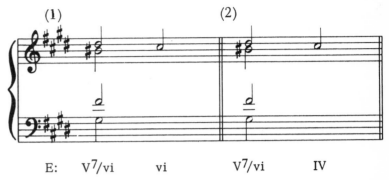

E: V^7/vi vi V^7/vi IV

202. Resolve the secondary dominant as indicated by the Roman numerals.

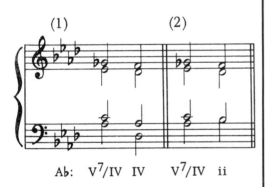

A♭: V^7/IV IV V^7/IV ii

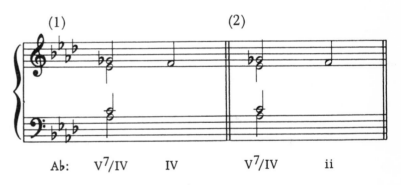

A♭: V^7/IV IV V^7/IV ii

203. Another unexpected resolution of a secondary dominant is shown below:

Chopin, *Mazurka*, Op. 67, No. 3

Allegro

C: I V^7/V

Altered Nonharmonic Tones and Secondary Dominants

viid7   I

The reiterated notes (C) in the bass constitute a pedal. The V^7/V resolves neither to the dominant nor deceptively to the mediant, but to an altered leading tone seventh chord. Since the leading tone seventh chord has the same harmonic function as the dominant triad or seventh chord, the substitution of one for the other does not change the basic harmonic movement. Chord choice in such a case is made at the discretion of the composer to achieve the desired color effect.

True.

The leading tone triad is a secondary triad of the dominant. (True/False) _____

204. The example below shows still another unexpected resolution of a secondary dominant:

Brahms, *An die Nachtigall*, Op. 46, No. 4

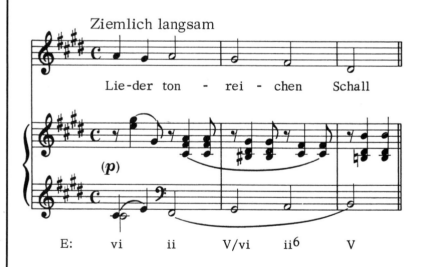

E: vi   ii   V/vi   ii⁶   V

second

In this case the root of the secondary dominant (G-sharp) progresses neither down a fifth, nor up a second, but down a _____.

205. A secondary dominant's chief function is to tonicize the chord which follows. Thus, the normal resolution of a V^7/V is as in (a); the resolution in (b) is merely a deceptive resolution of the secondary dominant.

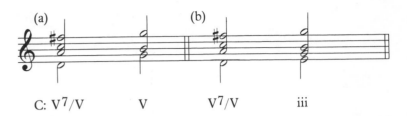

C: V^7/V V V^7/V iii

But still more unusual resolutions occur, and sometimes a potential secondary dominant may be analyzed better as another type of altered chord. You must be prepared for the fact that, in some cases, alternate interpretations are acceptable.

(No response.)

---

206. Complete the alto and tenor voices. Supply, also, the Roman numeral analysis.

Bach, Chorale: *Wie schön leuchtet der Morgenstern*

D: _____

D: vi V/vi IV iii⁶ IV⁶₅ vii°

I   ii⁶₅   V   I

It is an altered
passing tone.
(In your own words.)

207. On the first beat of the example in the preceding frame the G-sharp appears in the tenor. This note is not included in the D-major scale. How can you account for its presence? _____
_____

e: vii°6/IV   viid7/IV   IV6   viid7
              4
              3

i   V$^6_5$/V   V   I

208. **Analyze with Roman numerals the example below:**

Bach, Chorale: *Jesu, meine Freude*

e: ___ ___   ___ ___   ___ ___

209. A sequence of dominant seventh chords results when one secondary dominant resolves to another.

Chopin, *Mazurka,* Op. 33, No. 3

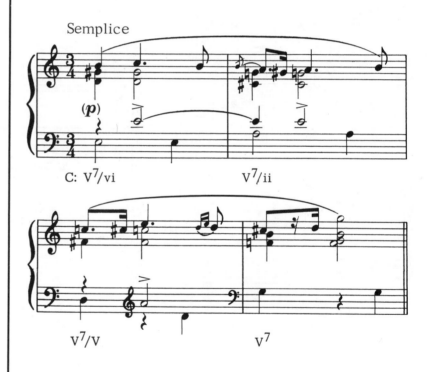

Semplice

(*p*)

C: V⁷/vi   V⁷/ii

V⁷/V   V⁷

Each of the secondary dominants resolves not to a simple triad, but to another secondary dominant. The progression of roots from each chord to the next is consistently down in (interval) _____.

fifths

Neither √

210. Check (√) the correct option:

1. All secondary dominants resolve to simple major or minor triads.
2. The root of a vii°/- usually progresses down a fifth.

True statements:
(1) _____   (2) _____   Both _____   Neither _____

(2) √

211. Check (√) the correct option:

1. The V^7/ii in the key of E major is F♯A♯C♯E.
2. The chord G♯BDF is the vii^{d7}/V in the key of D major.

True statements:
(1) _____   (2) _____   Both _____   Neither _____

(4).

212. Four resolutions of the V^7/V are shown below. Which of these is the most "likely" resolution? _____

Bb: V^7/V   iii   V$^6_5$/iii   vi^6 V

(3).

213. Although most secondary dominants resolve AS DOMI-NANTS (to a chord which relates to it as a tonic), they may resolve to *any* chord which serves the composer's purpose.

All of the resolutions of the vii^{d7}/ii shown below are possible. Indicate, however, the most "likely" one. _____

G: vii^{d7}/ii   V$^4_3$ vii$^{°6}$ ii   vii^{d7}/iii

SUMMARY.

Altered nonharmonic tones are easily absorbed by the prevailing tonality. As integral parts of altered chords, however, altered tones provide additional harmonic resources and expand the boundaries of tonality. Many altered chords result from the transfer of dominant function to other degrees of the scale. Such chords are called *secondary dominants*.

The chief function of secondary dominants is to increase the harmonic motion within the phrase. Dominant sonorities possess an inherent tension. This, plus the conditioned expectation for resolution to their tonic, is responsible for the unique motivation which dominant sonorities produce. Secondary dominants are encountered ever more frequently during the nineteenth century because composers grew to prefer dominant function to more stable sonorities. It is as if dominant function, once associated primarily with the cadence, is spread out over virtually the entire phrase. Secondary dominants also produce greater tonal variety, and often the effect of their unexpected color is most striking.

Secondary dominants elevate the status of diatonic triads to which they resolve. The reinforcement which they give to such triads is called "tonicization." Any diatonic triad (other than the tonic) which is major or minor may be embellished by a secondary dominant. The triad which is most frequently embellished, however, is the dominant.

4　Modulation to Closely Related Keys

Secondary dominants provide harmonic motivation and enlarge color resources. The gesture towards another tonality made by a secondary dominant is too fleeting to undermine the established key, but more extensive tonicization, involving several chords which function in the new key, causes the ear to be attracted to the new tonal center. This is particularly so, if the new key is confirmed by a cadence. The process of establishing a new tonality is called *modulation.* Used not only for additional tonal resources, modulation builds form by juxtaposing tonalities in various intervallic relations to one another.

214.　Secondary dominants are used to reinforce diatonic triads through the dominant (or leading tone) relationship which they bear to them. This is the process of *tonicization.* For a brief instant the triad which has been preceded by a secondary dominant assumes a tonic role.

Supply the Roman numeral analysis for the example below:

Bach, Chorale: *Ach Gott, wie manches Herzeleid*

A:　＿　＿　＿　＿　＿　＿

215.　Compare the example in the preceding frame with the one on the following page, which is taken from the same chorale. *(Play each of these examples at the piano.)*

Bach, Chorale: *Ach Gott, wie manches Herzeleid*

A:

half

The example in the preceding frame ends with an authentic cadence in A major. What type of cadence is used above? *(Listen carefully before answering.)* It is a _____ cadence.

E major.

216.   There is a similarity between the chords over which brackets have been placed in Frames 214 and 215. Notice, in particular, the chords at the asterisks. The crucial difference between these two examples is that whereas in Frame 214 the chord at the asterisk is a secondary dominant (V^6_5/V) which leads to an authentic cadence (V^7-I) in the key of A major, in Frame 215 the chord at the asterisk is followed by chords which produce a half cadence not in the tonic key of A major, but the key of the dominant. Name the key in which this phrase ends. _____

The chords following the secondary dominant must function in the original key.

217.   The phrase following that shown in Frame 215 continues in the key of E major, thus confirming the change of key.
    When followed by chords which do not function in the original key, secondary dominants may cause a shift from one tonal center to another. Whether or not a change of key occurs depends upon what happens after the secondary dominant. Actually, any secondary dominant is capable of propelling the music into a new key. Explain how secondary dominants may be held to the original key. _____
_____
_____

218.   Secondary dominants introduce a volatile element into music. They may function entirely within the original key, or the tonicization which they produce may be confirmed to the extent that a new key is established. *A change from one key to another is usually accomplished by introducing the dominant of the new key.* Thus, a close relationship exists

between secondary dominants and some of the processes by which music moves from one key to another. The act of establishing a new tonal center is called MODULATION.

Modulation occurs when the influence of one tonal center is supplanted by another. This implies that a new key must be established firmly enough, and endure long enough to cause the ear to reorientate itself to the new tonal center. The ear is often directed toward the new tonal center by the _____ chord of the new key.

dominant

---

219. Except for very short compositions, the effect of a single key tends to be monotonous. Modulations from the principal tonal center to other keys help to satisfy the need for greater tonal variety than can be supplied by a single key. Modulations may also contribute to the formal design of a composition. The sense of departure from, and return to a principal tonality often is instrumental in giving "shape" to the music.

In addition to contributing to formal design, modulations are necessary (especially in larger works) for the sake of tonal variety.

(No response.)

---

220. In modulation, one tonal center is replaced by another. An understanding of how a new tonality is established is important. This is not a simple matter, and several points must be discussed in this connection before we proceed to the actual processes of modulation. Except when modulating from a minor key to its relative major, the new key contains one or more tones which are not included as diatonic tones in the original key. The influence of the original key is undermined by the appearance of these new tones, which are instrumental in directing the ear toward the new tonal center.

Modulation causes the ear to accept a new tone as the _____.

tonic *(or key center)*

---

221. Circle the notes in the example below which are not included in the original key (D major).

Mozart, *Sonata*, K. 284

D:

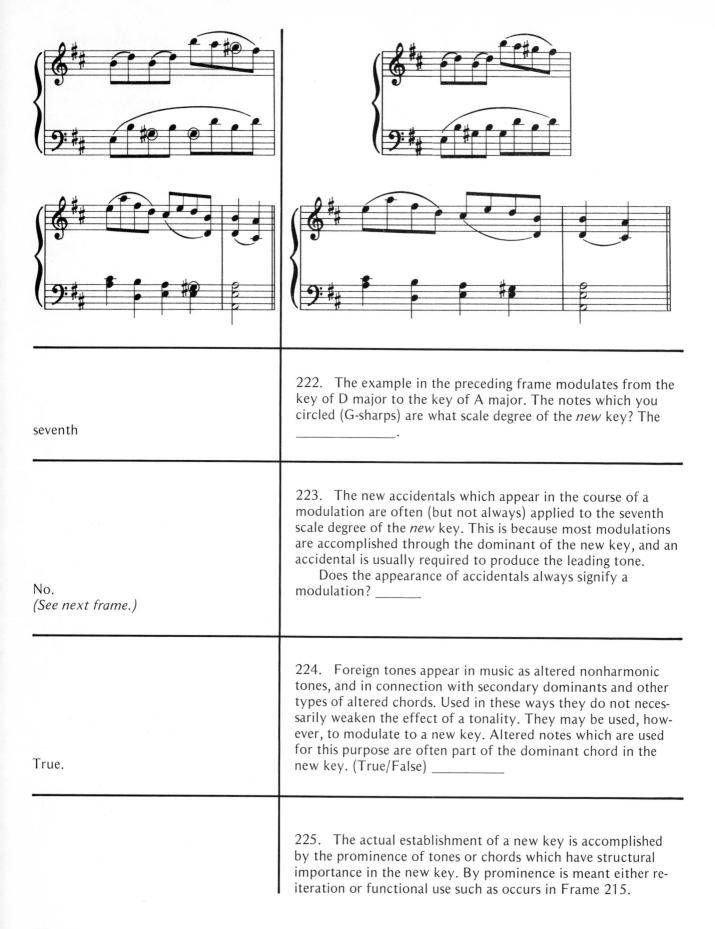

seventh

222. The example in the preceding frame modulates from the key of D major to the key of A major. The notes which you circled (G-sharps) are what scale degree of the *new* key? The _____.

No.
(See next frame.)

223. The new accidentals which appear in the course of a modulation are often (but not always) applied to the seventh scale degree of the *new* key. This is because most modulations are accomplished through the dominant of the new key, and an accidental is usually required to produce the leading tone.
     Does the appearance of accidentals always signify a modulation? _____

True.

224. Foreign tones appear in music as altered nonharmonic tones, and in connection with secondary dominants and other types of altered chords. Used in these ways they do not necessarily weaken the effect of a tonality. They may be used, however, to modulate to a new key. Altered notes which are used for this purpose are often part of the dominant chord in the new key. (True/False) _____

225. The actual establishment of a new key is accomplished by the prominence of tones or chords which have structural importance in the new key. By prominence is meant either re-iteration or functional use such as occurs in Frame 215.

Refer once again to the example in Frame 215. Is the new key (E major) established through reiteration of functional chords (notice that there are two dominant chords), or by the cadence used? _____

_____

(See next frame.)

226. Whatever opinion you expressed in the preceding frame you were correct. But, although the reiteration of the dominant chord is a factor in establishing the new key, the structural use of this chord in the cadence formula is even more important. The example in Frame 215 shows the importance of the dominant chord in establishing a new key.

(No response.)

227. Both the dominant and tonic chords are usually involved in the process of modulation, but the dominant is more important, and does not require resolution to the tonic to give a convincing impression of the new key.

The ability of the dominant chord to establish a key without *resolution to the tonic* is shown in the example below:

Brahms, *Waltz*, Op. 39, No. 9

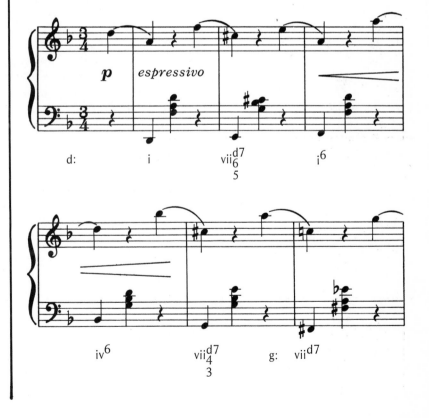

i   ii°⁶₅   V

half

The first section (at the double bar) closes with a _____ cadence in the key of G minor.

---

228.   Modulation can be likened to secondary dominants. But whereas secondary dominants produce merely momentary tonicizations, modulation causes a new tonal center to be established. Not all theorists are in agreement about the degree of emphasis needed to produce a modulation. All secondary dominants can be regarded as producing extremely brief modulations; many modulations, on the other hand, can be analyzed as extended tonicizations. In any case, you must judge whether or not a new key is actually established. The term "transient" modulation is sometimes used to refer to cases where the new key is established, but endures for only a short time.

Most modulations are made through the dominant chord of the *new* key. It is, in fact, difficult to establish a key without prominent use of dominant harmony. Once introduced, a new key is confirmed through the reiteration of chords which are functional in that key, or by a cadence. Cadences, remember, are usually not ambiguous as to tonality. In situations where the tonality is vague, *cadences often serve as the chief points of tonal reference.*

(No response.)

---

229.   In modulation, the relation of keys to one another is vital. Some keys are more remote to a given tonal center than others. The subject of this chapter is modulation to *closely related keys,* so we shall now define what is meant by this term.

Closely related keys are those whose signatures differ from one another by not more than one sharp or flat.

The closely related keys of C major are shown below:

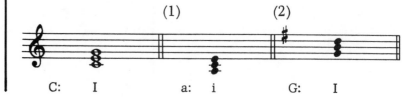

C: I   a: i   G: I

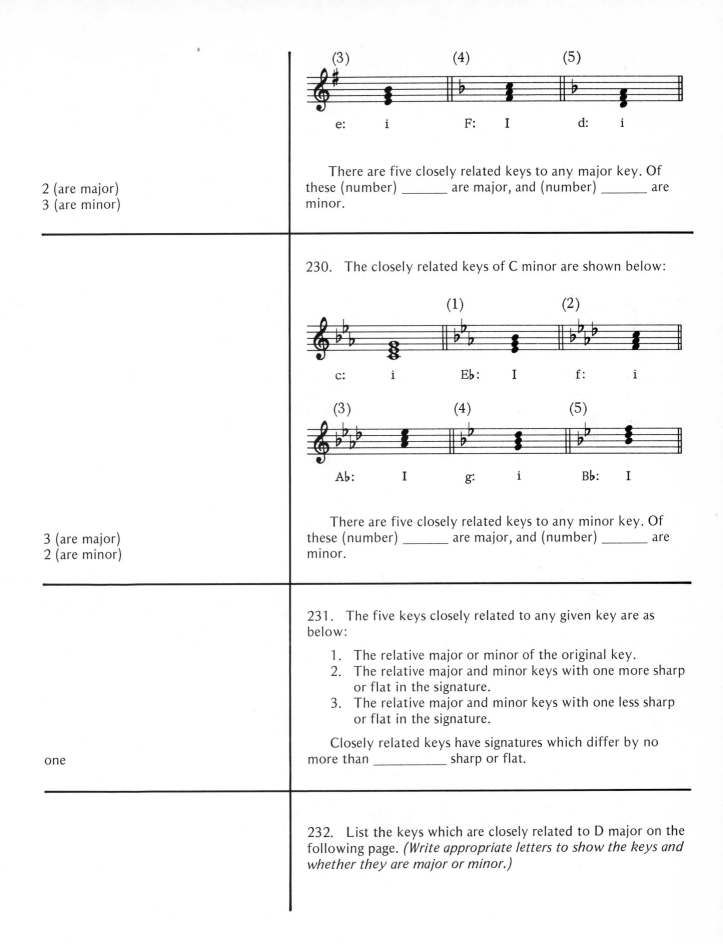

2 (are major)
3 (are minor)

There are five closely related keys to any major key. Of these (number) _____ are major, and (number) _____ are minor.

230. The closely related keys of C minor are shown below:

There are five closely related keys to any minor key. Of these (number) _____ are major, and (number) _____ are minor.

3 (are major)
2 (are minor)

231. The five keys closely related to any given key are as below:

1. The relative major or minor of the original key.
2. The relative major and minor keys with one more sharp or flat in the signature.
3. The relative major and minor keys with one less sharp or flat in the signature.

Closely related keys have signatures which differ by no more than _____ sharp or flat.

one

232. List the keys which are closely related to D major on the following page. *(Write appropriate letters to show the keys and whether they are major or minor.)*

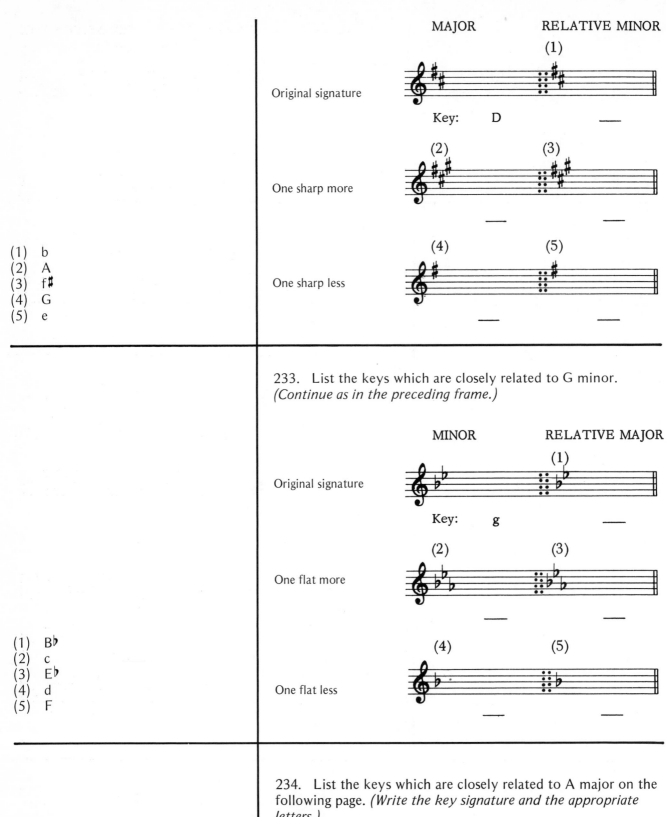

(1) b
(2) A
(3) f♯
(4) G
(5) e

233. List the keys which are closely related to G minor. *(Continue as in the preceding frame.)*

(1) B♭
(2) c
(3) E♭
(4) d
(5) F

234. List the keys which are closely related to A major on the following page. *(Write the key signature and the appropriate letters.)*

235. List the keys which are closely related to F minor. *(Continue as in the preceding frame.)*

236. There is another practical way to identify the five keys which are closely related to a given key: *find the keys of the subdominant and dominant, and the relative keys of these plus that of the tonic.*

	Major	Relative Minor
Original key	C	a
Subdominant key	F	d
Dominant key	G	e

Do the signatures of the keys listed above differ from the original key (C major) by more than one accidental? _____

No.

---

237. Complete the list of keys which are closely related to B-flat major.

M.	R.M.
B♭	g
E♭	c
F	d

	Major	Relative Minor
Original key	B♭	____
Subdominant key	____	____
Dominant key	____	____

---

238. Complete the list of keys which are closely related to E major.

M.	R.M.
E	c♯
A	f♯
B	g♯

	Major	Relative Minor
Original key	E	____
Subdominant key	____	____
Dominant key	____	____

---

239. Complete the list of keys which are closely related to A-flat major.

M.	R.M.
A♭	f
D♭	b♭
E♭	c

	Major	Relative Minor
Original key	A♭	____
Subdominant key	____	____
Dominant key	____	____

---

240. When the original key is minor, the notes of the *pure* minor scale must be used.

	Minor	Relative Major
Original key	c	E♭
Subdominant key	f	A♭
Dominant key	g	B♭

The keys which are closely related to a *minor* key include the subdominant and dominant keys plus the relative *major* keys of the tonic, subdominant, and dominant. In minor keys, the key of the dominant is a (major/minor) _____ key.

minor

241. Complete the list of keys which are closely related to B minor.

			Minor	Relative Major
		Original key	b	____
		Subdominant key	____	____
		Dominant key	____	____

M.   *R.M.*
b   D
e   G
f♯   A

---

242. Complete the list of keys which are closely related to G minor.

			Minor	Relative Major
		Original key	g	____
		Subdominant key	____	____
		Dominant key	____	____

M.   *R.M.*
g   B♭
c   E♭
d   F

---

243. Complete the list of keys which are closely related to E-flat minor.

			Minor	Relative Major
		Original key	e♭	____
		Subdominant key	____	____
		Dominant key	____	____

M.   *R.M.*
e♭   G♭
a♭   C♭
b♭   D♭

---

244. You now have two methods for determining which keys are closely related to a given key. The first of these is to find the relative major or minor of the original key, the relative major and minor keys with one more sharp or flat in the signature, and the relative major and minor keys with one less sharp or flat in the signature.

The second method is to find the keys of the subdominant and dominant, and the relative keys of these plus that of the tonic.

Use whichever method works best for you.

(No response.)

---

245. Which of the keys listed below are NOT closely related to B major? _____

    (1)   C♯ minor
    (2)   D major
    (3)   F♯ major
    (4)   G♯ minor
    (5)   A major

(2) and (5)

(1), (3) and (4).

246. Which of the keys listed below are NOT closely related to F minor? _____

    (1) G minor
    (2) B♭ minor
    (3) C major
    (4) D♭ minor
    (5) E♭ major

---

(2) and (5).

247. Which of the keys listed below are NOT closely related to E-flat major? _____

    (1) C minor
    (2) A♭ minor
    (3) B♭ major
    (4) F minor
    (5) D minor

---

(3) and (5).

248. Which of the keys listed below are NOT closely related to C-sharp minor? _____

    (1) B major
    (2) G♯ minor
    (3) F♯ major
    (4) A major
    (5) C♯ major

---

249. It was brought out in the preceding frame that the key of C-sharp major is *not* a closely related key of C-sharp minor. This is surprising because there is undoubtedly a close affinity between parallel major and minor keys as they have the same structural tones (the first, fourth and fifth scale degrees). One can not even refer to a change of key from C-sharp major to C-sharp minor as a modulation since the tonal center is the same. "Change of mode" is the expression usually used in such cases. Change of mode is an important device in modulation because parallel major and minor keys each have their own set of closely related keys. This fact facilitates modulations to more remote keys as will be seen in Chapter 9.

    Parallel keys have the same key center but are not closely related due to the difference of more than one sharp or flat between their signatures.

(No response.)

---

250. In music of the eighteenth century most modulations are to closely related keys. Such modulations do not seriously threaten the influence of the central tonality. Since modulations to closely related keys are, in fact, modulations to the various

diatonic major and minor triads, they perform on a larger scale the same function as secondary dominants, namely the raising in status of diatonic triads through the process of tonicization.

Modulations to closely related keys even tend to emphasize the structure of tonality. With this in mind, to what degree of the scale would you expect many modulations to be directed? To the _____.

fifth
(See next frame.)

---

251.   Modulations to the fifth scale degree (the dominant) occur frequently in order to emphasize the tonic-dominant axis which is the basis of tonal harmonic structure. This is especially true in major keys. In minor keys, the strong influence of the relative major results in a high proportion of modulations to the mediant.

Modulations result in a weakening of the tonal structure. (True/False) _____

False.
(Not necessarily—they may even strengthen tonal structure.)

---

252.   The tonic triads of closely related keys are all diatonic triads in the original key. (True/False) _____

True.

---

253.   We shall now examine the various means by which modulations are produced. Three basic types of modulation will be presented: PHRASE MODULATION, COMMON CHORD MODULATION, and CHROMATIC MODULATION.

Phrase modulation occurs at the beginning of a new phrase.

Mozart, *Sonata*, K. 331

C: (I)   I   V

Yes.

Are the two keys (as analyzed above) closely related? _____

254.   The ear readily accepts a change of key at the beginning of a phrase because of the pause provided by the cadence. Phrase modulation is shown in the example below. Identify the key of the second phrase and complete the Roman numeral analysis.

Bach, Chorale: *Es ist das Heil uns kommen her*

F: I⁶   V   IV⁶   I   V⁶

ii   V   I

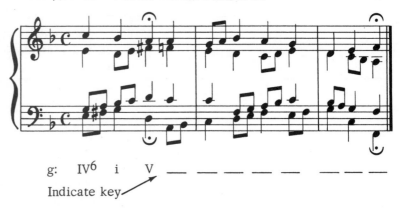

g: IV⁶   i   V __ __ __ __ __
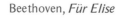
Indicate key

255.   A modulation occurs between the two phrases in the example below. Indicate the key of each phrase and supply the Roman numeral analysis.

Beethoven, *Für Elise*

Poco moto

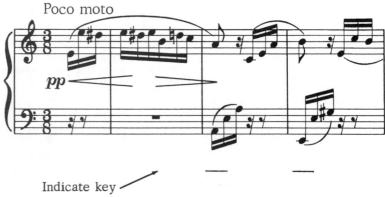

a: i   V

Indicate key __ __ __

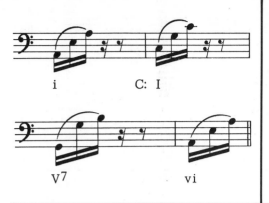

i   C: I

V7   vi

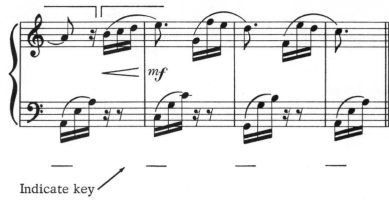

Indicate key

256. Supply the Roman numeral analysis for the example below. *(Remember to indicate the new key at the beginning of the second phrase.)*

Bach, Chorale: *Allein zu dir, Herr Jesu Christ*

d: i   -   V C: IV

V$\frac{4}{2}$ I^6 -   V   I

d: ___ ___ ___ ___

257. Supply the Roman numeral analysis for the example below. *(Remember to indicate the new key at the beginning of the second phrase.)*

Bach, Chorale: *Christe, du Beistand deiner Kreuzgemeine*

d: i   i^6 V^6 i   i^6

V a: i^6 V^6 i   iv^6 i$^6_4$

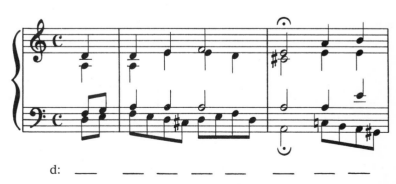

d: ___ ___ ___ ___

ii°⁶₅   V   i

258. Supply the Roman numeral analysis for the example below.

Beethoven, *Sonata*, Op. 10, No. 1

Allegro molto e con brio   ET

Ab:

Ab: V⁴₂   I⁶

V⁴₃   I   f: V⁴₂

i⁶   V⁴₃   i

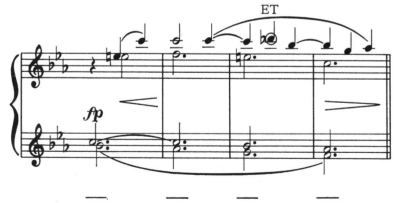

ET

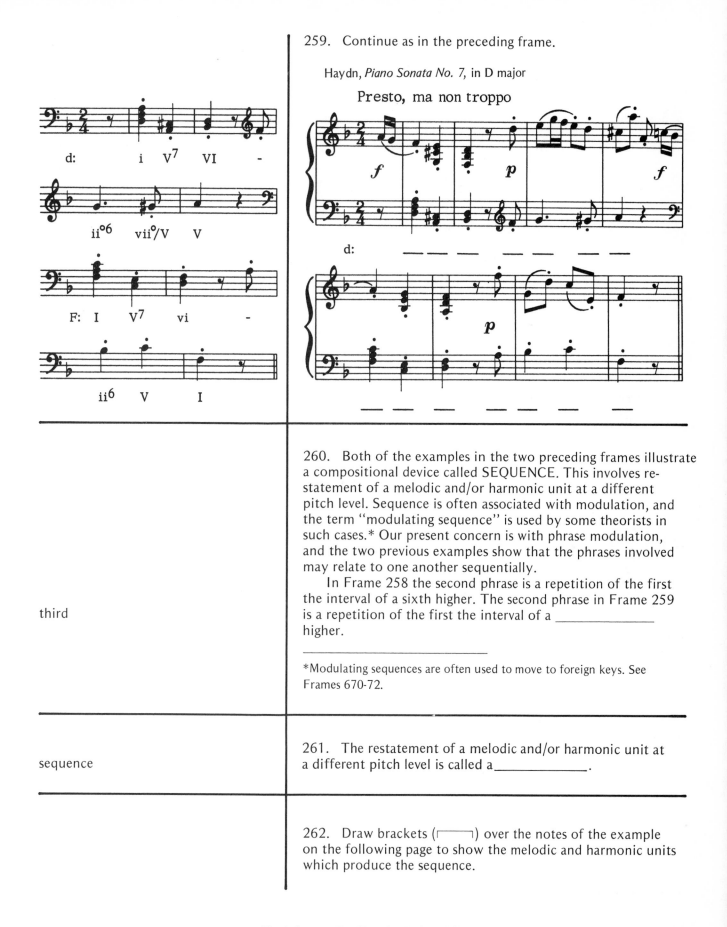

259. Continue as in the preceding frame.

Haydn, *Piano Sonata No. 7,* in D major

Presto, ma non troppo

260. Both of the examples in the two preceding frames illustrate a compositional device called SEQUENCE. This involves restatement of a melodic and/or harmonic unit at a different pitch level. Sequence is often associated with modulation, and the term "modulating sequence" is used by some theorists in such cases.* Our present concern is with phrase modulation, and the two previous examples show that the phrases involved may relate to one another sequentially.

third

In Frame 258 the second phrase is a repetition of the first the interval of a sixth higher. The second phrase in Frame 259 is a repetition of the first the interval of a _____ higher.

*Modulating sequences are often used to move to foreign keys. See Frames 670-72.

sequence

261. The restatement of a melodic and/or harmonic unit at a different pitch level is called a _____.

262. Draw brackets (⌐‾‾¬) over the notes of the example on the following page to show the melodic and harmonic units which produce the sequence.

Modulation To Closely Related Keys

89

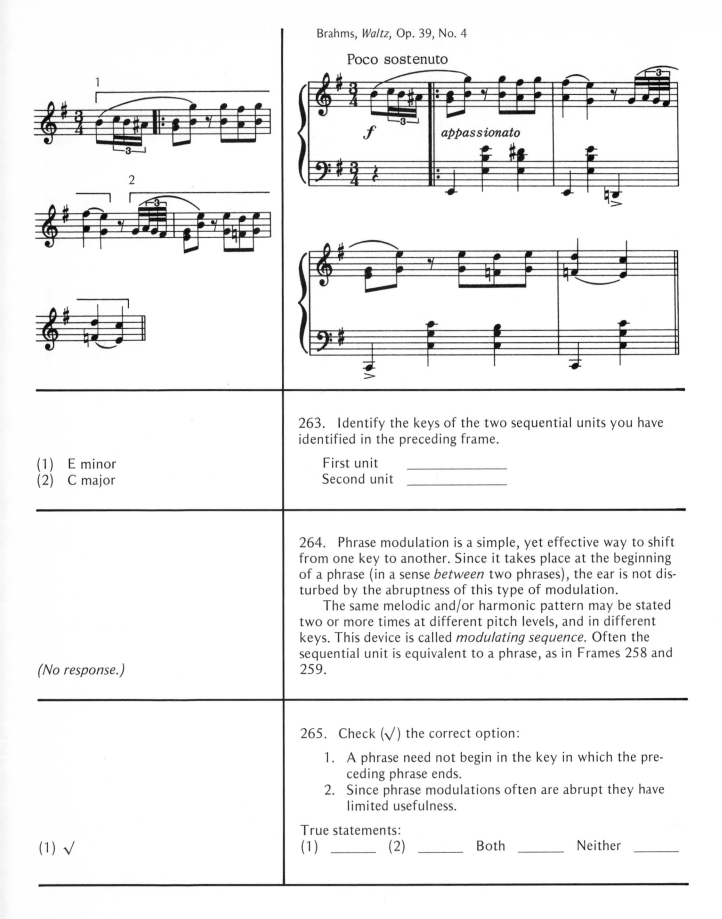

Brahms, *Waltz*, Op. 39, No. 4

Poco sostenuto

f   *appassionato*

(1) E minor
(2) C major

263. Identify the keys of the two sequential units you have identified in the preceding frame.

First unit   _____

Second unit   _____

(No response.)

264. Phrase modulation is a simple, yet effective way to shift from one key to another. Since it takes place at the beginning of a phrase (in a sense *between* two phrases), the ear is not disturbed by the abruptness of this type of modulation.

The same melodic and/or harmonic pattern may be stated two or more times at different pitch levels, and in different keys. This device is called *modulating sequence.* Often the sequential unit is equivalent to a phrase, as in Frames 258 and 259.

(1) √

265. Check (√) the correct option:

1. A phrase need not begin in the key in which the preceding phrase ends.
2. Since phrase modulations often are abrupt they have limited usefulness.

True statements:
(1) _____   (2) _____   Both _____   Neither _____

False.
*(The repetition must be
at a different pitch.)*

266.   The repetition of a melodic and/or harmonic pattern is a device called sequence. (True/False) _____

---

267.   In addition to occurring between phrases, modulations also take place within phrases. In such cases it is often desirable that the ear be led smoothly from one key to another, and one way to accomplish this is by COMMON CHORD MODULATION.

After playing at the piano the example below, supply the Roman numeral analysis to and including the chord at the asterisk. *(Do not go beyond this chord.)*

Bach, Chorale: *Jesu Leiden, Pein und Tod*

A: ___ ___ ___ ___ ___ ___

A: I   V   I⁶   V   I

No.

268.   Referring again to the example in the preceding frame, is the chord immediately following the one at the asterisk (BD♯F♯) a diatonic chord in the key of A major? _____

E

269.   The final two chords in Frame 267 produce an authentic cadence in the key of _____ major.

Yes.

270.   In Frame 267, the chord at the asterisk is a tonic triad (I) in the key of A major. Is this chord also a diatonic chord in the key of E major? _____

IV

271.   What Roman numeral is used to analyze this chord (AC♯E) in the key of E major? _____

272. Since the chord at the asterisk in Frame 267 (and below) is diatonic in both A major and E major, it is called a COMMON CHORD.*

Complete the analysis by supplying the proper Roman numerals *in the key of E major.*

Bach, Chorale: *Jesu Leiden, Pein und Tod*

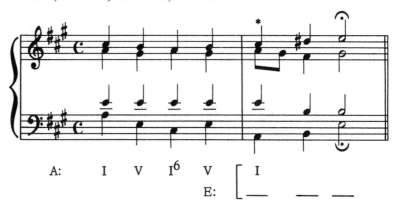

A: I   V   I⁶   V   [I
E: [___ ___ ___

_____

*The term *pivot* chord is sometimes used.

A: [I
E: [IV   V   I

---

common chord

273. Notice in the preceding frame that the common chord (at the asterisk) is analyzed twice, in both the "old" key of A major, and the "new" key of E major. The two Roman numerals are bracketed ([ ) to show the multiple function of the common chord, and the analysis continues at a different level as a visual representation of the "new" key.

A chord which is diatonic in two keys is called a _____ _____.

C: I   I⁶   I   IV   V$^4_2$ I⁶

274. We shall analyze with Roman numerals the phrase below. *(Follow instructions carefully.)*

Start with the first chord and proceed until you reach a chord which is NOT diatonic in the key of C major; *do not analyze this chord or any which follow.*

Bach, Chorale: *Ach Gott, wie manches Herzeleid*

C:

G major *(The phrase ends with a half cadence.)*	275. Now determine the key in which the phrase in the preceding frame ends. This example modulates from the key of C major to the key of _____.
Yes.	276. The last chord analyzed in Frame 274 is the tonic triad (I) in C major. Is this chord (CEG) diatonic in the key of G major? _____
common chord	277. Since the chord CEG is diatonic in both C major and G major, it is called a _____ _____.

278. Now complete the Roman numeral analysis. *(Observe the form established in Frame 272.)*

Bach, Chorale: *Ach Gott, wie manches Herzeleid*

279. The example below contains a common chord modulation. Supply the Roman numeral analysis by applying the methods presented in the preceding frames.

Bach, Chorale: *Wer nur den lieben Gott lässt*

280. Supply the Roman numeral analysis for the example below:

Mozart, *Sonata*, K. 284

D:

D:

A: vi⁶ / ii⁶ → I⁶

V⁷

I ii⁶ I⁶₄ V⁷ I

---

281. We shall pause now to make a few general observations regarding common chord modulation. It should be clear from the examples presented thus far that it is the dominant chord (in the new key) which propels the music out of the originally established key. The leading tone triad or seventh chord, of course, accomplishes the same purpose. The common chord provides a stepping-stone to the dominant, and is usually the first chord preceding it. Thus, as a rule, *the common chord immediately precedes the first chord encountered which is not diatonic in the old key.*

Which chord actually produces a modulation, the common chord or the dominant which follows? The _____.

dominant

---

282. Another point which has an influence on the selection of an appropriate common chord is the fact that since the common chord usually precedes a dominant chord, it is likely to be either a subdominant or supertonic chord (in the new key). Other possibilities include the tonic or submediant chords. Is this principle borne out by all of the examples of common chord modulation presented thus far (Frames 272, 278, 279, 280)? _____

Yes.

283.   The chords which are common to the key of C major and each of its closely related keys are shown below. Only the chords which occur in harmonic minor are shown here, but the chords derived from melodic minor are also available. These chords increase the number of common chords where minor keys are concerned.

In a common chord modulation, the common chord often is either a subdominant or supertonic chord in the NEW key. According to the chart above, there are two keys in which neither the subdominant nor supertonic chord is available. Name these keys. _____

F major; D minor.

DFA
(C: ii=d: i)

284. If neither the subdominant nor the supertonic chord (in the key to which a modulation is to be made) is available as a common chord, the tonic or submediant chords in the new key are acceptable. Actually, any chord which is common to two keys may be used in a common chord modulation, but it is desirable that your attention be directed first to the more useful possibilities.

Spell the chord which would *most likely* be used in a common chord modulation from C major to D minor. _____

---

285. On the lower staff write all of the triads which are common to the keys of D-flat and A-flat major. Indicate also the appropriate Roman numerals.

Db: I   ii   iii   IV   V   vi   vii°

Ab:

(left-frame answer:)

Ab: IV   vi   I   ii

Db FAb
(Db: I=Ab : IV)
Bb Db F
(Db :vi=Ab :ii)

286. Which two chords are common to the keys of D-flat and A-flat major (as identified in the preceding frame) would *most likely* be used as a common chord in a modulation? _____ _____

---

287. On the lower staff write all of the triads which are common to the keys of A major and C-sharp (harmonic) minor. Supply also the appropriate Roman numerals.

A: I   ii   iii   IV   V   vi   vii°

c#:

(left-frame answer:)

c#:   VI   i   iv

F♯AC♯
(A: vi=c♯:iv)

---

288. Spell the chord which would most likely be used as a common chord in modulating from the key of A major to C-sharp minor. _____

---

289. On the lower staff write all of the triads which are common to the keys of F major and G (harmonic) minor. Supply also the appropriate Roman numerals.

F: I   ii   iii   IV   V   vi   vii°

g:

g: i

GB♭D
(F:ii=g:i)

---

290. Spell the chord which would most likely be used as a common chord in modulating from the key of F major to G minor. _____

(c).
(E♭:vi=g:iv)
(See next frame.)

---

291. Which chord below would most likely be used as a common chord in modulating from the key of E-flat major to G minor? _____

(a)   (b)   (c)   (d)

(No response.)

---

292. Both (a) and (d) in the preceding frame are common chords, but do not lead to the dominant in G minor as effectively as the subdominant. Choice (b) is not appropriate at this time because this chord is not a diatonic chord in the original key of E-flat major.

(b).
(B: vi=F♯:ii)

---

293. Which chord on the following page would most likely be used as a common chord in modulating from the key of B major to F-sharp major? _____

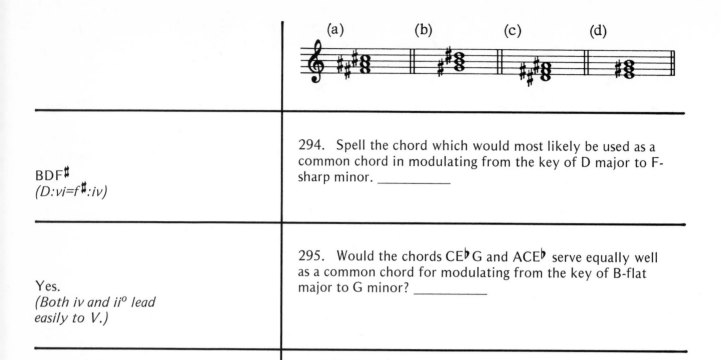

BDF♯ *(D:vi=f♯:iv)*	**294.** Spell the chord which would most likely be used as a common chord in modulating from the key of D major to F-sharp minor. _____
Yes. *(Both iv and ii° lead easily to V.)*	**295.** Would the chords CE♭G and ACE♭ serve equally well as a common chord for modulating from the key of B-flat major to G minor? _____
	296. The chords which are common to the key of C minor (harmonic form) and each of its closely related keys are shown below: 

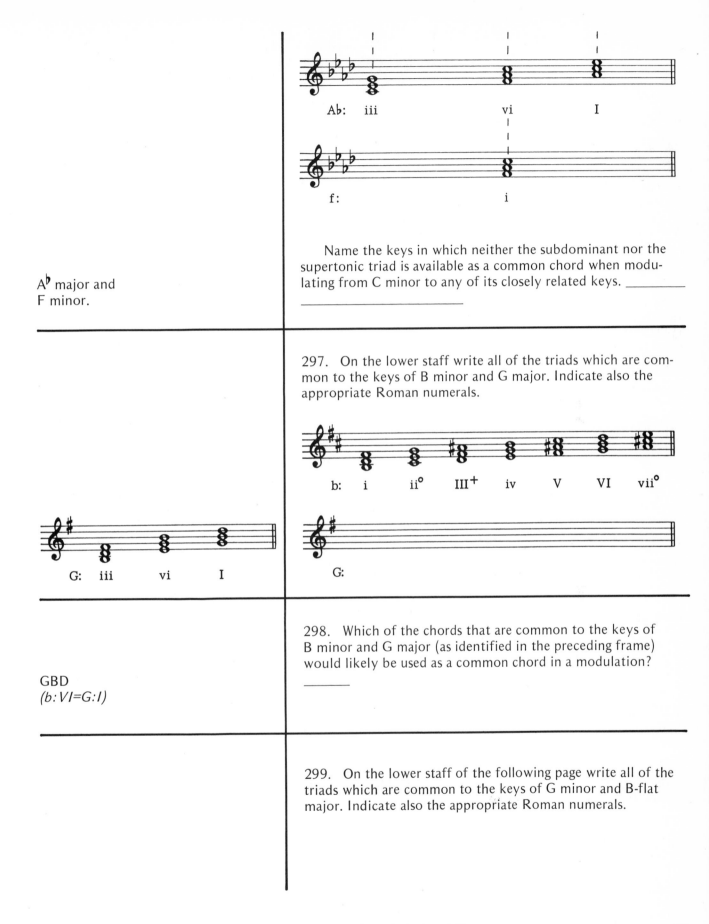

Ab: iii   vi   I

f: i

Name the keys in which neither the subdominant nor the supertonic triad is available as a common chord when modulating from C minor to any of its closely related keys. _____
_____

Ab major and
F minor.

297. On the lower staff write all of the triads which are common to the keys of B minor and G major. Indicate also the appropriate Roman numerals.

b: i   ii°   III⁺   iv   V   VI   vii°

G:

G: iii   vi   I

298. Which of the chords that are common to the keys of B minor and G major (as identified in the preceding frame) would likely be used as a common chord in a modulation?
_____

GBD
(b:VI=G:I)

299. On the lower staff of the following page write all of the triads which are common to the keys of G minor and B-flat major. Indicate also the appropriate Roman numerals.

g: i   ii°   III⁺   iv   V   VI   vii°

B♭:

B♭: vi vii° ii IV

CE♭G
(g:iv=B♭:ii)
E♭GB♭
(g: VI=B♭:IV)

300. Which two chords that are common to the keys of G minor and B-flat major (as identified in the preceding frame) would most likely be used as a common chord in a modulation? _____ _____

(b).
(f:iv=b♭:i)

301. Which chord below would most likely be used as a common chord in modulating from the key of F minor to B-flat minor? _____

(a)   (b)   (c)   (d)

(d).
(c♯:i=g♯:iv)

302. Which chord below would most likely be used as a common chord in modulating from the key of C-sharp minor to G-sharp minor? _____

(a)   (b)   (c)   (d)

EGB
(e:i=D:ii)

303. Spell the chord which would most likely be used as a common chord in modulating from the key of E minor to D major. _____

GB♭ D
(d:iv=F:ii)
B♭ DF
(d:VI=F:IV)

304. Spell the two chords which would most likely be used as a common chord in modulating from the key of D minor to F major. _____ and _____

---

305. To this point, in order to reduce the number of choices, chords have been limited to those which are derived from the harmonic minor scale. The melodic minor scale produces additional chords which may be used as common chords. On the lower staff write all of the triads which are common to the keys of C minor and G minor and supply the appropriate Roman numeral for each. *(Include all of the triads derived from the G melodic minor scale. There are seven common chords; try to find all of them.)*

(Triads derived from the C melodic minor scale.)

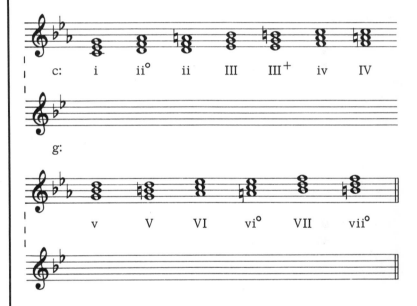

c: i   ii°   ii   III   III$^+$ iv   IV

g:

v   V   VI   vi°   VII   vii°

g: iv   v   VI   VII   i   ii°   III

---

306. The preceding frame shows that the melodic minor scale produces a large number of diatonic triads, which increases greatly the number of possible common chords (especially when both keys involved are minor keys). Although any chord which is common to two keys may serve as a common chord, those most often exploited are the subdominant or supertonic chords in the new key. If neither of these is available, either the tonic or submediant may be used. Most common chord modulations involve one of these chords; but you must be alert for other, less usual, practices. In any case, regardless of what chord is used, common chord modulations

(No response.)

F: I   IV   I   V

vi ⌈vii°⁶₅
d: ⌊ii°⁶₅   V   i

G: I   I   V⁶   I

⌈IV⁶
C:⌊I⁶   IV   V   I

produce a relatively smooth transition from one key to another. The common chord itself, since it functions in both keys, serves as a bridge between them.

307. Write the alto and tenor voices and supply the Roman numeral analysis.

Bach, Chorale: *Herr Christ, der ein'ge Gott's-Sohn*

F:

308. Write the alto and tenor voices and supply the Roman numeral analysis.

Bach Chorale: *Uns ist ein Kindlein heut' gebor'n*

G:

g: V
Bb: [i vi V6 I]

vi ii⁶₅ V I

309. Complete the alto and tenor voices and supply the Roman numeral analysis.

Bach, Chorale: *Auf meinen lieben Gott*

```
#    3  6  5  5  -  5  -  6  8  7
     3  3  -  3  -  3  -     5
     3  -  3  3
```

g:

310. Supply the Roman numeral analysis.

Brahms, *Waltz,* Op. 39, No. 15

(p)

Ab:

Ab: I vi I

vi I [iii⁶
c: [i⁶ V⁷]

i

F: I   vii°⁶   ⌈I⁶

C: ⌊IV⁶ V⁶

I   V⁷   I

311. Supply the Roman numeral analysis.

Beethoven, *Sonata*, Op. 2, No. 3

F:

312. Supply the Roman numeral analysis. *(In the second measure analyze a chord at each of the two asterisks.)*

D. Scarlatti, *Sonata*, in G minor

g:

g: i V V⁽⁷⁾ i - ⌈i⁶

F: ⌊ii⁶ vii°⁶₅

I⁶ ii⁷ V⁴₃ I - I⁶

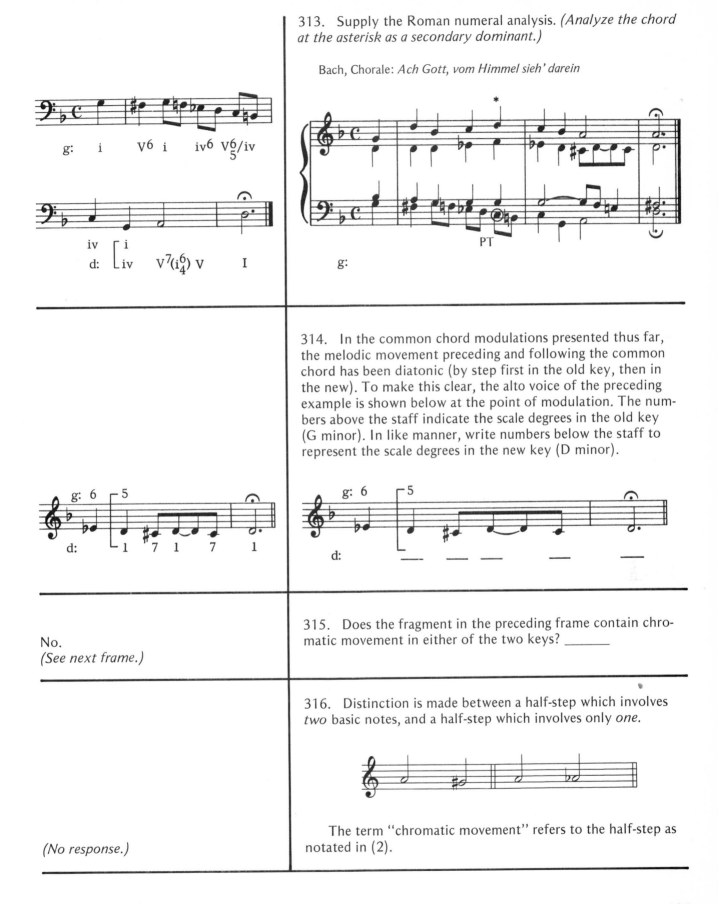

313. Supply the Roman numeral analysis. *(Analyze the chord at the asterisk as a secondary dominant.)*

Bach, Chorale: *Ach Gott, vom Himmel sieh' darein*

g: i   V⁶ i   iv⁶ V⁶₅/iv

iv ⌈ i
d: ⌊iv   V⁷(i⁶₄) V   I

g:

---

314. In the common chord modulations presented thus far, the melodic movement preceding and following the common chord has been diatonic (by step first in the old key, then in the new). To make this clear, the alto voice of the preceding example is shown below at the point of modulation. The numbers above the staff indicate the scale degrees in the old key (G minor). In like manner, write numbers below the staff to represent the scale degrees in the new key (D minor).

g: 6 ⌐5
d: ⌊1 7 1 7 1

g: 6 ⌐5
d: ⌊___ ___ ___ ___ ___

No.
(See next frame.)

315. Does the fragment in the preceding frame contain chromatic movement in either of the two keys? _____

(No response.)

316. Distinction is made between a half-step which involves *two* basic notes, and a half-step which involves only *one*.

The term "chromatic movement" refers to the half-step as notated in (2).

Yes.

317. A modulation which involves diatonic melodic movement in all voices, and in which the common chord is diatonic (not altered) in both the old and the new keys, is called a DIATONIC MODULATION. Stated simply, a diatonic modulation makes use only of tonal material which is diatonic—first in the old key, then in the new.

Does the modulation below qualify as a diatonic modulation? _____

Beethoven, *Quartet*, Op. 18, No. 3

No.
(See next Frame.)

318. One of the features of a diatonic modulation is the absence of chromatic movement in any of the voices immediately preceding and following the common chord. With this in mind, does the modulation from the key of F major to G minor in the phrase below qualify as a diatonic modulation? _____

Bach, Chorale: *O Ewigkeit, du Donnerwort*

319. We shall look closely at the example in the preceding frame. The chromatic movement in the bass at chord 3 (E-E♭) prevents the modulation from being diatonic. The change of key occurs suddenly, and the chromatic movement is the most striking feature.

(Play this example at the piano, and listen carefully to the effect of the modulation.)

(You may have chosen 2, 3, or 4. Continue with the next frame for explanation.)

Indicate (by number) the first chord you feel functions more strongly in the new key (G minor) than in the old (F major)._____

---

320.   You may have had difficulty deciding between chords 2, 3, and 4 in answering the question posed in the preceding frame. Chord 2 is actually a common chord (F: vii°=g: vi°), but its function in F major as a leading tone triad is stronger than its function in G minor as a submediant triad on the raised sixth degree. The problem, remember, was to identify the first chord which functions *more strongly* in the new key than the old.

Whereas chord 4 (B♭DF♯) clearly functions as III⁺ in G minor, chord 3 (ACE♭G) could be heard as either ii°⁷ in G minor or vii°⁷/IV in F major. *The choice between these two chords is based on aural impression.* Does the ear anticipate resolution of chord 3 in one key more strongly than the other, and if so, which key? There is no absolute answer to this question; but since the supertonic seventh chord occurs so frequently in key-defining cadence patterns—much more frequently than does the vii°⁷/IV—most of you probably hear the third chord in Frame 318 as ii°⁷ in G minor. Thus, it is Chord 3 which first asserts the new key.

(No response.)

---

321.   Care has been taken to identify the first chord in Frame 318 which functions in the new key to show that it coincides with the chromatic movement. Although chord 2 is a common chord, its function in the new key is weak, and *it is the chromatic bass line which actually pulls the ear away from the old key.* For these reasons the common chord is ignored, and the process is called a CHROMATIC MODULATION.

A modulation in which not all voices move diatonically is often called a _____ modulation.

chromatic

---

322.   On the following page, the harmonic analysis is shown to the point of modulation. Supply the remaining chord symbols.

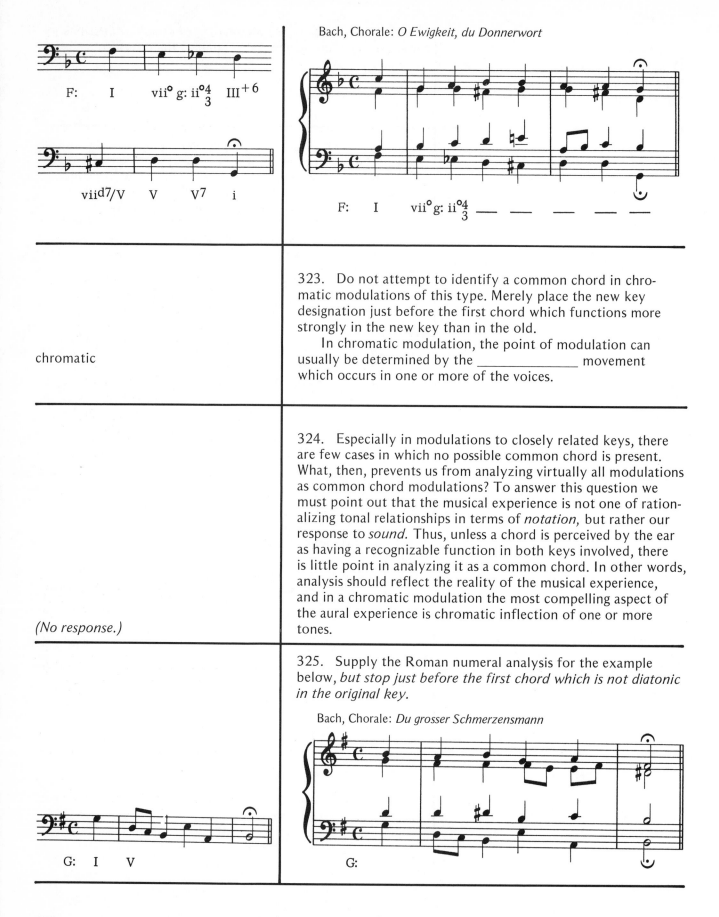

Bach, Chorale: *O Ewigkeit, du Donnerwort*

F: I   vii° g: ii°$^4_3$ III^{+6}

vii^{d7}/V   V   V^7 i

F: I   vii° g: ii°$^4_3$ _____ _____ _____ _____ _____

---

323. Do not attempt to identify a common chord in chromatic modulations of this type. Merely place the new key designation just before the first chord which functions more strongly in the new key than in the old.

In chromatic modulation, the point of modulation can usually be determined by the _____ movement which occurs in one or more of the voices.

chromatic

---

324. Especially in modulations to closely related keys, there are few cases in which no possible common chord is present. What, then, prevents us from analyzing virtually all modulations as common chord modulations? To answer this question we must point out that the musical experience is not one of rationalizing tonal relationships in terms of *notation*, but rather our response to *sound*. Thus, unless a chord is perceived by the ear as having a recognizable function in both keys involved, there is little point in analyzing it as a common chord. In other words, analysis should reflect the reality of the musical experience, and in a chromatic modulation the most compelling aspect of the aural experience is chromatic inflection of one or more tones.

(No response.)

---

325. Supply the Roman numeral analysis for the example below, *but stop just before the first chord which is not diatonic in the original key.*

Bach, Chorale: *Du grosser Schmerzensmann*

G: I   V

G:

E minor

---

326. The example in the preceding frame begins in the key of G major, but ends with a half cadence in the key of _____ _____.

Yes.
(See next frame.)

327. Refer again to the example in Frame 325. The last chord which could be analyzed as diatonic in the key of G major is the dominant (DF♯A). Can this chord be analyzed in the key of E minor? _____

---

328. The chord DF♯A is the dominant triad in the key of G major and the subtonic triad (VII) in the key of E minor. Thus, there actually is a common chord in the example of Frame 325. In spite of this, however, we shall call this progression a chromatic modulation. Here are the reasons: First of all, while the chord DF♯A has a strong function in the key of G major, its function in E minor is very weak; secondly, the chromatic movement in the tenor voice (D-D♯) is the feature which actually thrusts the music into the new key. Chromatic movement, then, is often the most compelling reason for deciding in favor of a chromatic modulation. So, we shall ignore the common chord for the two reasons stated above.
Complete the analysis.

Bach, Chorale: *Du grosser Schmerzensmann*

G: I   V   e:V   i   iv   V

G: I   V   e: __ __   __   __

329. Supply the Roman numeral analysis on the following page. *(Analyze the chord at the asterisk as a secondary dominant.)*

G: I   V⁶ V₂⁴/IV IV⁶ a:V₂⁴

i⁶   VI   iv   V⁷   i

Bach, Chorale: *Allein Gott in der Höh' sei Ehr'*

G:

Bb: I   ii⁶₅   V   g:V⁶   i

ii°⁶   i⁶₄   V   I

330.   Supply the Roman numeral analysis.

Bach, Chorale: *Das neugeborne Kindelein*

Bb:

---

331.   Supply the Roman numeral analysis.

Schubert, *Waltz*, Op. 27, No. 12

g:

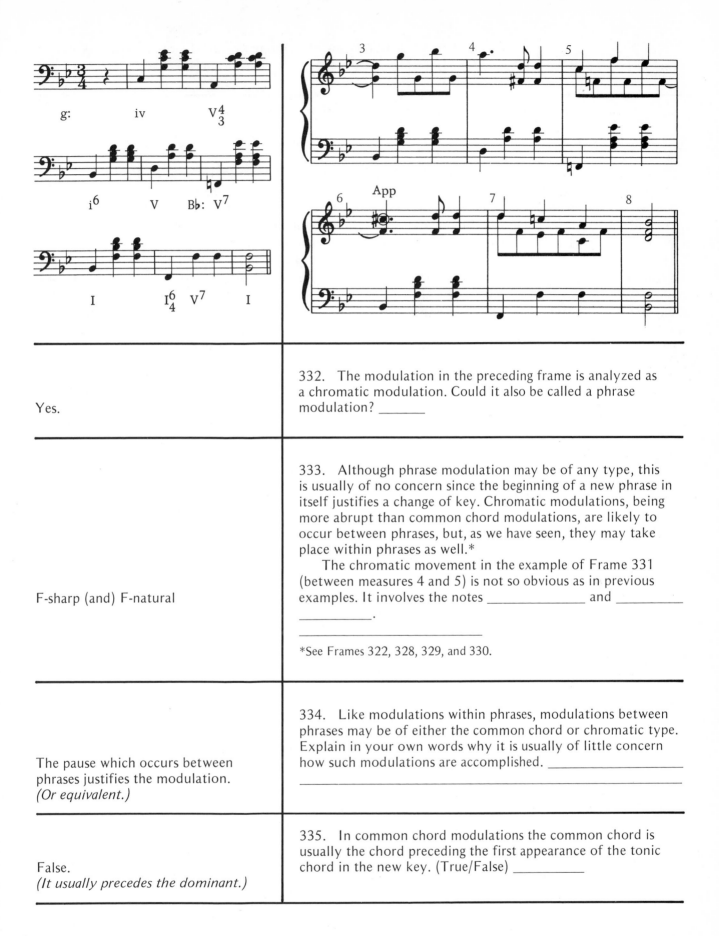

g: iv   V$\frac{4}{3}$

i^6 V   Bb: V^7

I   I$^6_4$ V^7 I

Yes.

332. The modulation in the preceding frame is analyzed as a chromatic modulation. Could it also be called a phrase modulation? _____

F-sharp (and) F-natural

333. Although phrase modulation may be of any type, this is usually of no concern since the beginning of a new phrase in itself justifies a change of key. Chromatic modulations, being more abrupt than common chord modulations, are likely to occur between phrases, but, as we have seen, they may take place within phrases as well.*

The chromatic movement in the example of Frame 331 (between measures 4 and 5) is not so obvious as in previous examples. It involves the notes _____ and _____ _____.

_____

*See Frames 322, 328, 329, and 330.

The pause which occurs between phrases justifies the modulation. (Or equivalent.)

334. Like modulations within phrases, modulations between phrases may be of either the common chord or chromatic type. Explain in your own words why it is usually of little concern how such modulations are accomplished. _____ _____

False.
(It usually precedes the dominant.)

335. In common chord modulations the common chord is usually the chord preceding the first appearance of the tonic chord in the new key. (True/False) _____

True.

336. In the case of a chromatic modulation, no attempt need be made to locate a common chord. (True/False) _____

SUMMARY.

The term phrase modulation does not refer to a *process,* but to the fact that the modulation occurs between phrases. The ear readily accepts a change of key at such points because of the momentary pause produced by structural divisions of music. The two actual processes presented in this chapter are common chord and chromatic modulation. Of these, common chord modulation ordinarily achieves smoother transition to a new key because of the "pivot" chord which functions simultaneously in both keys.

Diatonic common chord modulation results in diatonic melodic movement in all voices both preceding and following the common chord. Chromatic modulation, on the other hand, involves chromatic movement in one or more voices. This causes the new key to appear more suddenly than in the case of common chord modulation. Hardly a modulation can be written in which some kind of common chord does not exist. But if the common chord's harmonic function is weak in one or both of the keys, chromatic movement— often the most distinctive aural feature—causes the modulation to be classed as chromatic.

5   Borrowed Chords

Harmonic resources are expanded by exchanging diatonic chords between parallel major and minor keys. Chords which normally belong in one key but are used in a parallel key are called borrowed chords. Due to the alternate sixth and seventh degrees of the melodic minor scale, there are more diatonic chords available in minor keys than in major. Thus, most borrowed chords occur in major keys to supplement the comparatively limited array of chords provided by the major scale.

G♭ B♭ D♭ F

337.   The fourth chord in the example below is an altered chord. Spell this chord. _____

Bach, Chorale: *Christus, der ist mein Leben*

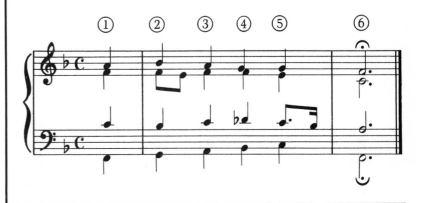

ii°⁶₅

338.   Although the chord GB♭ D♭ F is an *altered* chord in the key of F major, it is a *diatonic* chord in the key of F minor. Write the Roman numeral which is appropriate for this chord in F minor.

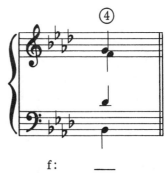

f: ____

339. Now supply the complete Roman numeral analysis using the symbol for the altered chord (4) which is appropriate for the key of F minor.

Bach, Chorale: *Christus, der ist mein Leben*

F: I vii°⁶ I⁶ ii°⁶₅ V I

F: — — — — — —

---

340. In the preceding frame the supertonic seventh chord (GB♭D♭F) is a diatonic chord in F minor. Used in F major it is called a BORROWED CHORD.

Most borrowed chords occur in major keys; they are "borrowed" from parallel _____ keys.

minor

---

341. The exchange of diatonic chords between parallel major and minor keys through the use of borrowed chords is sometimes called MODAL MIXTURE.

Most borrowed chords occur in major since the major scale provides considerably less tonal variety than the minor scale.

Select from the chords below those which are *borrowed chords* in the key of F major. (*Remember that while altered in one key, borrowed chords are diatonic in the parallel key.*)

(List by number.) _____

(2), (3), and (5).
(See next frame.)

KEY OF F MAJOR

secondary dominants

342. All of the chords in the preceding frame are altered chords in the key of F major, but only (2), (3), and (5) are borrowed chords. The remainder are all examples of another type of altered chord. These are called _____ _____.

---

343. The most common borrowed chords in major are shown below:

(a)   (b)   (c)   (d)   (e)

F: ii°   ii°7   iv   ♭VI   viid7

diminished

The symbols reflect the quality of the chords. In (d), the flat placed at the lower left-hand corner of the Roman numeral indicates that the *root* of the chord is flatted (it is a half-step lower than in its unaltered form). In (e), the symbol shows that the chord is a _____ seventh chord.

---

344. When a chord is built on an altered tone, the actual accidental used is included as part of the chord symbol.

(a)   (b)   (c)

A: ♮VI   B♭:   ♭VI   C: ♭III⁺

root

An accidental placed at the lower left-hand corner of a Roman numeral refers to the _____ of the chord.

---

345. Some of the diatonic triads and seventh chords in the key of B minor are shown in the example below. Select from these chords those which most likely would occur as *borrowed chords* in the key of B major. (You may refer to Frame 343. Also, take care not to include chords which are *diatonic* in both keys.)

(2), (3), (6), (10), and (12).

List by number. _____

(1)   (2)   (3)   (4)   (5)   (6)

b: i   ii°   ii°7   III   III⁺   iv

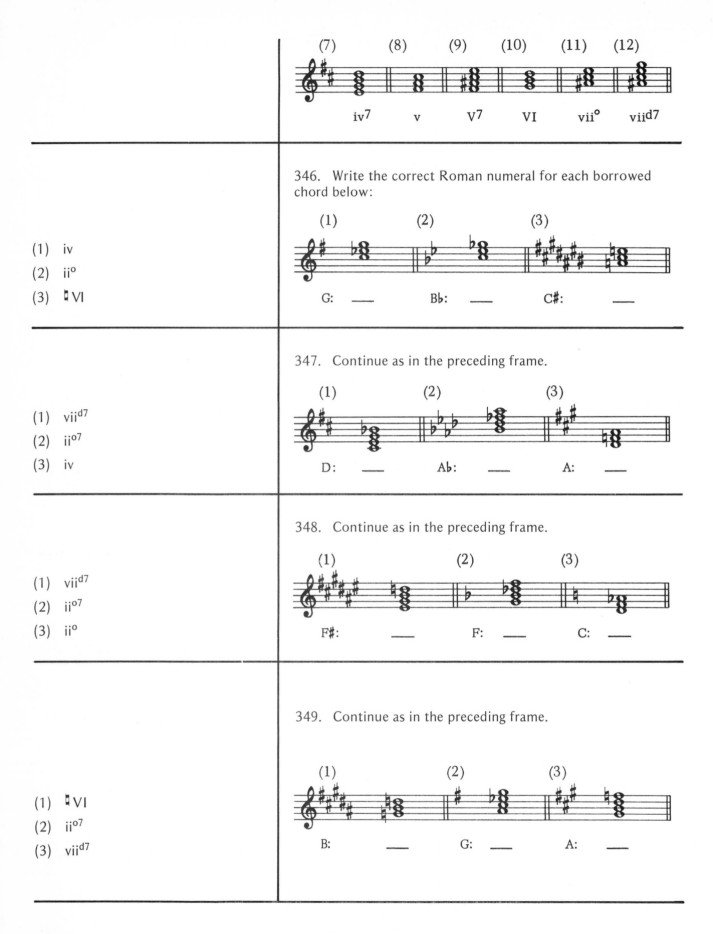

(7)   (8)   (9)   (10)   (11)   (12)

iv⁷   v   V⁷   VI   vii°   viid⁷

346. Write the correct Roman numeral for each borrowed chord below:

(1)   (2)   (3)

G: ____   B♭: ____   C♯: ____

(1) iv
(2) ii°
(3) ♮VI

347. Continue as in the preceding frame.

(1)   (2)   (3)

D: ____   A♭: ____   A: ____

(1) vii^{d7}
(2) ii^{o7}
(3) iv

348. Continue as in the preceding frame.

(1)   (2)   (3)

F♯: ____   F: ____   C: ____

(1) vii^{d7}
(2) ii^{o7}
(3) ii°

349. Continue as in the preceding frame.

(1)   (2)   (3)

B: ____   G: ____   A: ____

(1) ♮VI
(2) ii^{o7}
(3) vii^{d7}

350. Continue as in the preceding frame.

(1) ♭VI

(2) ii°

(3) iv

(1)   (2)   (3)

E♭: ___   E: ___   B♭: ___

351. Write on the staff the chords indicated by the Roman numerals.

(1)   (2)   (3)

(1)   (2)   (3)

F: ii°   D: ♭VI   G: viid7

352. Continue as in the preceding frame.

(1)   (2)   (3)

(1)   (2)   (3)

E♭: ii°7   A♭: iv   A: ii°7

353. Continue as in the preceding frame.

(1)   (2)   (3)

(1)   (2)   (3)

F: viid7   B♭: ♭VI   G: ii°

354. Most diatonic chords in a major key are available in the parallel minor as a result of the raised sixth and seventh degrees of the melodic minor scale. One exception is the major tonic triad. When this chord occurs at a cadence, the raised third is called the *"Picardy third."* The major quality of this chord is indicated by the large Roman numeral.

borrowed

The major tonic is the chief _____ chord which appears in a minor key.

(No response.)

355. Two other possible borrowed chords in minor are shown below:

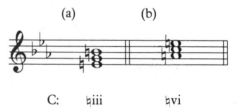

These chords are little used, but are available if an extreme mixture of modality is desired.

(No response.)

356. Borrowed chords are used primarily to introduce greater tonal variety into major keys. Few occur in minor due to the greater tonal resources of the melodic minor scale. The most common borrowed chord in minor is the major tonic. This chord occurs most frequently at the cadence where the major quality is often preferred to the minor. The third of this chord is called the *Picardy third.*

The most common borrowed chords in major are the diminished supertonic, the diminished-minor supertonic seventh chord, the minor subdominant, the major submediant (on the lowered sixth scale degree), and the diminished seventh chord on the leading tone.

The use of borrowed chords results in an exchange in quality between major and minor which is referred to as *modal mixture.*

357. Supply the Roman numeral analysis for the example below. *(Analyze the chord at the asterisk as a secondary dominant.)*

Bach, Chorale: *Herzliebster Jesu, was hast du verbrochen*

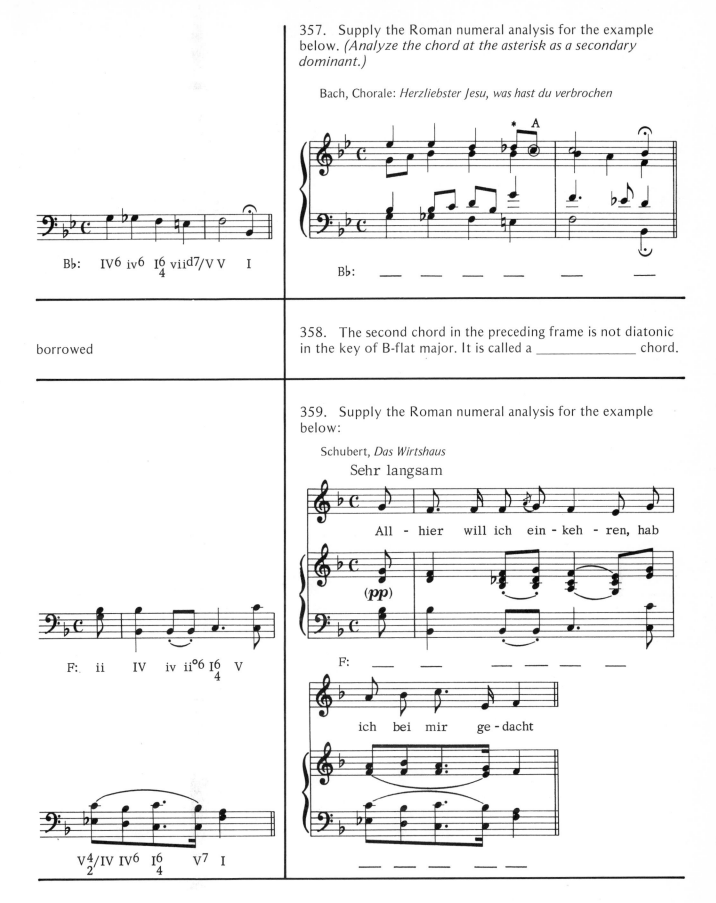

Bb: IV6 iv6 I6/4 viid7/V V   I

Bb: __ __ __ __ __ __

---

borrowed

358. The second chord in the preceding frame is not diatonic in the key of B-flat major. It is called a _____ chord.

---

359. Supply the Roman numeral analysis for the example below:

Schubert, *Das Wirtshaus*

Sehr langsam

F: ii   IV   iv   ii°6   I6/4   V

V4/2/IV   IV6   I6/4   V7   I

F: __ __ __ __ __ __

All - hier   will ich   ein - keh - ren, hab

ich bei mir   ge - dacht

__ __ __ __ __

360. Complete the Roman numeral analysis for the example below:

Mozart, *Sonata*, K. 330

C: V⁷/V   V⁴₃   I   i

ii°⁶₅   –   V⁶₅/V   –

V   –   V⁷   I⁶₄

Allegro moderato

(*p*)

C: V⁷/V ___   ___   ___

NT   PT   S

PT

___   –   ___   –   ___

361. Supply the Roman numeral analysis for the example below:

Schubert, *Symphony No. 5*, in B-flat major

Andante con moto

App

f   *p*

E♭:   ___   ___   ___

E♭:   I⁶₄   V   ♭VI

Deceptive.

362. What type of cadence is illustrated in the preceding frame? _____

363. The altered submediant triad (♭VI) produces an especially colorful effect when used in a deceptive cadence. Another example is shown below:

Bach, Chorale: *Vater unser im Himmelreich*

F: V⁶   I   vi   ii⁶₅ V ♭VI

Why is it necessary to double the third in the altered submediant triad (at the asterisk)? _____

_____

To avoid an augmented 2nd (E-D♭) in the alto.

364. The borrowed submediant and subdominant triads produce colorful effects in the example below:

Brahms, *Symphony No. 3*, Op. 90

C:

C: I   ♭VI   I   ♭VI

iv   I   I   I

Supply the Roman numeral analysis for the above example.

365. Supply the Roman numeral analysis for the example below:

Brahms, *Ballade*, Op. 10, No. 4

Andante con moto

B: _____ _____ _____

B: I   vii°7   I   vii°7
                                4
                                3

I6 V6 I   IV6 ii7 I6
    4

I6   V7   I
4

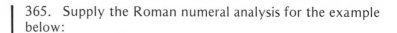

366. Complete the Roman numeral analysis for the example below:

Chopin, *Ballade*, Op. 52

Andante con moto

Ab: I   vii°7

I   vii°7

Ab: _____ _____ _____ _____

Chapter 5

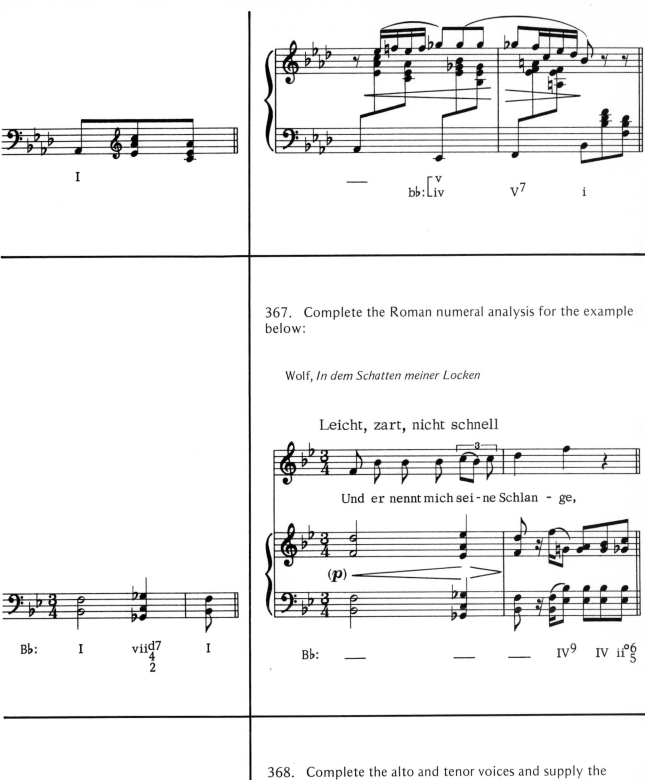

367. Complete the Roman numeral analysis for the example below:

Wolf, *In dem Schatten meiner Locken*

368. Complete the alto and tenor voices and supply the Roman numeral analysis on the following page. *(Analyze two chords at the asterisk.)*

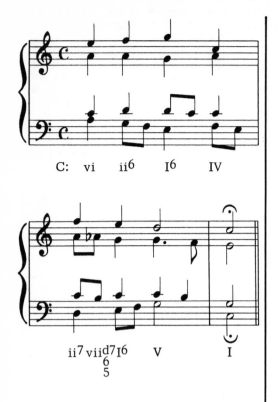

C: vi ii⁶ I⁶ IV

ii⁷ viiᵈ⁷I⁶ V I
    ⁶
    ⁵

Bach, Chorale: *Herr, ich habe missgehandelt*

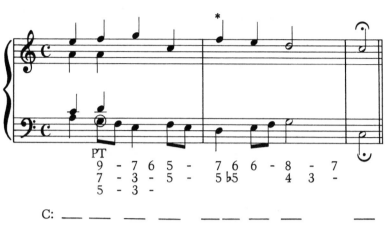

PT
9 - 7 6 5 - 7 6 6 - 8 - 7
7 - 3 - 5 - 5 ♭5   4 3 -
5 - 3 -

C: ___ ___ ___ ___ ___ ___ ___ ___ ___ ___ ___

(1) 1
(2) 3

369. The example below contains two altered chords. Indicate (by number) which chord is a secondary dominant and which is a borrowed chord.

Mozart, *Sonata*, K. 576

Adagio

A:

(1) Secondary dominant _____
(2) Borrowed chord _____

Chord 1: vii$^{\text{d7}}$/ii Chord 3: vii$^{\text{d7}}_{\frac{4}{3}}$	370. Write the proper Roman numeral for each of the altered chords in the preceding frame. Chord 1: _____ Chord 3: _____
5th.	371. Chord 1 in Frame 369 is an incomplete seventh chord. Which member of the chord is omitted? (Root/3rd/5th/7th) _____
True.	372. Chords 1 and 3 in Frame 369 are both diminished seventh chords. (True/False) _____
second	373. Chord 1 in Frame 369 is in root position; chord 3 is in _____ inversion.
	374. Complete the Roman numeral analysis for the example below: Brahms, *Symphony No. 1*, Op. 68

4 and 6.

natural *(or pure)*

C: I   V$^6_5$

V$^4_2$/iv   iv^6 i$^6_4$

V$^6_5$/V   V

change (of) mode

---

375. List (by number) the chords in the preceding frame which are not diatonic in the key of C major. _____

376. Chord 4 in Frame 374 is called the *subtonic* triad. It uses tones of the _____ minor scale.

377. An occasional borrowed chord in major results in only a fleeting sensation of the minor mode. Several used in succession, however, cause a more definite change of mode.
    Supply the Roman numeral analysis for the example below:

Mozart, *Mass in C Major,* K. 317

C: ___   ___   ___

378. Change of mode must not be confused with modulation. Whereas modulation involves a change of key center from one pitch to another, change of mode is merely a change from major to minor (or the reverse) *with the same tonal center retained*.
    Change from a major key to its *relative minor* is a modulation because a new key center is established; but change from a major key to its *parallel minor* is called _____ of _____.

379. The frequent use of borrowed chords and change of mode sometimes results in passages which are ambiguous as to mode.

Nielsen, *Sinfonia Espansiva*, Op. 27

Reprinted with permission of C.F. Peters Corporation, New York, sole agents for original publisher Engstroem & Soedering, Copenhagen.

The first part of this passage contains chords of both A major and minor. The key of D minor established in the fourth measure is less ambiguous, but notice the use of F-sharp in the next-to-the-last measure. Such blending together of the major and minor modes is an important feature of much late nineteenth-century music.

Does the frequent use of borrowed chords result in ambiguity of tonality? _____

(Ambiguity of modality, yes; but not necessarily tonality.)

For greater tonal
variety or color.

380. Borrowed chords have the same harmonic function as
their unaltered counterparts. A subdominant triad, for example,
tends to progress to the dominant, tonic, or supertonic chords
regardless of whether it is major or minor in quality. Since the
use of borrowed chords does not affect harmonic function,
what is the reason for using them? _____
_____

(c).

381. Which is the *least likely* chord (a, b, or c) to follow the
altered supertonic seventh chord below? _____

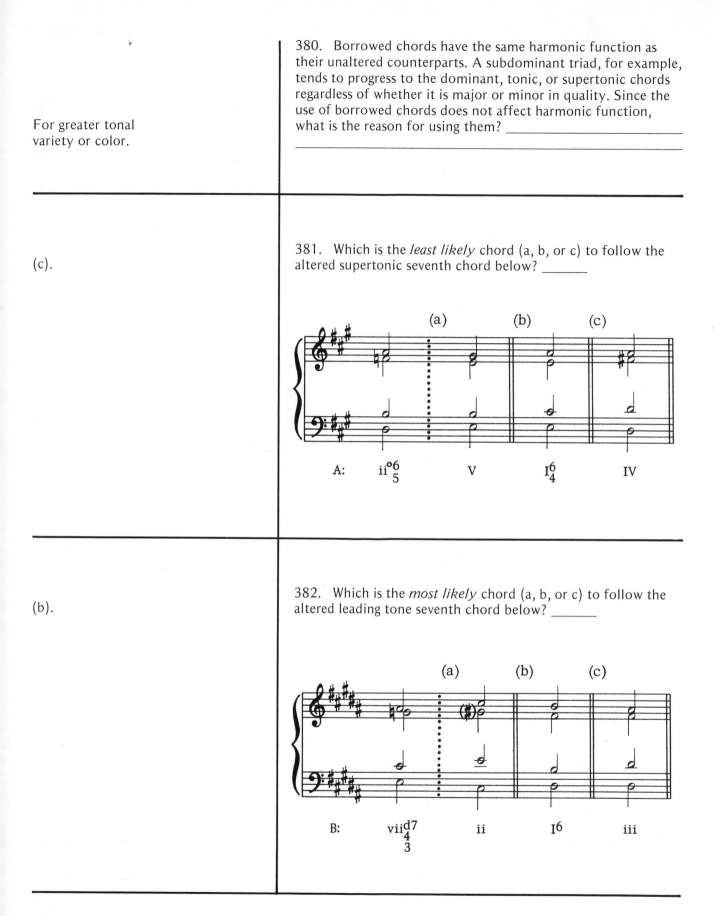

(b).

382. Which is the *most likely* chord (a, b, or c) to follow the
altered leading tone seventh chord below? _____

(a).
(Choice (b) produces a retrogression; choice (c) produces poor voice leading.)

(b).
(viiᵈ⁷-iv is a retrogression.)

(1) √

Both √

---

383. Which is the *most likely* chord (a, b, or c) to precede the altered submediant chord below? _____

Eb: V⁷   ii⁶   V⁶   bVI

---

384. Which is the *least likely* chord (a, b, or c) to precede the altered subdominant chord below? _____

G: IV   viiᵈ⁷₆₅   I⁶   iv

---

385. Check (√) the correct option:

1. Most borrowed chords occur in major keys.
2. Borrowed chords are taken from the relative minor (or major) key.

True statements:
(1) _____   (2) _____   Both _____   Neither _____

---

386. Check (√) the correct option:

1. Borrowed chords sometimes result in modal ambiguity.
2. Borrowed chords have the same harmonic function as their unaltered counterparts.

True statements:
(1) _____   (2) _____   Both _____   Neither _____

SUMMARY.

    Altered chords result from the use of tones which are not included in the diatonic scale. Whereas alterations which produce secondary dominants often change or intensify the function of a chord, those which produce borrowed chords do not. Borrowed chords tend to progress in the same way as their unaltered counterparts. They are used to introduce greater tonal variety than is contained solely in the diatonic scale.

    Borrowed chords are taken from parallel major or minor keys. The chief borrowed chords are listed below:

BORROWED CHORDS

Major	Minor
ii°, ii°7	I
♭III, ♭III+	
iv, iv7	
v	
♭VI	
viid7	

6   Augmented Sixth Chords

The term "augmented sixth chord" derives from the interval of an augmented sixth which occurs between the bass and an upper voice when these chords are in their most common position. Although, like triads and seventh chords, the notes of augmented sixth chords can be arranged in thirds, chromatic alteration is so extensive that the "written" root surrenders its influence to another tone which functions as the actual or "sounding" root. For this reason augmented sixth chords are approached as unique sonorities containing a variety of intervals.

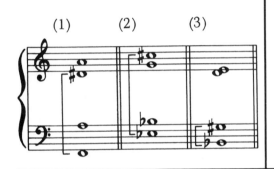

387. Each of the chords below contains the interval of an augmented sixth. Show with a bracket ([ ) the tones which produce this interval.

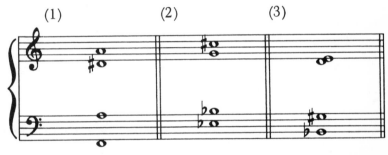

388. There are three types of augmented sixth chords, and the terms ITALIAN SIXTH, GERMAN SIXTH, and FRENCH SIXTH are used to identify them. Although the origin of these terms is unknown and their relevance is questionable, their use is so widespread that it is pointless not to avail ourselves of them.

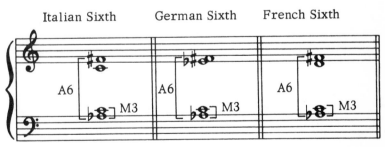

Italian Sixth   German Sixth   French Sixth

The example above shows that all three types of augmented sixth chords have two intervals in common: an augmented sixth, and a _____.

major third

389. Each of the three types of augmented sixth chords contains the intervals of an augmented sixth and a major third above the lowest note.

Write these two intervals above each note.

(1)   (2)   (3)   (4)

(1)   (2)   (3)   (4)

390. Write the intervals of an augmented sixth and a major third above each note.

(1)   (2)   (3)   (4)

(1)   (2)   (3)   (4)

391. Continue as in the preceding frame.

(1)   (2)   (3)   (4)

(1)   (2)   (3)   (4)

392. In the ITALIAN SIXTH chord, the major third above the bass is doubled by the fourth voice.

three

The Italian sixth is actually a chord of only _____ separate tones, one of which is doubled by the fourth voice.

393. Write the fourth voice in each of the *Italian sixth* chords below:

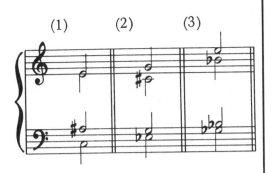

394. Write the alto and tenor voices in accordance with the figured bass symbols.

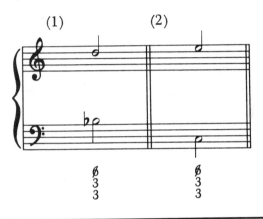

Yes.

395. Are both of the chords in the preceding frame Italian sixth chords? _____

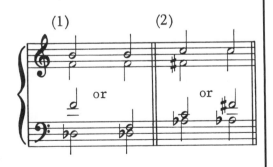

396. Write the alto and tenor voices in accordance with the figured bass symbols.

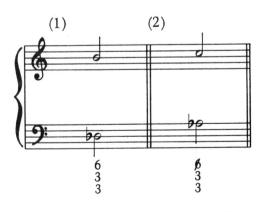

The third above the bass.

397. Italian sixth chords consist of the following intervals above the bass: an augmented sixth and a major third. In four-part writing which tone is doubled? _____

(a).

398. Since the interval of an augmented sixth is enharmonic with a minor seventh, the Italian sixth chord has the same aural effect as a major-minor seventh chord *with the fifth omitted.*

(a)   (b)

The two chords above sound the same. Which is notated as an Italian sixth chord? _____

---

(1)   (2)

399. You may wish to avail yourself of the similarity between the major-minor seventh chord and the Italian sixth chord to assist in spelling the latter. To spell an Italian sixth chord think first of a major-minor seventh chord; then omit the fifth and spell the seventh enharmonically as an augmented sixth.

Use this method to convert the major-minor seventh chords below into *Italian sixth* chords.

(1)   (2)

It6   It6

---

(1)   (2)

400. Continue as in the preceding frame.

(1)   (2)

It6   It6

False.
(Chord (c) is not.)

401. All of the chords on the following page are Italian sixth chords. (True/False) _____

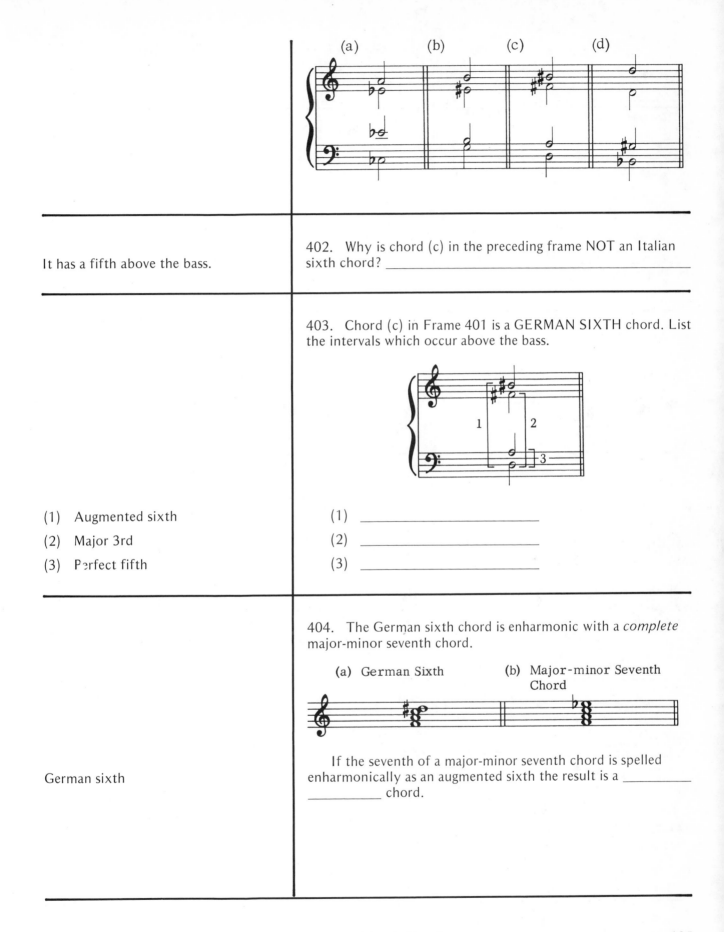

It has a fifth above the bass.

402. Why is chord (c) in the preceding frame NOT an Italian sixth chord? _____

403. Chord (c) in Frame 401 is a GERMAN SIXTH chord. List the intervals which occur above the bass.

(1) Augmented sixth

(2) Major 3rd

(3) Perfect fifth

(1) _____

(2) _____

(3) _____

German sixth

404. The German sixth chord is enharmonic with a *complete* major-minor seventh chord.

(a) German Sixth

(b) Major-minor Seventh Chord

If the seventh of a major-minor seventh chord is spelled enharmonically as an augmented sixth the result is a _____ _____ chord.

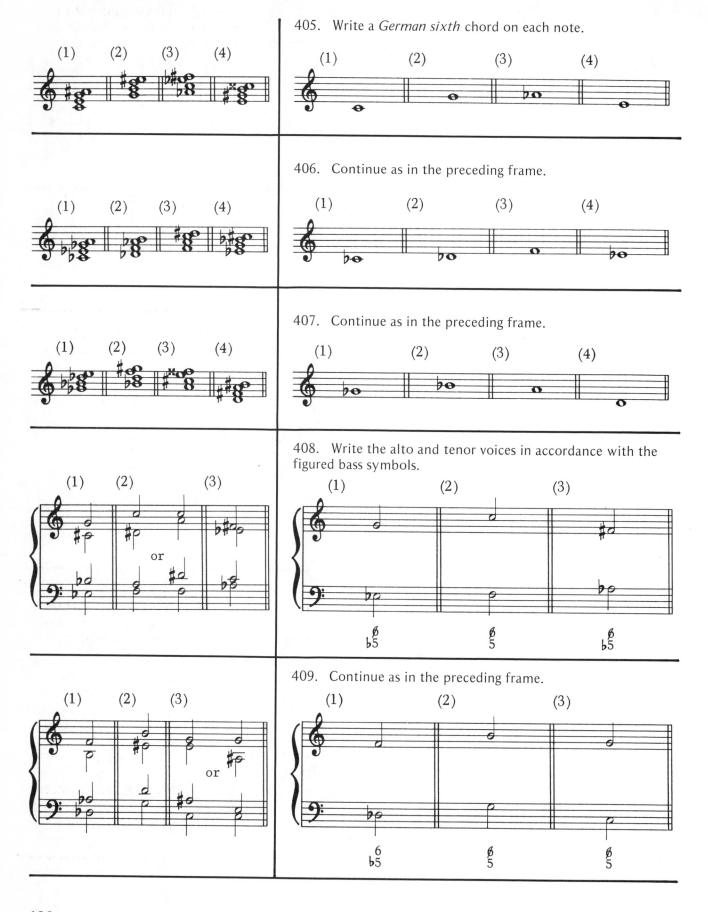

405. Write a *German sixth* chord on each note.

406. Continue as in the preceding frame.

407. Continue as in the preceding frame.

408. Write the alto and tenor voices in accordance with the figured bass symbols.

409. Continue as in the preceding frame.

6 (and) 5

410. The figured bass symbol which represents the Italian sixth chord includes the numbers 6 and 3; the symbol which represents the German sixth chord includes the numbers _____ and _____.

---

411. List each chord according to the categories provided below:

(a)   (b)   (c)   (d)   (e)   (f)

(1) Italian sixth   _____
(2) German sixth   _____
(3) Neither of these _____

(1) (b), (d)
(2) (a), (c), (f)
(3) (e)

---

412. Chord (e) in the preceding frame is a FRENCH SIXTH chord. List the intervals which occur above the bass. *(Be specific.)*

(1) _____
(2) _____
(3) _____

(1) Augmented 6th
(2) Major 3rd
(3) Augmented 4th

---

413. The FRENCH SIXTH CHORD contains an augmented sixth, a major third, and an augmented fourth above the bass.
    The chords below are all French sixth chords. *(Check each interval before responding.)* (True/False) _____

False.
(See next frame.)

(a)   (b)   (c)   (d)   (e)

(d)   Italian sixth
(e)   German sixth

414.   Chords (d) and (e) in the preceding frame are not French sixth chords. Chord (d) is a(n) _____ chord and chord (e) is a(n) _____ chord.

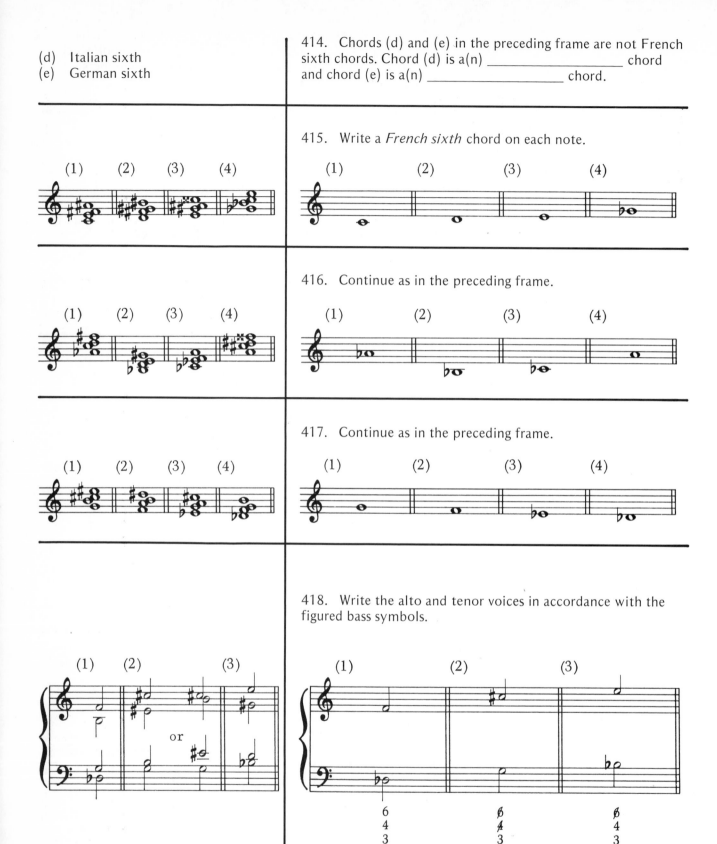

415.   Write a *French sixth* chord on each note.

(1)   (2)   (3)   (4)

416.   Continue as in the preceding frame.

(1)   (2)   (3)   (4)

417.   Continue as in the preceding frame.

(1)   (2)   (3)   (4)

418.   Write the alto and tenor voices in accordance with the figured bass symbols.

(1)   (2)   (3)

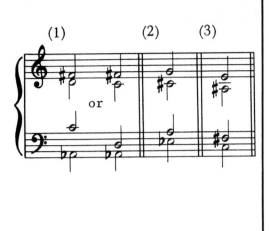

419. Continue as in the preceding frame.

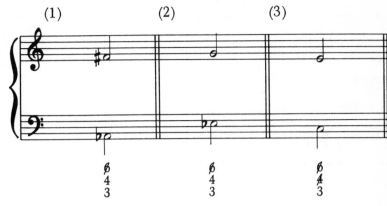

420. Because of the numbers which appear in the figured bass symbols, augmented sixth chords are sometimes identified as follows:

Italian sixth   - *Augmented six-three*
German sixth - *Augmented six-five*
French sixth - *Augmented six-four-three*

By referring to the figured bass symbols, list the proper name, (Italian, German, or French sixth) of each chord below:

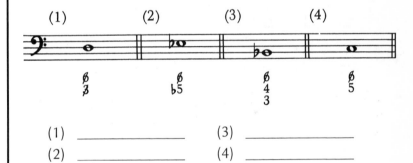

(1) Italian sixth
(2) German sixth
(3) French sixth
(4) German sixth

(1) _____   (3) _____

(2) _____   (4) _____

421. Continue as in the preceding frame.

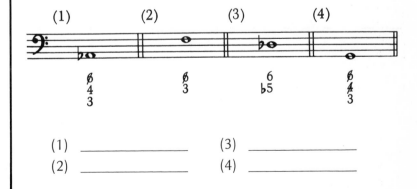

(1) French sixth
(2) Italian sixth
(3) German sixth
(4) French sixth

(1) _____   (3) _____

(2) _____   (4) _____

422. We shall continue to identify augmented sixth chords by their proper names. For the purpose of analysis use the abbreviations It^6, G^6, and F^6.

Utilizing these symbols, indicate the type of each chord.

(1)   (2)   (3)   (4)

(1) F^6

(2) It^6

(3) G^6

(4) F^6

___   ___   ___   ___

423. Continue as in the preceding frame.

(1)   (2)   (3)   (4)

(1) It^6

(2) G^6

(3) F^6

(4) G^6

___   ___   ___   ___

424. The name augmented sixth chord derives from the interval of an augmented sixth which usually appears between the bass and an upper voice. These chords occur in other positions which cause the augmented sixth through inversion to become a diminished third.

The three types of augmented sixth chords are called Italian sixth, German sixth, and French sixth. The Italian sixth contains the intervals of an augmented sixth and a major third above the bass, and is enharmonic with a major-minor seventh chord with the fifth omitted. The German sixth contains the intervals of an augmented sixth, a major third, and a perfect fifth above the bass, and is enharmonic with a complete major-minor seventh chord. The French sixth has no counterpart in the diatonic chord vocabulary. Its tones could be derived from the whole-tone scale, and its aural effect is extremely colorful. The intervals which produce the French sixth are an augmented sixth, a major third, and an augmented fourth.

(No response.)

425. You should now be able to spell and identify the various types of augmented sixth chords. Our task from this point will be to examine their use.

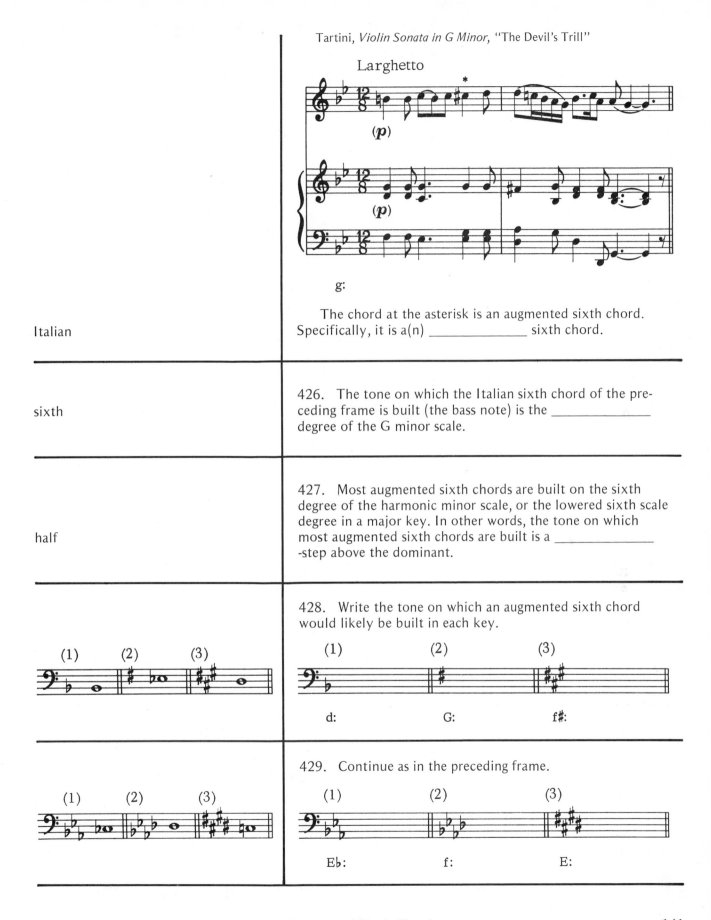

Tartini, *Violin Sonata in G Minor,* "The Devil's Trill"

Larghetto

g:

The chord at the asterisk is an augmented sixth chord. Specifically, it is a(n) _____ sixth chord.

Italian

---

sixth

426. The tone on which the Italian sixth chord of the preceding frame is built (the bass note) is the _____ degree of the G minor scale.

---

half

427. Most augmented sixth chords are built on the sixth degree of the harmonic minor scale, or the lowered sixth scale degree in a major key. In other words, the tone on which most augmented sixth chords are built is a _____ -step above the dominant.

---

(1)   (2)   (3)

428. Write the tone on which an augmented sixth chord would likely be built in each key.

(1)   (2)   (3)

d: G: f#:

---

(1)   (2)   (3)

429. Continue as in the preceding frame.

(1)   (2)   (3)

Eb: f: E:

430. Augmented sixth chords have been presented as unique sonorities which are not constructed entirely of thirds. The purpose of this approach is to cause you to build these chords on the note which usually appears in the bass *and which has the aural effect of the root.*

The tones of augmented sixth chords may, in fact, be arranged in thirds; but the lowest note will not sound as the root, especially in the case of the Italian and German sixth chords.

The Italian sixth chord from the example in Frame 425 is shown with the notes arranged in thirds (a) and as it actually appears in the music (b).

(Play each of these chords at the piano.)

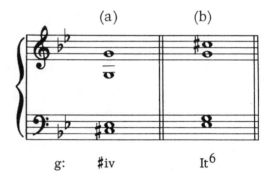

Comparison of the aural effect of the two chords above should make it clear that the note C-sharp does not sound like the root. The "sounding" root is E-flat, the note on which we consider the chord to be built. The chord symbol in (a) shows that the chord is an altered subdominant triad. The designation It[6] in (b), however, is the symbol which shall be used to identify this chord.

(No response.)

431. Compare the three types of augmented sixth chords which are arranged in thirds in the example below:

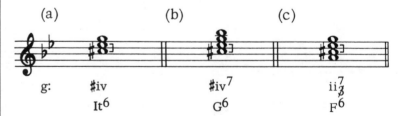

Arranged in this way the interval of the augmented sixth becomes through inversion a diminished third (bracketed in the example above). The Italian sixth may be regarded as an altered subdominant triad, the German sixth as an altered subdominant seventh chord, and the French sixth as an altered supertonic seventh chord. With this in mind, to what chord would you expect these chords to progress? To the
_____.

dominant *(or V)*

432. Augmented sixth chords (when built on the sixth degree of the harmonic minor scale, or the lowered sixth degree of the major scale) progress to the dominant triad or seventh chord or the tonic triad in a cadential six-four figure.

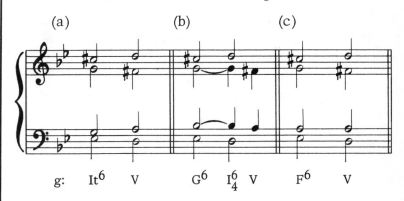

(a)   (b)   (c)

g: It^6 V   G^6 I$^6_4$ V   F^6 V

Because of their unusual color and highly active character, augmented sixth chords provide exceptional motivation to the dominant. They are used at points in musical form where this motivation is required. They often serve to focus attention on dominant harmony immediately prior to an important return of the tonic such as at the end of the development section in sonata form.

In each case above, the interval of an augmented sixth occurs between the _____ and _____ voices.

bass (and) soprano

---

433. Notice in the preceding frame that the interval of an augmented sixth expands outward to an octave.

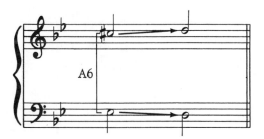

A6

This is the most characteristic feature in the resolution of augmented sixth chords. The remaining voices find their places in the following chord quite smoothly provided the augmented sixth resolves in this way.

The voices in the example above move by the interval of a _____ -step.

half

434. Complete the progression in each case. *(Be sure that the augmented sixth expands outward to an octave.)*

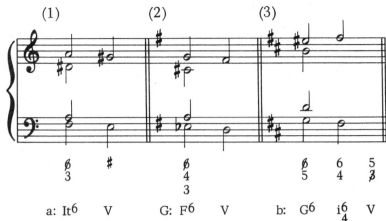

$$\begin{array}{ccc} \overset{6}{\underset{3}{\emptyset}} \quad \# & \overset{6}{\underset{\underset{3}{4}}{\emptyset}} & \overset{6}{\underset{5}{\emptyset}} \quad \overset{6}{\underset{4}{}} \quad \overset{5}{\underset{\cancel{3}}{}} \end{array}$$

a: It⁶   V   G: F⁶   V   b: G⁶   i⁶₄   V

435. Continue as in the preceding frame.

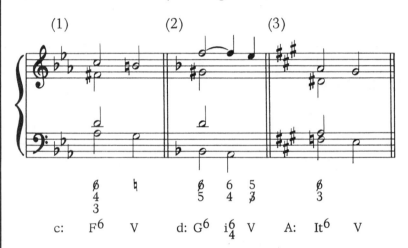

$$\begin{array}{ccc} \overset{6}{\underset{\underset{3}{4}}{\emptyset}} \quad \natural & \overset{6}{\underset{5}{\emptyset}} \quad \overset{6}{\underset{4}{}} \quad \overset{5}{\underset{\cancel{3}}{}} & \overset{6}{\underset{3}{\emptyset}} \end{array}$$

c: F⁶   V   d: G⁶   i⁶₄   V   A: It⁶   V

436. Continue as in the preceding frame.

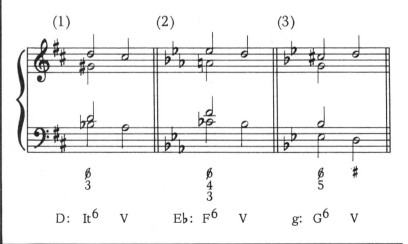

$$\begin{array}{ccc} \overset{6}{\underset{3}{\emptyset}} & \overset{6}{\underset{\underset{3}{4}}{\emptyset}} & \overset{6}{\underset{5}{\emptyset}} \quad \# \end{array}$$

D: It⁶   V   E♭: F⁶   V   g: G⁶   V

Parallel perfect fifths occur
between the bass and the tenor.

437.   What is the abnormality of part writing in the answer given for (3) of the preceding frame? _____
_____

438.   When the German sixth chord progresses directly to the dominant, parallel perfect fifths result. *These are not considered a mistake unless they occur between the bass and soprano voices.*

Draw lines between notes in the two chords at the asterisks to show the parallel fifths in the example below:

Chopin, *Nocturne*

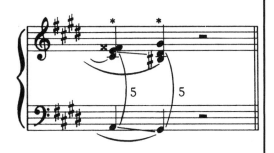

439.   Although parallel perfect fifths may occur when the German sixth chord progresses directly to the dominant, they are usually avoided or at least disguised by melodic movement.

Schubert, *Mass in G Major,* "Sanctus"

The chord at the asterisk is a German sixth chord. The melodic movement in the tenor from F-natural to D reduces the effect of parallel perfect fifths. Because of the melodic movement, the chord on the second beat (immediately following the asterisk) is an _____ sixth chord.

Italian

440. For the sake of avoiding parallel perfect fifths, the German sixth chord often progresses first to the tonic triad in second inversion.

Mozart, *Sonata*, K. 284

a: G⁶   -   I⁶₄   V⁷   i

Yes.

Does the interval of the augmented sixth resolve "normally" in the example above? _____

441. Complete the Roman numeral analysis for the following example:

Schubert, *Der Doppelgänger*

Sehr langsam

so   man - che Nacht,   in

b: ___   ___   ___

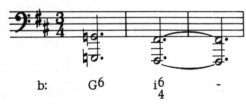

b: G⁶   i⁶₄   -

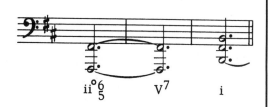

al - - - ter Zeit?

ii°⁶₅ V⁷ i

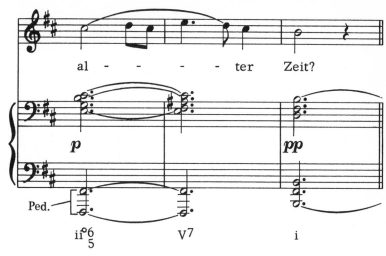

p *pp*

Ped.

ii°⁶₅ V⁷ i

442. When the German sixth chord progresses to the tonic triad in second inversion in a major key, an alternate spelling is sometimes used.

Complete the Roman numeral analysis for the example below:

Schumann, *Dichterliebe*, Op. 48, No. 12

Zeimlich langsam

B♭:   G⁶

p

Am   leuch - ten-den

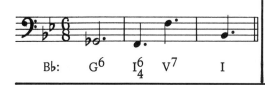

B♭:   G⁶   I⁶₄   V⁷   I

443. The harmonic progression of the example in the preceding frame is shown in simplified form below:

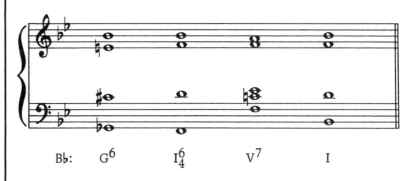

Bb: G^6 I$^6_4$ V^7 I

How does the German sixth chord above differ from the
usual spelling? _____

_____

D-flat is spelled enharmonically
as C-sharp.

---

444. The German sixth chord as spelled in the preceding frame
is sometimes called the *doubly augmented six-four-three.* It
contains these intervals: an augmented sixth, a major third,
and a doubly-augmented fourth.

Bracket ( ]) the voices which produce the interval of the
doubly augmented fourth.

---

445. The reason for the alternate spelling of the German sixth
chord is to avoid the chromatic melodic movement which otherwise would occur when the following chord is a tonic six-four.
Observe the tenor voice in the two examples below:

(a)   (b)

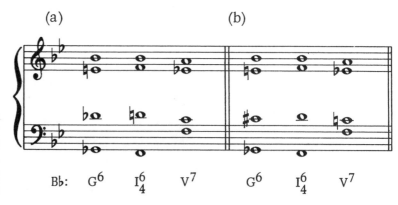

Bb: G^6 I$^6_4$ V^7 G^6 I$^6_4$ V^7

doubly augmented
six-four-three

In (a) the German sixth chord is spelled "normally." Its resolution to the tonic in second inversion results in chromatic movement in the tenor. This is avoided in (b) by spelling D-flat enharmonically as C-sharp. The German sixth chord in (b) is sometimes called a _____

_____ chord.

---

446.   The alternate spelling of the German sixth chord (doubly augmented six-four-three) is not always used.

Haydn, *Quartet*, Op. 64, No. 5

A: IV   I⁶₄   G⁶   I⁶₄

V⁷   I

major

Composers show a lack of consistency in notating German sixth chords. When spelled as a doubly augmented six-four-three it is for the purpose of avoiding a chromatic melodic progression when resolving to the tonic six-four chord in a _____ key.

Change C-natural
to B-sharp

447.   If the German sixth chord in the preceding frame were to be spelled as a doubly augmented six-four-three, what change would be required? _____

_____

No.	
	448. Would you expect to encounter the doubly augmented six-four-three chord in a minor key? _____

Eb: V$^4_2$

I^6 IV^6 F^6 V

449. Supply the Roman numeral analysis for the example below:

Beethoven, *Sonata*, Op. 13

Allegro

Eb: ___   ___   ___ ___ ___

German

450. The example in the preceding frame illustrates the use of a French sixth chord. Sometimes the term augmented six-four-three is used to refer to the French sixth chord.

Do not confuse the augmented six-four-three with the doubly augmented six-four-three chord. The former is a French sixth, while the latter is a _____ sixth chord with an enharmonic spelling.

g: V$^4_2$/IV IV^6 F^6 i$^6_4$ V

451. Supply the Roman numeral analysis for the example below:

Mozart, *Symphony No. 40*, K. 550

Allegro molto

g: ___   ___   ___   ___   ___

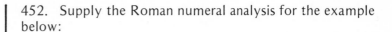

452. Supply the Roman numeral analysis for the example below:

Schumann, *Papillons*, Op. 2

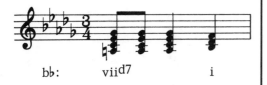

bb: viid7   i

          iv⁶   G⁶   F⁶   V

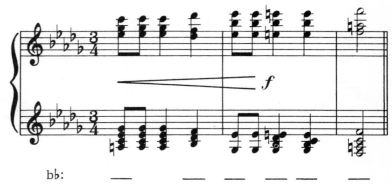

bb: ___ ___ ___ ___ ___ ___

453. Augmented sixth chords occur frequently in the music of some late nineteenth-century composers. Used in combination with nonharmonic tones they often produce strikingly colorful effects.

Taking into account the nonharmonic tones which have been circled, supply the Roman numeral analysis for the example below:

Wagner, *Tristan und Isolde*, "Prelude"

Langsam und schmachtend

a: ___   ___

a: F⁶   V⁷

g: i   i   It⁶ V   i⁶ i⁷

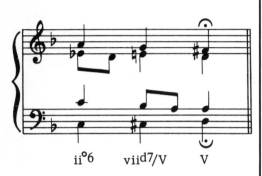

ii°6   viid7/V   V

454. Complete the alto and tenor voices and supply the Roman numeral analysis.

Bach, Chorale: *Ich hab' mein' Sach' Gott heimgestellt*

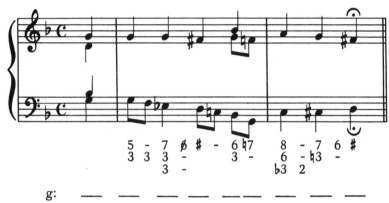

$$\begin{matrix} 5 & - & 7 & \flat & \# & - & 6 & \natural 7 & 8 & - & 7 & 6 & \# \\ 3 & 3 & 3 & - & & & 3 & - & 6 & - & \natural 3 & - \\ & & 3 & - & & & & & \flat 3 & 2 & & \end{matrix}$$

g: — — — — — — — — — —

d: V⁶ i iv⁶₅ VII III IV⁶₅ vii°

(V/III)

i   G⁶   i⁶₄ viid7/V V

455. Complete the alto and tenor voices and supply the Roman numeral analysis.

Bach, Chorale: *Befiehl du deine Wege*

$$\begin{matrix} 6 & - & 3 & - & 6 & 8 & - & 6 & & 9 & \flat & 6 & 7 & \# \\ 6 & 5 & 3 & - & 5 & 5 & - & 5 & 3 & & 5 & 4 & \natural 3 \\ & & & & & 3 & - & 3 & 3 & \end{matrix}$$

d: — — — — — — —

456. A high degree of harmonic motivation is achieved through the use of various types of altered chords in the example below. There are two secondary dominants and one augmented sixth chord. Complete the Roman numeral analysis.

Bach, Chorale: *Wer nur den lieben Gott lässt*

a: v

a: v   i⁷   ii°   V⁶₅   V⁴₂/IV

IV⁶   F⁶   i⁶₄   V⁶/V   V   (V⁷)   i

457. All of the augmented sixth chords presented to this point have been in the "normal" position—*the interval of an augmented sixth has appeared between the bass and an upper part.* When the raised fourth scale degree is in the bass, the augmented sixth becomes by inversion a diminished third.

Tchaikovsky, *Eugene Onegin,* Act II, No. 17

Andante, assai adagio

He sends as well the dark,   dark night.

e: ii°⁷   i⁶   iv⁷   G⁶   V⁷   i

Use a bracket ( ]) to identify the diminished third in the German sixth chord above.

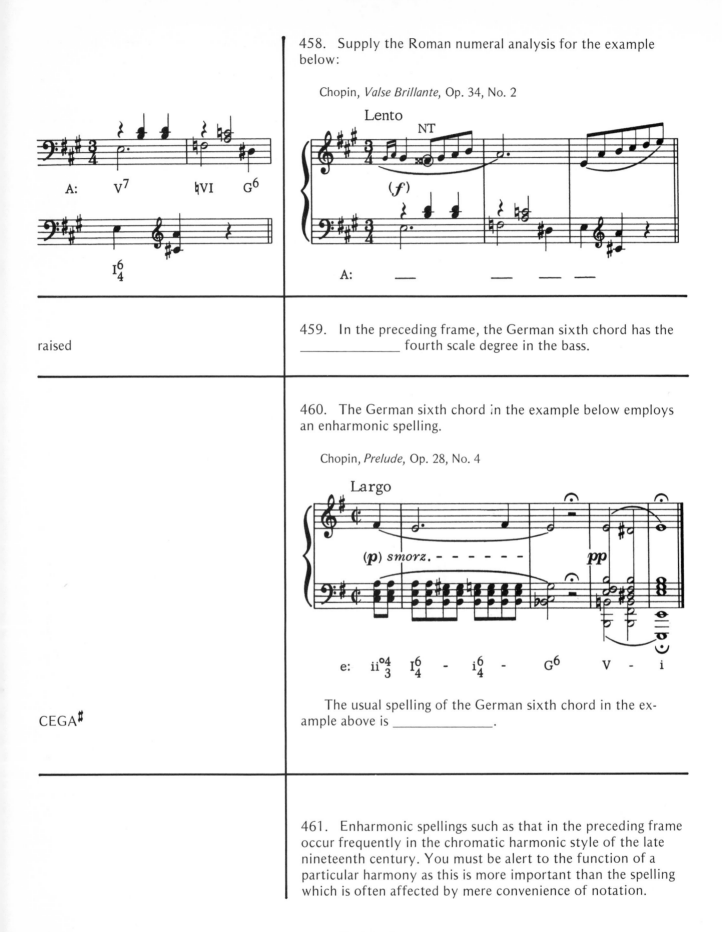

458. Supply the Roman numeral analysis for the example below:

Chopin, *Valse Brillante*, Op. 34, No. 2

A: V⁷   ♮VI   G⁶

I^6_4

A: ___   ___ ___ ___

---

raised

459. In the preceding frame, the German sixth chord has the _____ fourth scale degree in the bass.

---

460. The German sixth chord in the example below employs an enharmonic spelling.

Chopin, *Prelude*, Op. 28, No. 4

e: ii°$^4_3$ I^6_4 - i$^6_4$ -   G⁶   V - i

The usual spelling of the German sixth chord in the example above is _____.

CEGA♯

---

461. Enharmonic spellings such as that in the preceding frame occur frequently in the chromatic harmonic style of the late nineteenth century. You must be alert to the function of a particular harmony as this is more important than the spelling which is often affected by mere convenience of notation.

3rd

The aural effect of the German sixth chord when the raised fourth degree is in the bass (Frames 457, 458, and 460) is the same as a major-minor seventh chord in (1st/2nd/3rd) _____ inversion.

462. Augmented sixth chords may be found in any position, but the two most common are shown below:

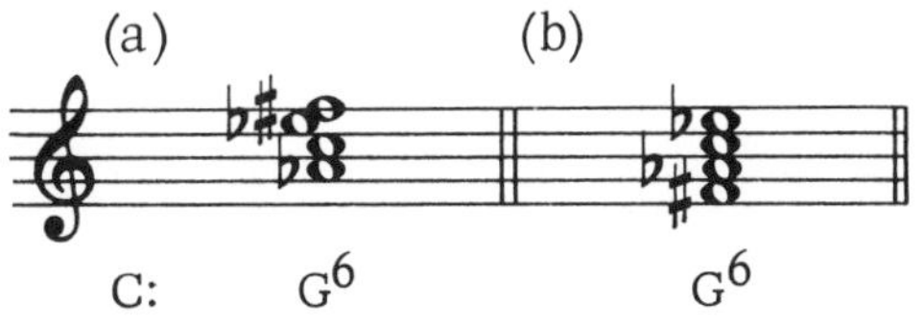

In (a), the lowered sixth scale degree is in the bass and the interval of an augmented sixth occurs between the bass and an upper part; in (b), the raised fourth scale degree is in the bass and the augmented sixth, through inversion, now appears as a _____ third.

diminished

463. Since augmented sixth chords rarely occur in positions other than the two shown in the preceding frame, only a few examples will be cited. In the example below, the German sixth chord is spelled as a doubly augmented six-four-three.

Franck, *Symphony in D Minor*

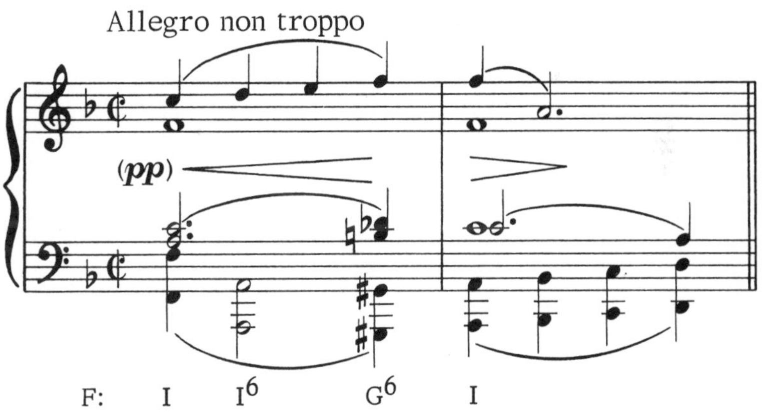

In the German sixth above, the note in the bass (G-sharp) is the "sounding" (root/3rd/5th/7th) _____ of the chord.

5th

464. Augmented sixth chords are exploited by some composers for their novel color effects. The example on the following page makes effective use of a German sixth chord spelled enharmonically as a major-minor seventh chord.

Dvořák, *Symphony No. 9*, "From the New World," Op. 95

c#:   i   G⁶   i   G⁶

i   I

The colorful effect of this passage is due, in part, to the unusual resolution of the German sixth to the tonic triad in root position.

Augmented sixth chords (when built on the sixth scale degree) usually progress to the dominant triad or seventh chord, or to the tonic triad in _____ inversion.

second

3rd

465. The German sixth chord at the asterisk has the first scale degree in the bass. This note (D) is the "sounding" (root/3rd/5th/7th) _____ of the chord.

Franck, *Symphony in D Minor*

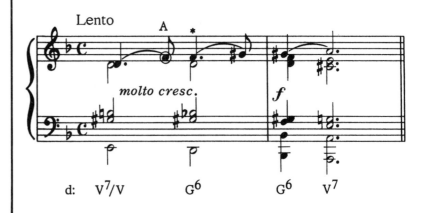

d: V⁷/V   G⁶   G⁶   V⁷

466. All of the augmented sixth chords presented to this point are built on the note which is a half-step above the dominant (the sixth scale degree in harmonic minor, or the lowered sixth-scale degree in major). But augmented sixth chords occur on other scale degrees as well.

We have learned that augmented sixth chords are highly active and that their usual resolution is to the dominant (a chord whose root is a half-step below the note on which the augmented sixth chord is built). This strong tendency to resolve in a particular way leads to a use of these chords which is analogous to secondary dominants. *Thus chords other than the dominant may be attended by augmented sixth chords.* Reference is occasionally made to the "augmented sixth of the supertonic," etc. Augmented sixth chords used in this manner are usually part of a highly chromatic style of writing as will be seen in examples which follow.

(No response.)

---

467. The augmented sixth chord below precedes a secondary dominant.

Brahms, *Symphony No. 1, Op. 68*

The Italian sixth chord in this example relates to the chord which follows as if both were in the key of _____ major.

G

468. Supply the Roman numeral analysis for the example below:

Beethoven, *Sonata,* for violin and piano, Op. 23

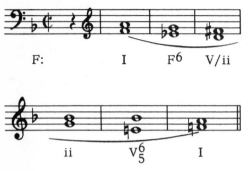

469. The analogous function possessed by secondary dominants and augmented sixth chords is made especially clear in the example below. Here the supertonic triad is preceded by both a secondary dominant (V_3^4/ii) and a French sixth chord.

Wolf, *Wiegenlied*

Does the interval of the diminished third resolve "normally" in the example above? _____

Yes.

470. Check (√) the correct option:

    1. Like secondary dominants, augmented sixth chords may relate to various triads in the key.
    2. In augmented sixth chords the interval of an augmented sixth always occurs between the bass and an upper voice.

True statements:
(1) _____   (2) _____   Both _____   Neither _____

(1) √

---

471. The French sixth chord at the asterisk is built on E-flat, and thus would tend to resolve to the mediant (vi). It progresses instead to the subdominant in first inversion (IV^6).

Wolf, *Biterolf*

Does the interval of the augmented sixth resolve in the "normal" way? _____

Yes.

472. In the preceding frame there are three borrowed chords. To review your knowledge of these chords, show them with chord symbols in the order of their occurrence.

(1) _____   (2) _____   (3) _____

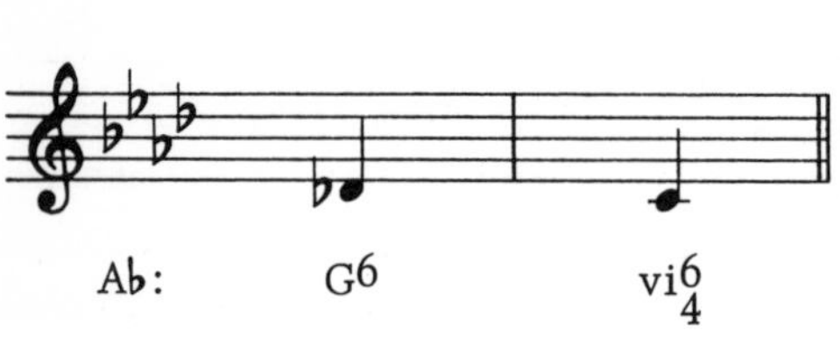

(1) iv   (2) ii°   (3) ii°⁷

473. Complete the Roman numeral analysis for the example below:

Wagner, *Lohengrin,* Act I

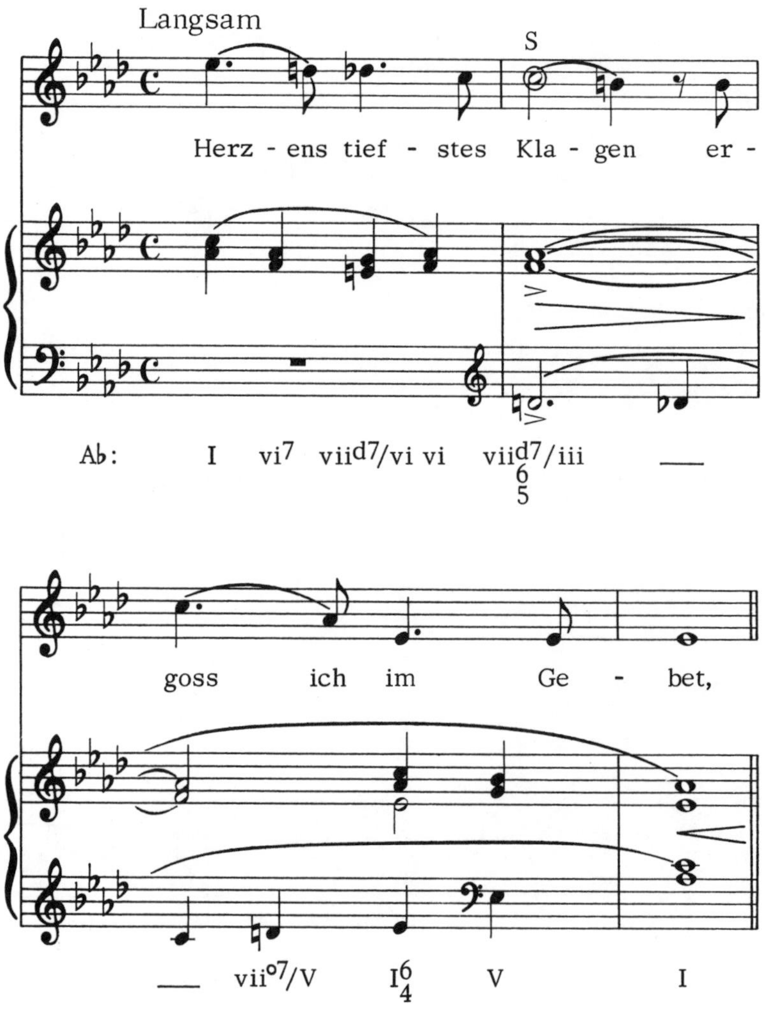

474. Augmented sixth chords are less active than secondary dominants. (True/False) _____

False.
(Both are highly active.)

second

(c). The French sixth.

475. Most augmented sixth chords are built on the sixth degree of the harmonic minor scale or the lowered sixth degree of the major scale. They are also used in a manner similar to secondary dominants to embellish various diatonic triads. Two other uses remain to be examined: (1) built on the lowered second scale degree in major and minor, and (2) built on the fourth scale degree in major.

    The chord at the asterisk is a French sixth built on the lowered _____ degree of the E minor scale.

Brahms, *Symphony No. 4*, Op. 98

Allegro energico e passionato

e: i   iv^6 V^7/V   i^6 F^6 I

476. When built on the lowered second scale degree, augmented sixth chords usually resolve to the tonic in root position.

(a)   (b)   (c)

C: It^6 I   G^6 I   F^6 I

    As usual, the interval of an augmented sixth expands outward to the octave. Progression to the tonic causes these chords to have dominant function. Which of the chords above could be regarded as an altered dominant seventh chord? _____

_____

477. When built on the lowered second scale degree, the French sixth may rightly be considered a dominant seventh chord with a lowered fifth. This is made clear by arranging the chord in (c) of the preceding frame in thirds.

V$^7_{\flat 5}$

(F^6)

leading tone

Similarly, the Italian sixth in (a) of the preceding frame could be analyzed as an altered _____ _____ triad.

478. Augmented sixth chords built on the lowered second scale degree are often used at the cadence. Complete the Roman numeral analysis for the example below:

Fauré, *Au bord de l'Eau*, Op. 8, No. 1

479. Supply the Roman numeral analysis for the example below:

Sibelius, *Finlandia*, Op. 26

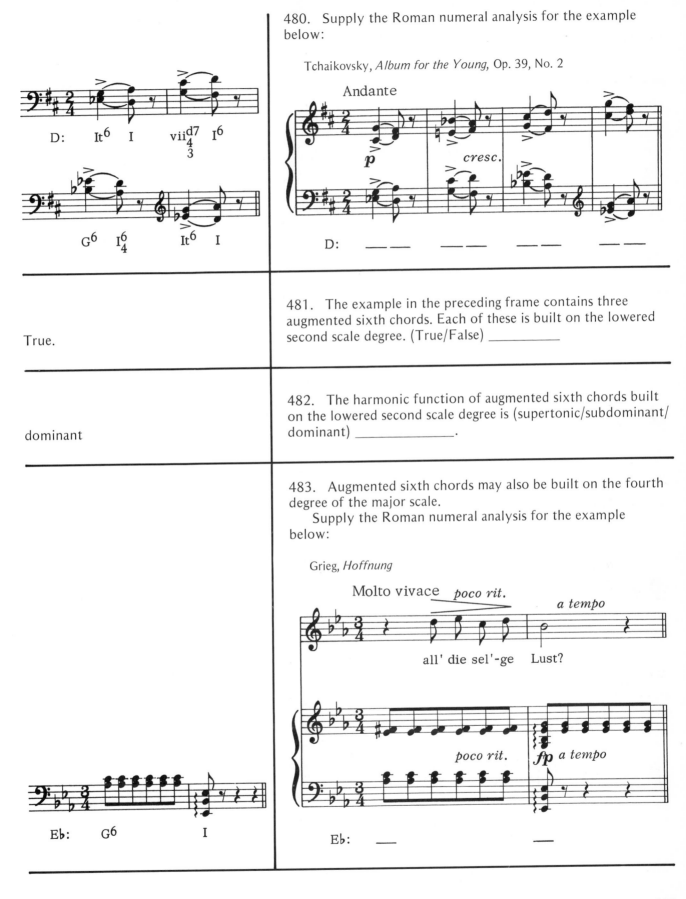

480. Supply the Roman numeral analysis for the example below:

Tchaikovsky, *Album for the Young*, Op. 39, No. 2

Andante

D: __ __ __ __ __ __

D: It⁶ I vii°⁷₄₃ I⁶

G⁶ I⁶₄ It⁶ I

True.

481. The example in the preceding frame contains three augmented sixth chords. Each of these is built on the lowered second scale degree. (True/False) _____

dominant

482. The harmonic function of augmented sixth chords built on the lowered second scale degree is (supertonic/subdominant/dominant) _____.

483. Augmented sixth chords may also be built on the fourth degree of the major scale.
  Supply the Roman numeral analysis for the example below:

Grieg, *Hoffnung*

Molto vivace *poco rit.*   *a tempo*

all' die sel'-ge Lust?

poco rit. *fp a tempo*

Eb: G⁶ I

Eb: __ __

Augmented Sixth Chords

163

484. When built on the fourth scale degree, augmented sixth chords usually resolve to a tonic triad in root position. The effect of this progression is somewhat like a plagal cadence.

Complete the Roman numeral analysis for the example below:

Grieg, *First Meeting*

C: V$\frac{4}{3}$/IV   — — — —

C: vii°7/V   G^6 I

485. Complete the Roman numeral analysis for the example below:

Gounod, *Faust*, "Introduction"

E♭:   I   ii°$\frac{6}{5}$ — — — —

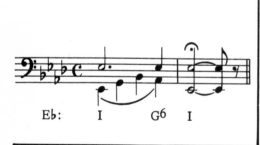

E♭:   I   G^6 I

SUMMARY.

The most common use of augmented sixth chords is to heighten the appearance of the dominant chord by providing a chromatic approach to it. Used in this manner, they are altered subdominant or supertonic chords. In the chromatic harmonic styles of some nineteenth-century composers these chords embellish diatonic chords other than the dominant, and even other altered chords such as secondary dominants.

Augmented sixth chords also appear on the lowered second scale degree as altered leading tone or dominant chords. They perform the same function as their diatonic counterparts, which is to progress to the tonic. When built on the fourth degree of the major scale, augmented sixth chords usually progress to the tonic triad in root position. The result is an effect similar to the plagal cadence.

Augmented sixth chords may be found which do not conform to any of the uses described in this chapter. In such cases their use may be termed "nonfunctional" (the result of chromatic nonharmonic tones), or merely the composer's desire to exploit the particular color which they possess.

7 The Neapolitan Sixth, Altered Dominants, and Diminished Seventh Chords

Three types of altered chords are presented in this chapter: the Neapolitan sixth—an altered supertonic triad, dominants with increased activity due to alterations of the fifth, and two diminished seventh chords which do not have dominant function. All of these chords are used sparingly; they are saved for moments when their distinctive tonal qualities are most appropriate. Like all highly-colored sonorities, over use of these chords diminishes their effectiveness.

486. The chord at the asterisk is called a NEAPOLITAN SIXTH chord.

Chopin, *Valse Brillante*, Op. 34, No. 2

a: i   N⁶   V⁷   VI

The Neapolitan sixth chord above is in _____ inversion.

first

487. Although the origin of the term "Neapolitan sixth" is unknown, its use is universally accepted. The second part of this term (sixth) refers to the fact that the chord is usually in first inversion.

The word "sixth" in the term Neapolitan sixth chord refers to the interval of a sixth which occurs above the bass in any triad which is in _____ inversion.

first

488. We shall use the symbol N^6 to represent the Neapolitan sixth chord. In the very few cases when it is in root position or second inversion the symbol will be N or N_4^6.

(a)   (b)   (c)

a: N^6 N N_4^6

a: $\flat II^6$ $\flat II$ $\flat II_4^6$

In (a) the chord is in first inversion (its usual position); (b) and (c) show the chord in root position and second inversion. The alternate analysis indicates that the Neapolitan sixth chord is a major triad built on the lowered second degree of the scale.

(No response.)

---

489. The earliest examples of the Neapolitan sixth chord are in minor keys, but they may occur in major keys as well. In either case, the chord is a major triad built on the lowered second degree of the scale. In the key of G minor, for example, the Neapolitan sixth chord is spelled $A\flat C E\flat$.

Spell the Neapolitan sixth chord in the key of C minor. _____

$D\flat F A\flat$

---

490. Since the majority of Neapolitan sixth chords occur in first inversion, we shall write them on the staff with the third as the lowest note. In the key of A major, for example, the chord is spelled $B\flat DF$. Written on the staff it appears as below:

A: N^6

Why is it necessary to place a natural sign before the note F in the example above? _____

_____

To produce a major triad.

---

491. Write the chord indicated. (Remember that the third is the lowest note.)

(1)   (2)   (3)

(1)   (2)   (3)

F: N^6 b: N^6 c: N^6

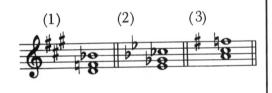

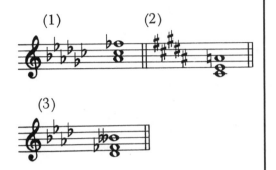

492. Continue as in the preceding frame.

(1) c#: N⁶   (2) Db: N⁶   (3) F#: N⁶

493. Continue as in the preceding frame.

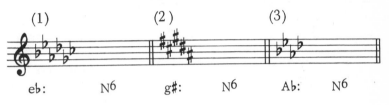

(1) eb: N⁶   (2) g#: N⁶   (3) Ab: N⁶

494. Continue as in the preceding frame.

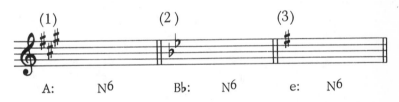

(1) A: N⁶   (2) Bb: N⁶   (3) e: N⁶

495. Since the Neapolitan sixth chord is an altered supertonic triad, it normally progresses to a dominant chord.

Beethoven, *Sonata,* Op. 27, No. 2

c#: V^6_5 i

The Neapolitan Sixth, Altered Dominants, and Diminished Seventh Chords   167

$$N^6 \qquad V^7 \qquad\qquad i$$

In the Neapolitan sixth chord above, the (root/3rd/5th) _____ is in the bass.

3rd

---

496.   The Neapolitan sixth chord produces a distinctive and colorful effect. The effect is most pronounced when the Neapolitan sixth chord is followed immediately by a dominant chord (as in the preceding frame). This is due to the tritone relationship which exists between the roots of the two chords.

Beethoven, *Sonata*, Op. 27, No. 2

(Adagio)

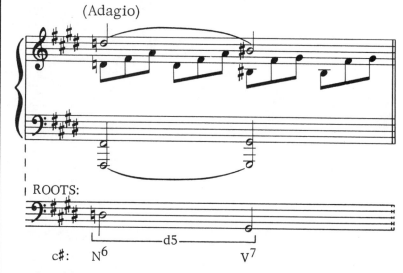

ROOTS:

$$c\sharp: \qquad N^6 \xleftarrow{\;\;d5\;\;} V^7$$

In addition to the tritone relationship between the roots of these chords, the melodic line contains an unusual interval (D-natural to B-sharp). Name this interval. _____

Diminished third.

---

497.   The unusual features mentioned in the preceding frame are eliminated if a tonic six-four chord occurs between the Neapolitan sixth chord and the dominant.

Complete the Roman numeral analysis for the example on the following page.

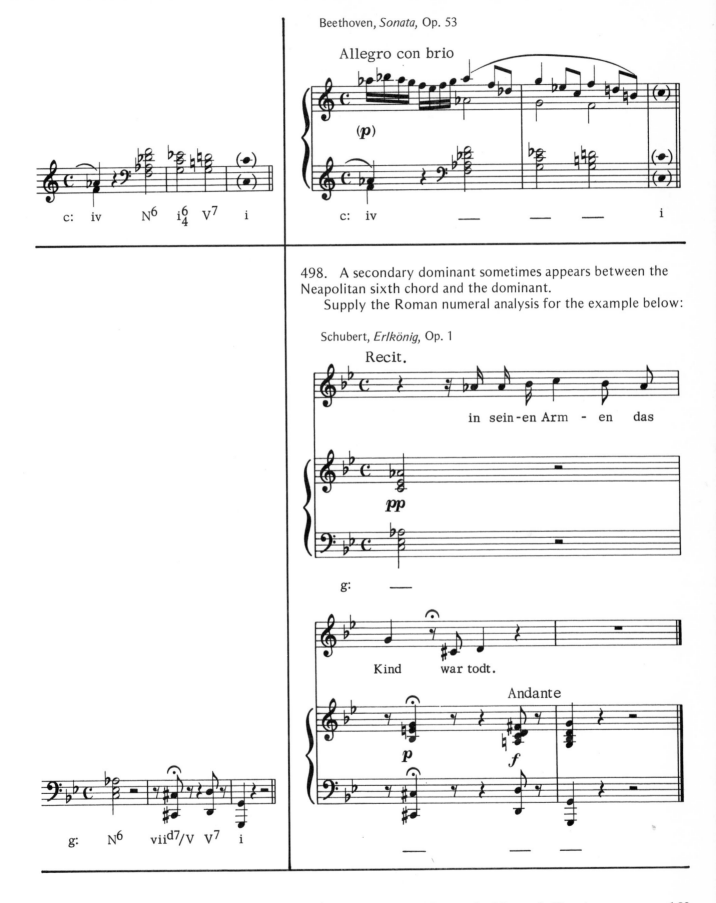

498. A secondary dominant sometimes appears between the Neapolitan sixth chord and the dominant.

Supply the Roman numeral analysis for the example below:

Schubert, *Erlkönig*, Op. 1

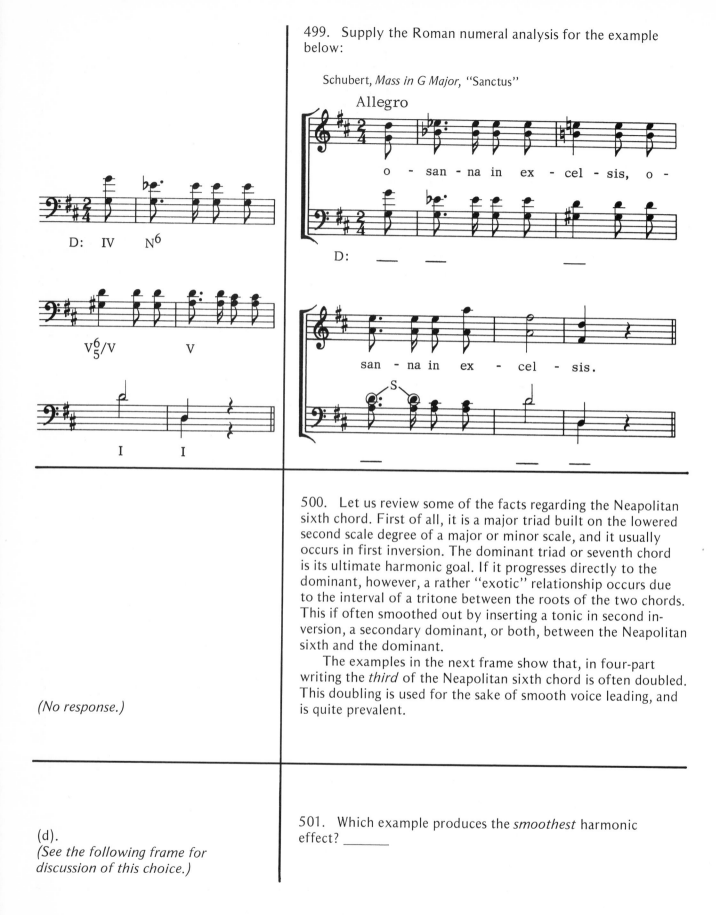

499. Supply the Roman numeral analysis for the example below:

Schubert, *Mass in G Major*, "Sanctus"

D: IV   N⁶

V^6_5/V   V

I   I

(No response.)

(d).
(See the following frame for discussion of this choice.)

500. Let us review some of the facts regarding the Neapolitan sixth chord. First of all, it is a major triad built on the lowered second scale degree of a major or minor scale, and it usually occurs in first inversion. The dominant triad or seventh chord is its ultimate harmonic goal. If it progresses directly to the dominant, however, a rather "exotic" relationship occurs due to the interval of a tritone between the roots of the two chords. This if often smoothed out by inserting a tonic in second inversion, a secondary dominant, or both, between the Neapolitan sixth and the dominant.

The examples in the next frame show that, in four-part writing the *third* of the Neapolitan sixth chord is often doubled. This doubling is used for the sake of smooth voice leading, and is quite prevalent.

501. Which example produces the *smoothest* harmonic effect? _____

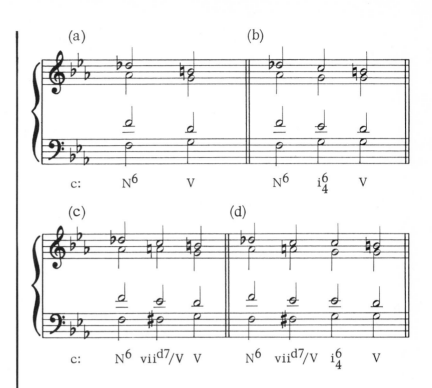

502. The progression in (d) of the preceding frame provides the smoothest effect, because the Neapolitan sixth and the dominant chords are separated by a greater number of chords than in either (b) or (c). Thus the dissonant effect caused by the tritone root relationship is considerably lessened.

Maximum smoothness, of course, is not always desired. The tritone relationship is often exploited for expressive purposes. Such a case is shown in the example below. Supply the Roman numeral analysis.

Chopin, *Prelude,* Op. 28, No. 20

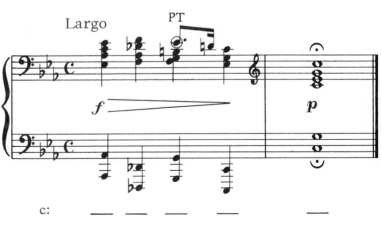

It is in root position.

503. 503. How does the Neapolitan sixth chord in the preceding frame differ from all those previously shown? _____
_____

504. Supply the Roman numeral analysis for the example below:

Brahms, *Intermezzo*, Op. 119, No. 3

Grazioso e giocoso

C: ___ ___ ___

C: I   N   -

___ ___ ___

♭VI⁶   iv⁶   iv   I

505. The chords in the third and fourth measures of the preceding example are altered chords. Name the type of altered chord to which these chords belong. They are _____ chords.

borrowed

506. Another example of the Neapolitan sixth chord in root position is shown below. Supply the Roman numeral analysis.

Wagner, *Die Walküre*, Act I, Scene 2

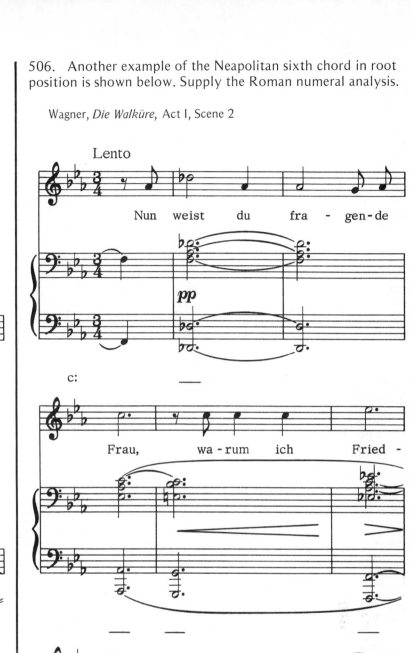

Nun weist du fra - gen - de Frau, wa - rum ich Fried - mund nicht heis - se!

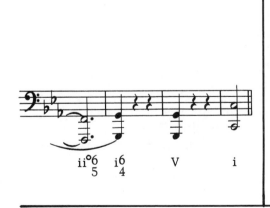

c: N -

VI   V$\frac{4}{3}$/iv   iv^7

ii$^{\circ}$$\frac{6}{5}$ i$\frac{6}{4}$ V   i

507. Although quite rare, the Neapolitan sixth chord may appear with the fifth in the bass. Supply the Roman numeral analysis.

Mozart, *Quintet*, K. 515

C: N⁶₄ ___ V⁷ vi

C: ___ ___ ___

Both √

508. Check (√) the correct option:

1. Neapolitan sixth chords are altered supertonic triads.
2. One or more chords may appear between the Neapolitan sixth chord and the dominant, which is its ultimate goal.

True statements:
(1) _____ (2) _____ Both _____ Neither _____

subdominant

509. The Neapolitan sixth chord may occur at any point in a phrase where its special color makes an appropriate effect. But because it is so distinctive, it should not be overused.

The harmonic function of the Neapolitan sixth chord is most like that of the (tonic/leading tone/subdominant/submediant) _____ triad.

510. We shall now turn to a species of altered chords called *altered dominants.* Like the Neapolitan sixth chord, altered dominants are highly colored, thus should be used with discretion.

Harmonic activity is heightened when a chord's urgency to resolve is increased. Dominant chords—active because of their position in the structure of tonality—are made more so by chromatic alterations of the fifth. The example on the following page shows the dominant triad and seventh chord with *raised* fifth.

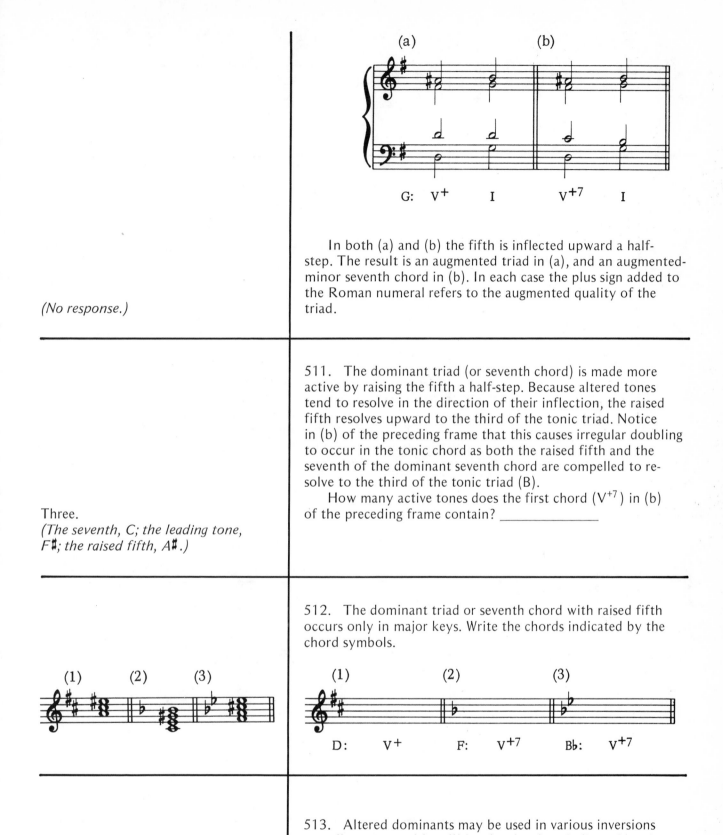

(a)   (b)

G: V⁺   I   V⁺⁷   I

In both (a) and (b) the fifth is inflected upward a half-step. The result is an augmented triad in (a), and an augmented-minor seventh chord in (b). In each case the plus sign added to the Roman numeral refers to the augmented quality of the triad.

(No response.)

---

511.   The dominant triad (or seventh chord) is made more active by raising the fifth a half-step. Because altered tones tend to resolve in the direction of their inflection, the raised fifth resolves upward to the third of the tonic triad. Notice in (b) of the preceding frame that this causes irregular doubling to occur in the tonic chord as both the raised fifth and the seventh of the dominant seventh chord are compelled to resolve to the third of the tonic triad (B).

How many active tones does the first chord (V⁺⁷) in (b) of the preceding frame contain? _____

Three.
(The seventh, C; the leading tone, F♯; the raised fifth, A♯.)

---

512.   The dominant triad or seventh chord with raised fifth occurs only in major keys. Write the chords indicated by the chord symbols.

(1)   (2)   (3)

(1)   (2)   (3)

D: V⁺   F: V⁺⁷   B♭:   V⁺⁷

---

513.   Altered dominants may be used in various inversions as well as root position. Write the chords as indicated by the chord symbols on the following page.

The Neapolitan Sixth, Altered Dominants, and Diminished Seventh Chords   175

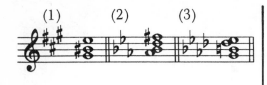

A: V⁺⁶   E♭:   V⁺⁴₂   A♭:   V⁺⁶₅

514. Continue as in the preceding frame.

C: V^{+6}_{4} G: V^{+4}_{3} E: V^{+7}

515. The activity of a dominant triad or seventh chord is increased by inflecting its fifth upward a half-step. It is important to remember that notes which are altered chromatically tend to resolve in the direction of their inflection.

Write the alto and tenor voices in accordance with the figured bass symbols. Supply, also, the Roman numeral analysis. *(Use close structure.)*

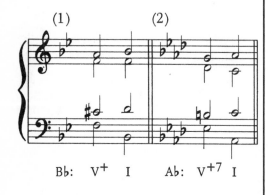

B♭: V^{+} I   A♭: V^{+7} I

B♭: ___   ___   A♭: ___   ___

516. Write the alto and tenor voices in accordance with the figured bass symbols. Supply, also, the Roman numeral analysis. *(Use open structure.)*

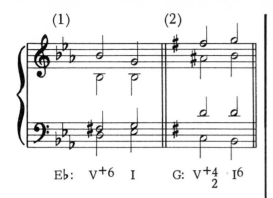

Eb: V+6   I   G: V+4/2   I6

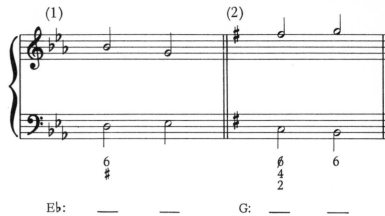

6
#

Eb: ___ ___   G: ___ ___

Bb: V+6   I   V+6   I

517. Supply the Roman numeral analysis for the example below:

Brahms, *Piano Concerto No. 2,* Op. 83

Allegretto grazioso

p

Bb: ___ ___ ___ ___

Ab: V+7   I

518. Supply the Roman numeral analysis for the final two chords in the example below:

Wolf, *Wo wird einst. . .*

Langsam

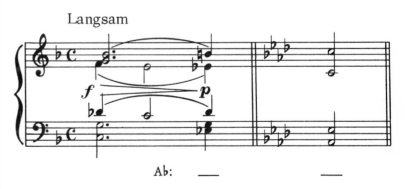

f   *p*

Ab: ___   ___

The Neapolitan Sixth, Altered Dominants, and Diminished Seventh Chords

519. The raised fifth in the dominant triad or seventh chord often appears in a manner similar to a chromatic passing tone. Such a case is shown below. Supply the Roman numeral analysis.

Schubert, *Erlkönig*, Op. 1

520. Altered dominant chords such as those shown in the previous few frames may also be used as secondary dominants. In the example below, the subdominant is embellished by an altered dominant. Complete the Roman numeral analysis.

Strauss, *Till Eulenspiegels lustige Streiche*, Op. 28

3rd

521. The dominant triad or seventh chord with raised fifth normally progresses to a *major* tonic triad; the raised fifth resolves up a half-step to the (root/3rd/5th) _____ of the tonic chord.

522. The dominant triad or seventh chord sometimes contains a *lowered* fifth, and these chords may occur in either a major or minor key.

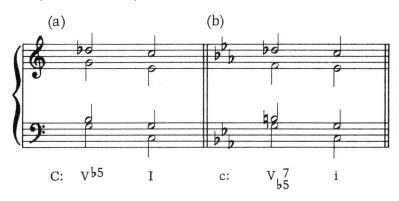

C: V♭5   I   c: V 7♭5   i

Is the altered dominant triad in (a) above (GBD♭) one of the four diatonic triad types (major, minor, diminished, or augmented)? _____

No.

523. Since the triad which results when the fifth of a dominant triad is lowered a half-step is not one of the four diatonic triad types, there is no symbol to express its quality. The altered tone is shown by an accidental applied to the chord symbol.

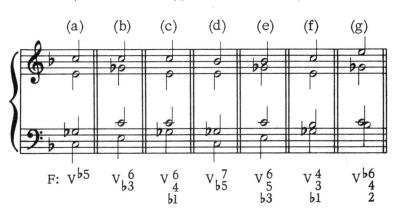

F: V♭5   V 6♭3   V 6 4 ♭1   V 7♭5   V 6 5 ♭3   V 4 3 ♭1   V ♭6 4 2

The altered note is represented variously as ♭5, ♭3, ♭1, or ♭6 according to the inversion, but in each case the altered note is the _____ of the chord.

fifth

524. When in second inversion as in (f) of the preceding frame, the dominant seventh with lowered fifth consists of the same notes as one of the augmented sixth chords built on the lowered second scale degree. Name this chord. _____ sixth.

French

525. The chord in (f) of Frame 523 is the same as a French sixth built on the lowered second scale degree, and may be analyzed as such. In most cases this analysis is preferred.

Write the chords indicated by the chord symbols. *(Remember: raise the seventh scale degree in minor.)*

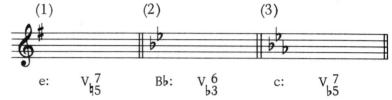

$$\text{e:} \quad V\,^{7}_{\natural5} \qquad \text{B}\flat\text{:} \quad V\,^{6}_{\flat3} \qquad \text{c:} \quad V\,^{7}_{\flat5}$$

526. Continue as in the preceding frame.

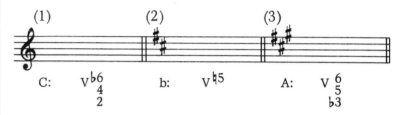

$$\text{C:} \quad V\,^{\flat6}_{\substack{4\\2}} \qquad \text{b:} \quad V\,^{\natural5} \qquad \text{A:} \quad V\,^{6}_{\substack{5\\\flat3}}$$

527. Supply the Roman numeral analysis.

c#:   i   N^6 V$^{7}_{\natural5}$

i

Chopin, *Nocturne,* Op. 27, No. 1

Larghetto

p

c#:   ___   ___   ___   ___

528. As the harmonic vocabulary evolved during the nineteenth century, composers placed more and more stress upon chords of dominant function. The restless activity produced by increased numbers of dominant chords was appropriate to the subjective character of their music. This preoccupation with dominant harmonic activity caused an increase in the level of tension. Not only used more frequently, dominant chords were altered chromatically to increase their activity.

The dominant chord with raised fifth is one example of such alteration; the dominant chord with lowered fifth is another. All of these chords possess greater tension than do the same chords without alteration. The use of such chords adds to harmonic activity and provides additional color resources.

Extensive use of altered dominants is characteristic of late nineteenth-century music, and this style of writing is also encountered in music of a semi-popular vein in the twentieth century. By now, the sonorities—and harmonic function—of these chords are so familiar, that their usefulness in serious composition is limited. Like all highly-colored effects, they should be used sparingly and with discretion.

(No response.)

(b).
(See next frame.)

529. In which case is the dominant seventh chord with raised fifth resolved most satisfactorily? _____

(a)   (b)

Ab: V$^{+6}_{5}$ I   V$^{+6}_{5}$ I

The seventh does not resolve by step downward.

530. Why is the part writing weak in (a) of the preceding frame? _____

_____

(a).
(In (b), the seventh does not resolve properly.)

531. In which case is the dominant seventh chord with lowered fifth resolved most satisfactorily? _____

(a)   (b)

b: V$_{\flat5}^{7}$ i   V$_{\flat5}^{7}$ i

---

532. Check (√) the correct option:

1. The dominant seventh chord with lowered fifth contains the same notes as a German sixth built on the lowered second scale degree.
2. Altered tones tend to resolve in the direction of their inflection.

True statements:
(1) _____ (2) _____ Both _____ Neither _____

(2) √

---

533. Check (√) the correct option:

1. The chord GB♮DF is an altered dominant seventh in the key of C minor.
2. The chord C♯E♯G♯B is a dominant seventh with raised fifth in the key of F-sharp major.

True statements:
(1) _____ (2) _____ Both _____ Neither _____

Neither √

---

534. We shall now turn from altered dominants to examine two diminished seventh chords which function in a unique manner.

The diminished seventh chord, as either a leading tone seventh or secondary dominant, has dominant function. Its root is a half-step below the root of the following chord to which it relates. The two chords below do not function in this way.

In (a), the SUPERTONIC SEVENTH CHORD WITH RAISED ROOT AND THIRD progresses to the tonic triad in first inversion; in (b), the SUBMEDIANT SEVENTH CHORD WITH RAISED ROOT AND THIRD progresses to the dominant seventh chord in _____ inversion.

first

---

535. Which of the chords below is a *supertonic seventh chord with raised root and third*? _____

KEY OF A-FLAT MAJOR

(c).

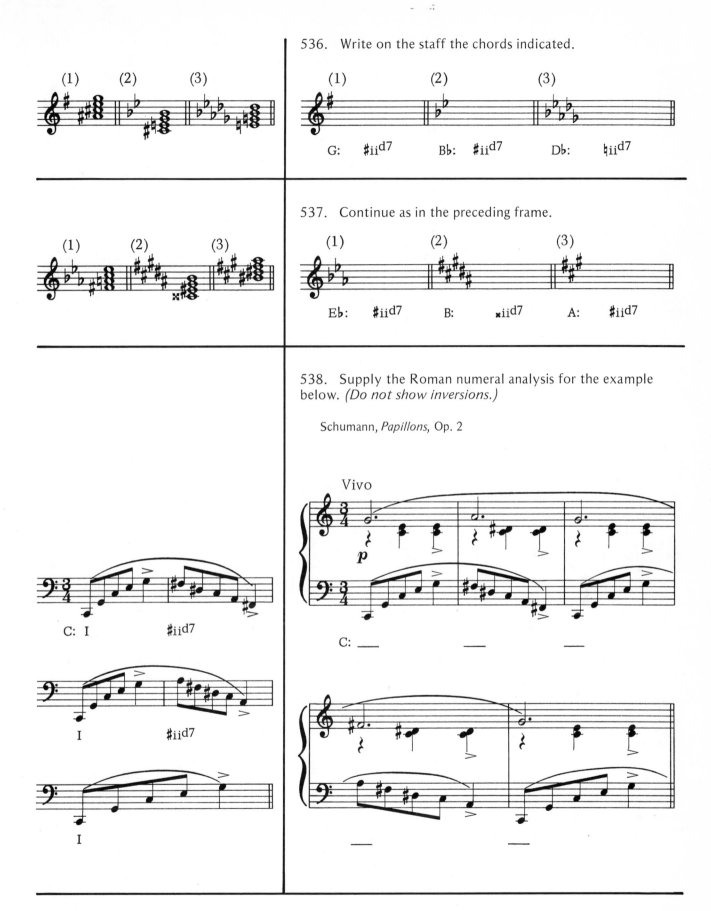

536. Write on the staff the chords indicated.

(1)   (2)   (3)

G: #ii d7   Bb: #ii d7   Db: ♮ii d7

537. Continue as in the preceding frame.

(1)   (2)   (3)

Eb: #ii d7   B: ×ii d7   A: #ii d7

538. Supply the Roman numeral analysis for the example below. *(Do not show inversions.)*

Schumann, *Papillons,* Op. 2

Vivo

C: ____   ____   ____

____   ____

C: I   #ii d7

I   #ii d7

I

third

539. The supertonic seventh chord with raised root and third may appear in various inversions. In the example below, this chord (at the asterisk) is in _____ inversion.

Rossini, *William Tell*, "Overture"

540. Chord symbols may show inversions if desired.

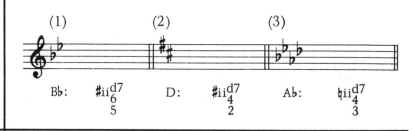

(a)	(b)	(c)	(d)

$$G: \quad \sharp ii^{d7} \qquad \sharp ii^{d7}_{\substack{6\\5}} \qquad \sharp ii^{d7}_{\substack{4\\3}} \qquad \sharp ii^{d7}_{\substack{4\\2}}$$

Write the chords as indicated.

(1)   (2)   (3)

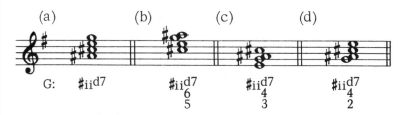

(1)   (2)   (3)

$$Bb: \quad \sharp ii^{d7}_{\substack{6\\5}} \qquad D: \quad \sharp ii^{d7}_{\substack{4\\2}} \qquad Ab: \quad \natural ii^{d7}_{\substack{4\\3}}$$

$$G: IV^{6}_{4} \qquad\qquad \sharp ii^{d7}_{\substack{4\\2}}$$

541. Supply the Roman numeral analysis for the example below. *(Indicate inversions.)*

Mozart, *Sonata*, K. 545

Andante

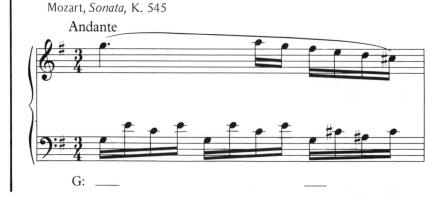

G: _____   _____

I

542. Supply the Roman numeral analysis for the example below. *(Indicate inversions.)*

Chopin, *Grande Valse Brillante,* Op. 18

Ab: I   I

♮ii°⁷₄₂   I

♮ii°⁷₆₅   I⁶₄

V⁷   I

Ab: ⎯   ⎯

⎯   ⎯   ⎯

⎯   ⎯   ⎯

The Neapolitan Sixth, Altered Dominants, and Diminished Seventh Chords   185

B-flat

543. As often is the case with diminished seventh chords, enharmonic spellings are used to simplify notation. In the example below, the altered supertonic seventh chord contains an enharmonic spelling of one note. The root, which normally would be spelled A-sharp, is notated as _____.

Brahms, *String Quintet*, Op. 111

544. The chord symbol used in the preceding frame for the altered supertonic seventh chord needs to be explained. The sharp placed to the left of the Roman numeral refers to the root (A♯) which is spelled enharmonically as a B-flat. It follows, then, that a symbol is used which expresses the chord as *normally spelled*.

Each chord on the following page is a supertonic seventh chord with raised root and third but contains an enharmonic spelling. Supply the correct Roman numeral analysis in each case. *(Do not indicate inversions.)*

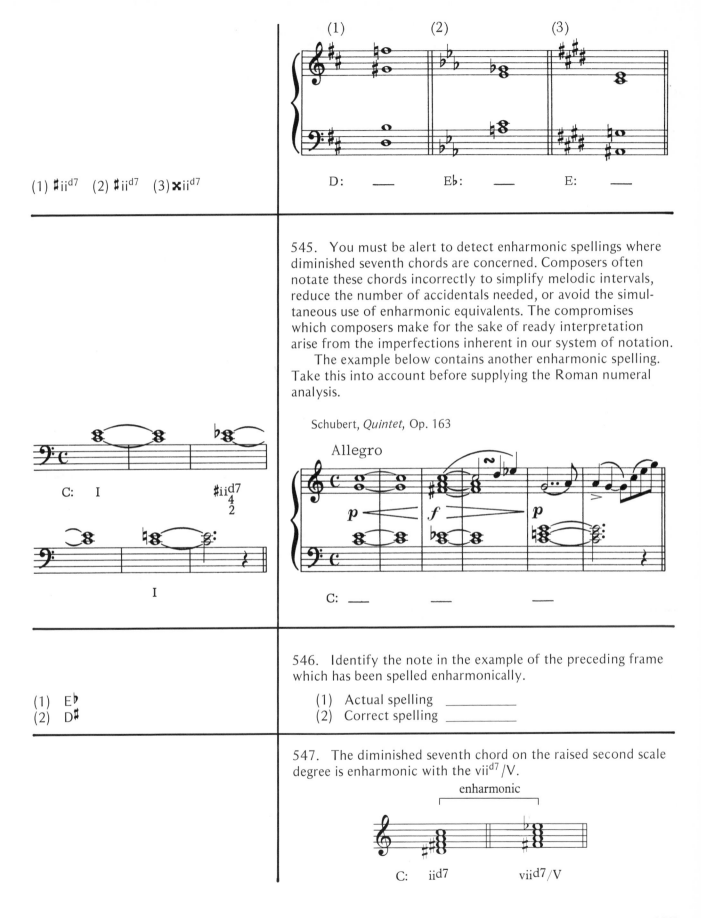

(1) ♯ii^{d7} (2) ♯ii^{d7} (3) 𝄪ii^{d7}

D: ____   E♭: ____   E: ____

C: I   ♯ii^{d7}_{4/2}

                    I

545. You must be alert to detect enharmonic spellings where diminished seventh chords are concerned. Composers often notate these chords incorrectly to simplify melodic intervals, reduce the number of accidentals needed, or avoid the simultaneous use of enharmonic equivalents. The compromises which composers make for the sake of ready interpretation arise from the imperfections inherent in our system of notation.

The example below contains another enharmonic spelling. Take this into account before supplying the Roman numeral analysis.

Schubert, *Quintet*, Op. 163

Allegro

C: ____   ____   ____

546. Identify the note in the example of the preceding frame which has been spelled enharmonically.

(1) E♭
(2) D♯

(1) Actual spelling _____
(2) Correct spelling _____

547. The diminished seventh chord on the raised second scale degree is enharmonic with the vii^{d7}/V.

enharmonic

C: ii^{d7}   vii^{d7}/V

(No response.)

The resolution determines the analysis of enharmonic chords. Regardless of the spelling, the chord above is analyzed as vii^{d7}/V if resolved to the dominant; if resolved to the tonic, it is analyzed as ♯ii^{d7}.

---

548. In addition to being built on the raised second scale degree, the diminished seventh chord also appears on the raised sixth degree.

C: ♯vi^{d7} V$^6_5$ I

dominant

Whereas the supertonic seventh chord with raised root and third progresses to the tonic triad, the submediant seventh chord with raised root and third progresses to the _____ triad or seventh chord.

(d).

549. Which of the chords below is a *submediant seventh chord with raised root and third?* _____

KEY OF D MAJOR

(a)   (b)   (c)   (d)

---

(1)   (2)   (3)

550. Write on the staff the chords indicated.

(1)   (2)   (3)

F: ♯vi^{d7} D: ♯vi^{d7} B: 𝄪vi^{d7}

551. Continue as in the preceding frame.

(1)　　　　(2)　　　　(3)

A:　×vi^{d7}　　Db:　♮vi^{d7}　　Eb:　♯vi^{d7}

C: V⁷　IV⁶　♯vi^{d7}　V⁶₅　I

552. Supply the Roman numeral analysis for the example below.

Schumann, *Dichterliebe*, Op. 48, No. 7

Nicht zu schnell

langst.

Pedal

C: ___　___　___　___

C: ♯vi^{d7}   V⁷

553. Complete the Roman numeral analysis below:

Wagner, *Die Meistersinger* "Vorspiel"

Sehr mässig bewegt

C: V⁷   vii^{d7}/V V⁹   ___ ___

A: I - - V$^6_5$ I - V$^6_5$ I

V$^6_5$ - - ⨯vi^{d7} V$^6_5$ - ⨯vi^{d7} V$^6_5$

(Note the omission of the 5th in the altered submediant seventh chord.)

554. Supply the Roman numeral analysis for the example below:

Beethoven, *Quartet*, Op. 131

Adagio ma non troppo e semplice

A: ___ - ___ - ___ - ___

___ - ___ - ___ - ___

7th

555. Like the altered supertonic seventh, the submediant seventh chord with raised root and third may appear in various inversions. The bass note of the chord at the asterisk is the (root/3rd/5th/7th) _____ of the chord.

Tchaikovsky, *Nutcracker Suite, "Valse des Fleurs"*

D: V   ♯vi d7   V   V

556. Enharmonic spellings frequently occur. Identify the note in the chord at the asterisk which is spelled enharmonically.

Beethoven, *Symphony No. 2*, Op. 36

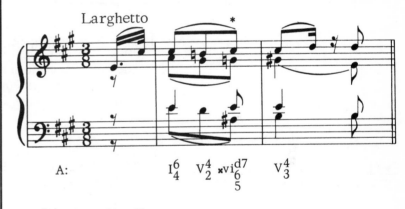

A: I$^6_4$ V$^4_2$ x vi d7$^6_5$ V$^4_3$

(1) G♮
(2) F𝄪

(1) Actual spelling _____
(2) Correct spelling _____

557. Supply the Roman numeral analysis for the example on the following page.

The Neapolitan Sixth, Altered Dominants, and Diminished Seventh Chords   191

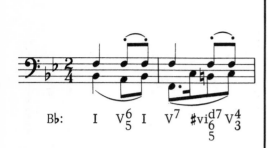

Bb: I   V$^6_5$ I   V^7 #vi$^{d7}_{\substack{6\\5}}$ V$^4_3$

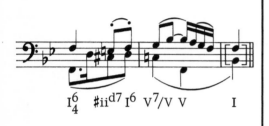

I$^6_4$ #ii^{d7} I^6 V^7/V V   I

Both are diminished,
not perfect fifths.

Beethoven, *Quartet*, Op. 18, No. 3

Andante con moto

Bb: ⸺ ⸺ ⸺

⸺   ⸺

558. One of the most important principles to observe when using altered chords is the proper resolution of altered tones. The supertonic and submediant seventh chords with raised root and third each contain two altered tones; these should continue in the same direction as their inflection (upwards).

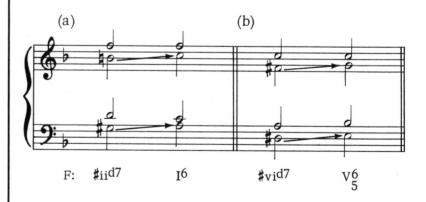

F: #ii^{d7} I^6 #vi^{d7} V$^6_5$

There are parallel fifths between the bass and tenor in (b). Why is this not an error? _____

_____

559. Write the alto and tenor voices in accordance with the figured bass symbols. Supply, also, the Roman numeral analysis. *(Indicate inversions.)*

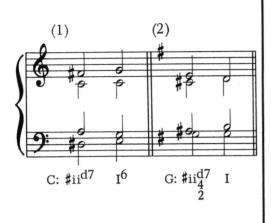

C: #ii d7   I⁶   G: #ii d7 ⁴₂   I

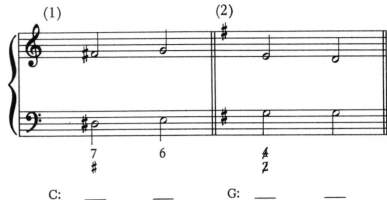

(1)   (2)

7   6   4
2

C: ___   ___   G: ___   ___

560. Continue as in the preceding frame. *(Use open structure.)*

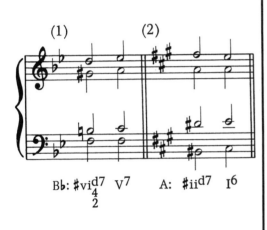

Bb: #vi d7 ⁴₂   V⁷   A: #ii d7   I⁶

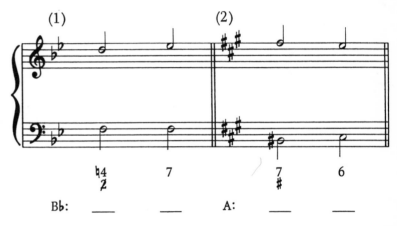

(1)   (2)

♮4   7   7   6
2   #

Bb: ___   ___   A: ___   ___

561. Continue as in the preceding frame.

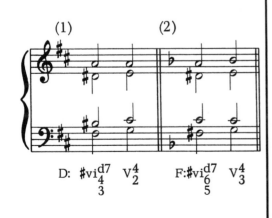

D: #vi d7 ⁴₃   V⁴₂   F: #vi d7 ⁶₅   V⁴₃

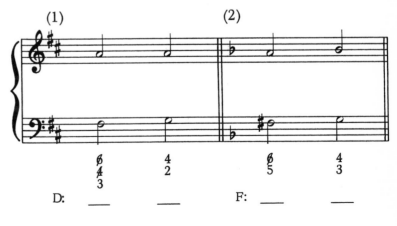

(1)   (2)

⁶₄₃   ⁴₂   ⁶₅   ⁴₃

D: ___   ___   F: ___   ___

The Neapolitan Sixth, Altered Dominants, and Diminished Seventh Chords

SUMMARY.

The Neapolitan sixth is a colorful, but not especially active chord; it functions like any other supertonic triad—its normal resolution is to the dominant. Altered dominants, on the other hand, are highly active due to the raised or lowered fifth, which provides an additional active tone. Like most chromatically altered tones, the raised or lowered fifth tends to resolve in the direction of inflection.

The resolution of diminished seventh chords on the raised second and sixth scale degrees is unlike that of most other diminished seventh chords. These two chords do not function as leading tone seventh chords, but rather as colorful embellishments of the tonic or dominant. The root of the diminished seventh chord (as usually spelled) progresses down an augmented second to the root of the following chord, and it is this relationship which gives these progressions their distinctive character.

8   Chromatic Third-Relation Harmony

During the nineteenth century, composers increasingly exploited root movement by thirds. Because the third is the basic constructive unit of chords in the tertian system, it follows that root relations by thirds should have a "fundamental" character. They do, in fact, generally produce an aurally pleasing effect. Limited to diatonic chords, third-relation harmony is pleasing, but does not expand the tonal horizon. *Chromatic* third relations, however, lead to chords which are quite foreign to the tonality, yet may be used in such a way that the tonal center is not seriously undermined. The result is not necessarily tonal instability, but tonal expansion.

562. Mediant and submediant chords are called "mediants" because they are half-way between the tonic and either the dominant or subdominant.

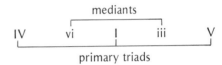

From this we can assert that any two chords whose roots are the interval of a third apart are in a "mediant" relationship with one another. The mediant and submediant triads relate to the tonic in this manner.

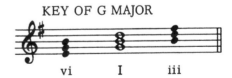

Extending this principle a step further, we can state that vii° and iii are in a "mediant" relation to the dominant.
Which two chords are in a "mediant" relationship with the subdominant?

(1) Submediant
(2) Supertonic

(1) _____

(2) _____

563. Which chords have a mediant relationship to the D major triad on the following page? *(Don't be misled by inversions.)*

(a) and (c).

_____

KEY OF D MAJOR

(a) (b) (c) (d)

(b) and (d).

564. Which chords have a mediant relationship to the F major triad below? _____

KEY OF F MAJOR

(a) (b) (c) (d)

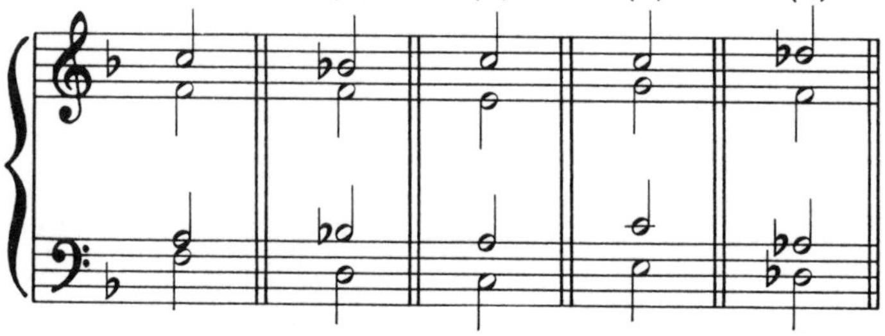

---

third

565. Within a tonality, mediant chords are built on the third and sixth scale degrees. (The mediant lies halfway between the tonic and dominant; the submediant lies halfway between the subdominant the tonic.) The roots of mediant triads are related to the tonic by the interval of a _____.

(No response.)

566. Whereas root relationships of fifths and seconds predominate in the music of earlier composers, mediant relationships (roots a third apart) are an important feature of many works by composers of the Romantic and post-Romantic eras. Of special importance is the use by these composers of *chromatic* mediant relationships. These, of course, involve the use of tones which are not part of the diatonic scale, and produce altered chords.

567. Limited to only major and minor triads, the mediants (both diatonic and altered) of the C major triad are shown in the diagram on the following page.

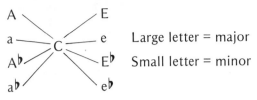

Large letter = major

Small letter = minor

Only two of these mediant triads are *diatonic* in the key of C major. Spell these chords.

(1) _____

(2) _____

(1) ACE

(2) EGB

(Any order.)

---

chromatic

568. With the exception of the A minor and E minor triads, all of the mediant triads in the preceding frame bear a _____ mediant relation to the C major triad.

---

569. Write the second chord in each case as directed. *(Observe the principles of correct voice leading and doubling.)*

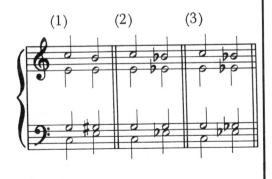

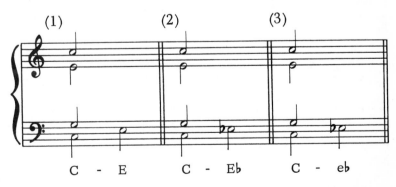

C - A   C - Ab   C - ab

---

570. The chords you wrote in the preceding frame are the chromatic (sub)mediants of the C major triad.

    Write the second chord in each case as directed. *(Continue to employ correct part writing procedures.)*

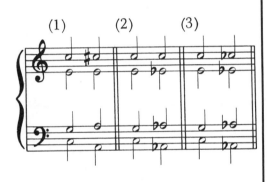

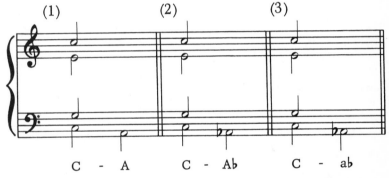

C - E   C - Eb   C - eb

---

third

571. The root of a chromatic mediant may be either a major or minor _____ from the root of the chord to which it relates.

572. It is chiefly major and minor triads which take part in chromatic mediant progressions. Diminished and augmented triads do not produce the novel tonal effect associated with this kind of writing and usually are best analyzed as some other type of altered chord. Seventh chords, on the other hand, sometimes are used in this manner, but we shall limit ourselves at this point to major and minor triads.

The mediant triads (both diatonic and altered) of the C minor triad are shown in the diagram below:

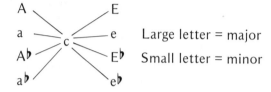

Large letter = major

Small letter = minor

Spell the two mediant triads which are *diatonic* in the key of C minor.

(1) A♭CE♭

(2) E♭GB♭
(The note B♭ derives from natural minor.)

(1) _____

(2) _____

573. Write the second chord in each case as directed. *(Observe the principles of correct voice leading and doubling.*

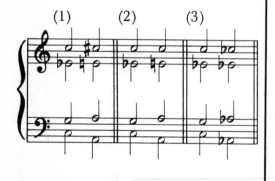

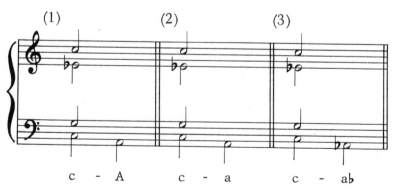

c – A   c – a   c – ab

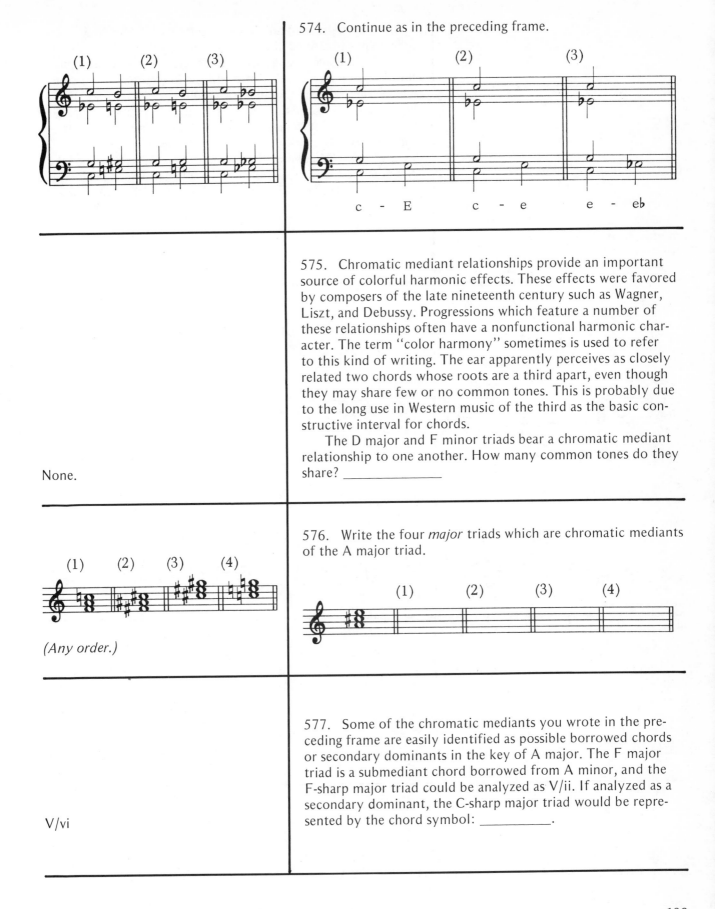

574. Continue as in the preceding frame.

(1)   (2)   (3)

c – E   c – e   e – e♭

None.

575. Chromatic mediant relationships provide an important source of colorful harmonic effects. These effects were favored by composers of the late nineteenth century such as Wagner, Liszt, and Debussy. Progressions which feature a number of these relationships often have a nonfunctional harmonic character. The term "color harmony" sometimes is used to refer to this kind of writing. The ear apparently perceives as closely related two chords whose roots are a third apart, even though they may share few or no common tones. This is probably due to the long use in Western music of the third as the basic constructive interval for chords.

The D major and F minor triads bear a chromatic mediant relationship to one another. How many common tones do they share? _____

(Any order.)

576. Write the four *major* triads which are chromatic mediants of the A major triad.

(1)   (2)   (3)   (4)

V/vi

577. Some of the chromatic mediants you wrote in the preceding frame are easily identified as possible borrowed chords or secondary dominants in the key of A major. The F major triad is a submediant chord borrowed from A minor, and the F-sharp major triad could be analyzed as V/ii. If analyzed as a secondary dominant, the C-sharp major triad would be represented by the chord symbol: _____.

578. Chromatic mediants may sometimes be identified as other types of altered chords. But when used as color sources rather than in accordance with functional harmonic principles, they open up new tonal relationships and effects. Progressions which contain a large number of such relationships take on a novel aspect. Chromatic mediants greatly enlarge the tonal vocabulary without necessarily undermining the stability of the tonality.

In Frame 576 one of the chromatic mediants given for the A major triad is the C major triad. Could this chord be analyzed as either a borrowed chord or a secondary dominant in the key of A major? _____

Yes.
(It is a diatonic triad in A (pure) minor. Thus it could be a borrowed chord.)

---

579. Write the two *minor* triads which are chromatic mediants of the A major triad. (Remember: *triads which are diatonic in the key of A major are excluded.*)

(1)   (2)

---

580. Write the four *minor* triads which are chromatic mediants of the G minor triad.

(1)   (2)   (3)   (4)

---

581. Write the two *major* triads which are chromatic mediants of the G minor triad. (Remember: *triads which are diatonic in the key of G minor are excluded.*)

(1)   (2)

---

582. The chord symbol used to represent a chromatic mediant is determined by the quality of the chord and the scale degree on which it is built. The first chord in the example on the following page is a major triad on the third degree of the D-flat major scale. Thus a large Roman numeral (III) is used.

Liszt, *Sonetto 47 del Petrarca*

Db: III   V(13) V⁷   I

Explain why the chord at the asterisk should not be analyzed as a secondary dominant (V/vi). _____
_____
_____

It does not function as a secondary dominant. As such, it would progress to vi.

---

583. Observe the chord symbols used for each of the chords below:

   (a)   (b)   (c)   (d)

D: vi   VI   bVI   bvi

Chord (a) is a diatonic (unaltered) submediant triad. A large Roman numeral is used in (b) to reflect the major quality of the chord. The flats placed at the lower left-hand corner of the Roman numerals in (c) and (d) indicate the lowered root in each case. What feature of the chord symbol in (d) indicates that the chord is a *minor* triad? _____
_____

A small Roman numeral is used.

---

584. Write the proper chord symbol for each chord.

  (1)   (2)   (3)

  (1)   (2)   (3)

Eb: iii   bIII   bvi

Eb: ___   ___   ___

---

585. All of the chords in the preceding frame are chromatic mediants. (True/False) _____

False.
(Chord (1) is diatonic.)

Chromatic Third-Relation Harmony   *201*

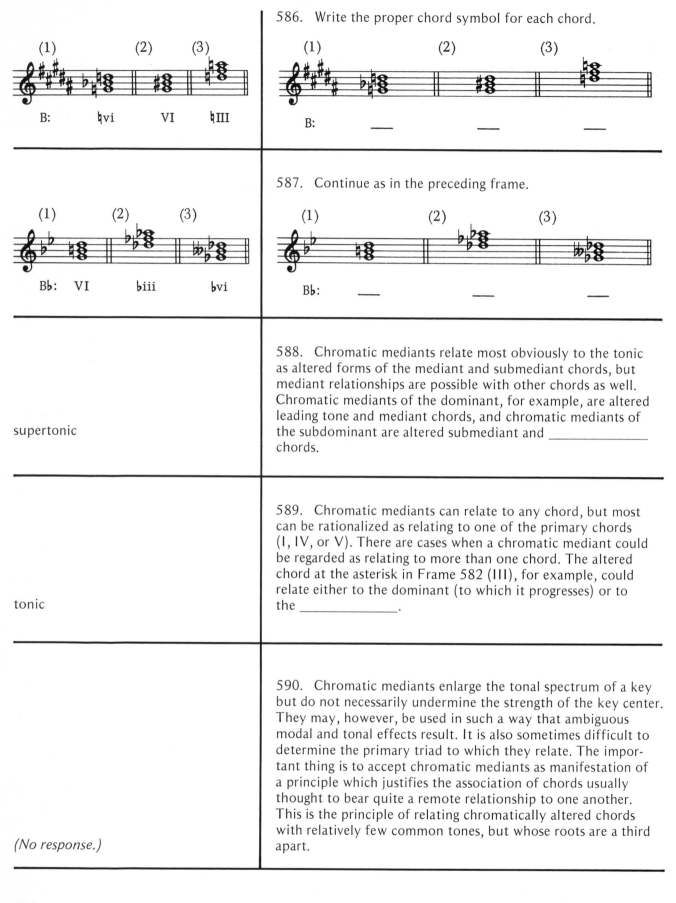

(1) **(2)** **(3)**

B: ♮vi   VI   ♮III

586. Write the proper chord symbol for each chord.

(1) **(2)** **(3)**

B: _____   _____   _____

---

(1) **(2)** **(3)**

B♭:   VI   ♭iii   ♭vi

587. Continue as in the preceding frame.

(1) **(2)** **(3)**

B♭: _____   _____   _____

---

supertonic

588. Chromatic mediants relate most obviously to the tonic as altered forms of the mediant and submediant chords, but mediant relationships are possible with other chords as well. Chromatic mediants of the dominant, for example, are altered leading tone and mediant chords, and chromatic mediants of the subdominant are altered submediant and _____ chords.

---

tonic

589. Chromatic mediants can relate to any chord, but most can be rationalized as relating to one of the primary chords (I, IV, or V). There are cases when a chromatic mediant could be regarded as relating to more than one chord. The altered chord at the asterisk in Frame 582 (III), for example, could relate either to the dominant (to which it progresses) or to the _____.

(No response.)

590. Chromatic mediants enlarge the tonal spectrum of a key but do not necessarily undermine the strength of the key center. They may, however, be used in such a way that ambiguous modal and tonal effects result. It is also sometimes difficult to determine the primary triad to which they relate. The important thing is to accept chromatic mediants as manifestation of a principle which justifies the association of chords usually thought to bear quite a remote relationship to one another. This is the principle of relating chromatically altered chords with relatively few common tones, but whose roots are a third apart.

Chapter 8

nonfunctional

591. The use of chromatic mediants usually results in (functional/nonfunctional) _____ harmony.

592. A passage which illustrates the vague or ambiguous tonal effect which may result from the use of chromatic mediant relationships is the "eternal sleep motive" from Wagner's opera, *Die Walkure*.

Wagner, *Die Walküre*, Act III, Scene 3

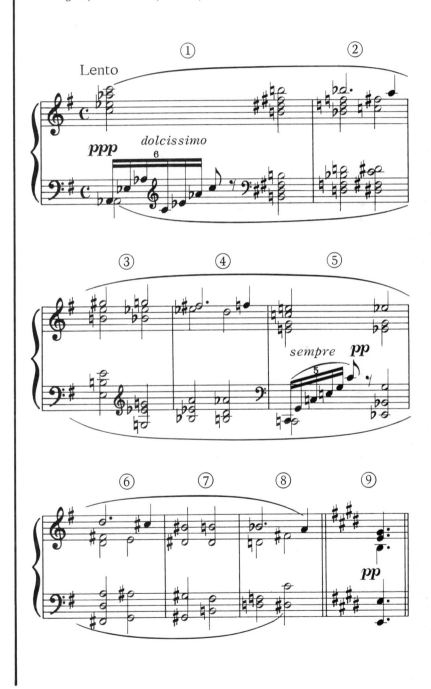

E

Harmony such as this is naturally open to a variety of interpretations. We shall discuss briefly one possibility in the next few frames.

One aspect of this passage is fairly obvious: the tonality established in measure nine is the key of _____ major.

(No response.)

593. In spite of the highly chromatic character of the passage in the preceding frame, it may be regarded as being entirely in the key of E major. Many of the chords can be explained as chromatic mediants, and these are the chords which concern us here. Melodically, this passage consists of a descending chromatic scale extending for more than an octave. It is organized rhythmically into a sequence which repeats every two measures.

---

third

594. Although the harmony varies, it is organized in accordance with the melodic sequence mentioned above. The units which comprise this sequence begin in measures 1, 3, 5, and 7. The last chord in the example (E major) closes the sequence. Obviously the chords which begin each unit of a sequence such as this have special significance. The example below shows the root progression of these chords. (Numbers refer to measures.)

①　　　　③　　　　⑤　　　　⑦　　　　⑨

The notes are written in order to make clear their relation to one another. The root progression in each case is down a major _____.

---

augmented

595. Chromatic mediants are often spelled enharmonically. The first chord of the example in Frame 592, for example, is an A-flat major triad. It is considered to have a chromatic mediant relation to the E major triad because the interval of a diminished fourth (A♭-E) is the aural equivalent of a major third (G♯-E).* You must not be misled by enharmonic spellings, for these occur frequently in highly chromatic music. Sound is more important than notation, which is often merely a matter of convenience.

The descending pattern of roots shown in Frame 594 outlines the _____ triad.

---

*Chord 1 in Frame 592 can be viewed equally well as related to the dominant (B major triad) which follows.

596. The progression of chords which serves as the harmonic framework for the passage in Frame 592 is shown below:

E: III   I   ♮VI   III   I

mediants

All of these chords are easily related to the key of E major as either the tonic triad (I) or chromatic _____.

597. The specific progressions in the example of Frame 592 which feature chromatic mediant relationships are shown below. *(Numbers refer to measures.)* Supply the proper chord symbols. *(Note the indication of C major in (b).)*

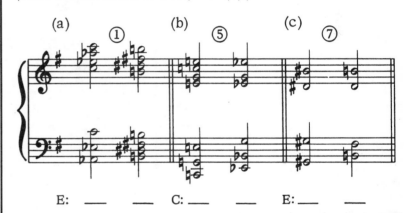

E: ___ ___   C: ___ ___   E: ___ ___

(a) E: III V

(b) C: I ♭III

(c) E: III V

598. You were asked to analyze the chords in (b) of the preceding frame in the key of C major as this makes them easier to comprehend. Even though the over-all tonal structure of Wagner's motive is in the key of E major, the momentary presence of other keys can be felt. This excerpt provides a good example of how the basic harmonic scheme can be endowed with extraordinarily colorful effects through chromatic mediants which suggest, but do not necessarily confirm, other keys.

Of course, the tonal fluidity produced in this manner can also result in actual changes of key. Whether or not keys are felt to be "established" is left to the discretion of the analyst. It is generally desirable to absorb as many chords as possible into a given tonality in order to obtain as large a view of the tonal organization as possible.

True.

All chromatic mediants are potentially in some key other than that in which they appear. (True/False) _____

599.   The harmony in the example below consists of major triads built on a series of roots which ascend in minor thirds.

Brahms, *Immer leiser wird mein Schlummer,* Op. 105, No. 2

No.
(See next frame.)

Is the third chord (B♭ D♯ F♯) as closely related to the key of E major as the second (G♯ B D♯)? _____

600. Chord 3 in the preceding frame is a tritone removed from the tonal center of E major. This is the most remote tonal relationship possible. Note that B-flat divides the octave E-E into two equal parts.

Such relations are called "symmetrical," and they tend to obliterate tonal distinctions.

(No response.)

---

601. The tonality of the progression in Frame 599 is ambiguous. Not only does the exclusive use of major triads provide the ear nothing to differentiate between, but furthermore, the sequence of roots quickly reaches a point which is so remote from the key of E major that it lies outside the orbit of this key.

Chromatic mediant relationships can be used to undermine the strength of a tonality. Do you think this is desirable? _____

It is not possible to give a simple yes or no answer. It depends upon circumstances.

---

602. The term FALSE RELATION* applies to chromaticism which occurs between two *different* voices. Compare the two examples below:

In (a), the chromaticism (D-D♯) occurs in the same voice. In (b), however, it not only occurs between the two voices but is displaced by the interval of an octave. *(Play these two examples at the piano.)*

Which example produces the "smoother" effect? _____

(a).
(There should be no difference of opinion in this case.)

_____

*The term "cross relation" is also used.

603. False relations cause rather "harsh" effects. For this reason they are often avoided by means of careful part writing which limits chromatic movement to the same voice (as in (a) of the preceding frame). Sometimes false relations are exploited for their peculiar expressive value, particularly when a sudden, unexpected change of harmony is desired. Such a case is shown below:

Wolf, *Biterolf*

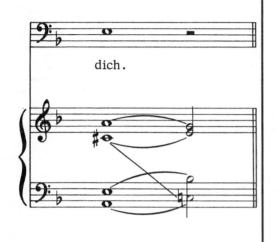

Find the false relation and draw a line connecting the notes which produce it.

(b) and (c).

604. Which example(s) contains a false relation? _____

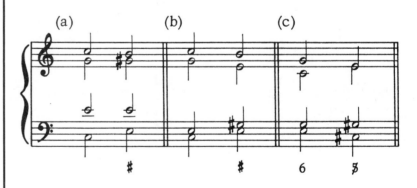

605. Chromatic mediants bring about many false relations. These sometimes are exploited for their expressive value, but at other times are eliminated through careful part writing.

No.
(The chromaticism D♯-D♮ occurs in the same voice.)

A chromatic mediant relationship occurs in the example below between the second and third chords. Does this passage contain a cross relation? _____

Chopin, *Prelude*, Op. 28, No. 9

606. Supply the Roman numeral analysis for the example below. Analyze the chords at the asterisks as chromatic mediants.

Franck, *Chorale No. 1*

607. In each of the two examples below, the B major triad is used as a different type of altered chord. Taking into account its function, indicate to what type each belongs.

KEY OF D MAJOR

(a) Secondary dominant

(b) Chromatic mediant

(a) _____

(b) _____

---

608. Check (√) below the type of altered chord shown in the example.

Db:

(b) √

(a) Altered dominant _____

(b) Chromatic mediant _____

(c) Borrowed chord _____

(d) None of these _____

---

609. The chord in the preceding frame could also be a secondary dominant (depending upon its use). Write the chord symbol which would be appropriate in such a case.

V/vi

_____

SUMMARY.

Chords whose roots are separated by the interval of a major or minor third are said to be in a mediant relationship to one another. Chromatic mediants employ tones which are foreign to the key, and greatly enlarge the harmonic material of a particular tonality. Used with discretion (clearly related to primary triads), they do not undermine the strength of the key center. They may, however, depending upon the frequency of occurrence and the root relationships involved, cause ambiguity of modality and obscure the tonal center. Some chords can be analyzed either as chromatic mediants or other types of altered chords. The way a particular chord is used determines its classification.

Although chromatic mediants generally are not used as frequently as some of the other types of altered chords, they are capable of producing striking effects which cannot be achieved by other means. They are especially prevalent in music of late nineteenth-century composers who frequently exploited the third relation of roots to achieve novel tonal effects.

9   Modulation to Foreign Keys 1

Extensive use of altered chords is generally accompanied by expansion of tonality beyond the limitations of closely related keys. The various techniques of modulation presented in this and the following chapter make available all of the tonal relationships contained in the chromatic scale; any key—no matter how remote—may be reached with ease. Due to the many ways diminished seventh chords can be resolved, they are especially mobile. In this chapter, we shall examine the use of these chords as springboards into distant tonal realms.

F minor.

610. Two keys whose signatures differ by more than one sharp or flat are called FOREIGN KEYS.* Although the techniques of modulation presented in this chapter may be used to modulate to closely related keys, they are associated chiefly with modulations to foreign keys.

Which of the keys listed below is *not* closely related to B-flat major? _____

C minor	E-flat major
F minor	G minor

_____

*The terms *remote* keys, and *distant* keys are also used.

---

foreign

611. Since the signature of B-flat major contains two flats and that of F minor four flats, these two keys are not closely related; they are called _____ keys.

D minor (and) B major

612. Identify the two keys listed below which are foreign to the key of E minor. _____ and _____.

D minor	A minor
G major	B major

---

two

613. Modulations to foreign keys produce greater tonal variety than do modulations to closely related keys. This is because fewer tones are shared by foreign keys than by closely related keys. The signatures of foreign keys differ by at least _____ sharps or flats.

---

614. The example below shows there are six common tones between the keys of D major and F-sharp minor (pure form).

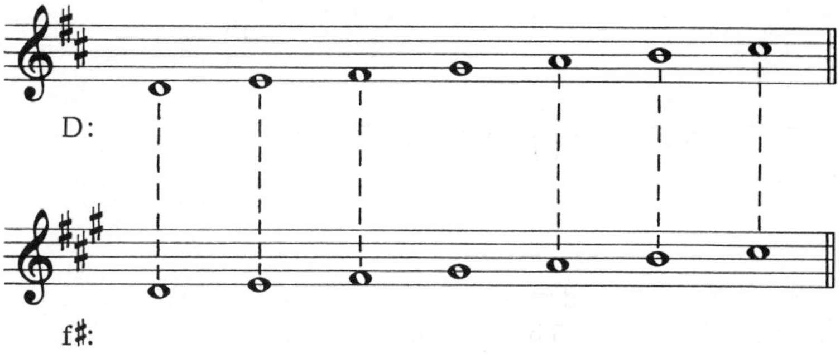

D:

f#:

closely

D major and F-sharp minor are _____ related keys.

Three.

615. How many common tones are there between the foreign keys of D major and F-sharp major? _____

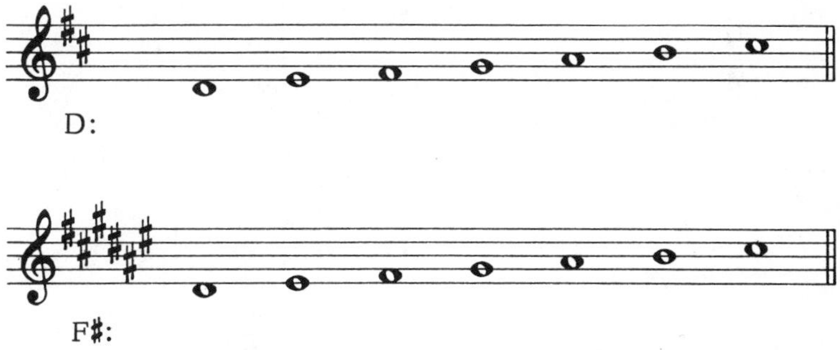

D:

F#:

No.
(G major and G minor are foreign keys.)

616. Are all of the keys listed below closely related to G major? _____

    D major   B minor
    E minor   G minor

No.

617. Parallel major and minor keys are not closely related because of the difference of three sharps or flats between their signatures. Their identify is very close, however, due to the fact that they share the same tonic, subdominant, and dominant notes. The difference between them is of mode (quality) rather than key. Is it logical to speak of "modulating" from the key of G major to G minor? _____

Yes.

618. Modulation involves a shift of the tonal center from one pitch to another. Thus a change from a major key to its parallel minor (or the reverse) is not a modulation. This is called a *change of mode*.
      Does change of mode result in tonal variety? _____

(No response.)

619. Change of mode is a useful device for introducing tonal variety into music. Because parallel major and minor keys share the same structural tones, the ear readily accepts a change from one to the other. While this in itself is not modulation, it leads to an expansion in the area of closely related keys, and interchangeability of mode makes available the closely related keys of both the major and minor in a given tonality.

620. Interchange of mode expands tonality to include most of the tones of the chromatic scale. The composite modal structure thus created also possesses a greatly enlarged set of closely related keys. The diagram below shows the keys which are available to C major or minor as closely related keys through change of mode.

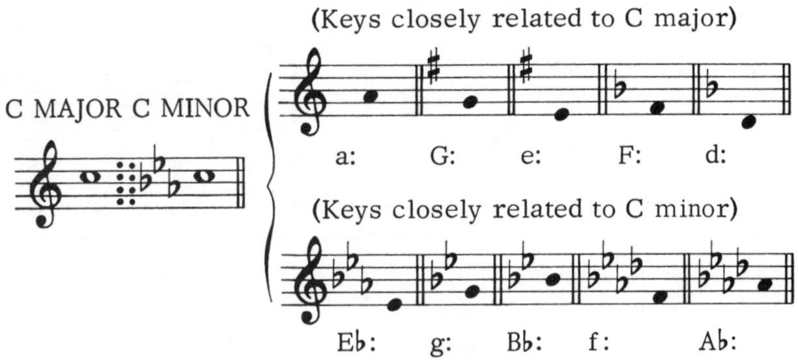

ten

      Interchange of mode leads to a total of _____ keys which can easily be brought within the orbit of a single tonality.

621. The example on the following page demonstrates how change of mode can be used to lead to a foreign key. The first phrase shown is in F major. The second phrase begins with a change of mode to F minor, and quickly modulates to D-flat major, followed by B-flat minor.

Mozart, *Sonata*, K. 533

F minor

The keys of D-flat major and B-flat minor are both foreign to F major, but they are closely related to the key of _____ _____.

622. Change of mode accounts for the ease with which the ear accepts the key of G minor in the second half of the example below.

Beethoven, *Sonata,* Op. 2, No. 3

The key of G minor is closely related to (C major/C minor)?

_____

C minor.

Chapter 9

(No response.)

---

623. Change of mode is not a modulation, but introduces tonal variety through contrast of major and minor modes. Further, change of mode has an important bearing upon modulation since it may serve as a steppingstone to more remote keys. In effect, change of mode increases the number of closely related keys from five to ten.

---

(1) √

624. Check (√) the correct option:

1. Modulations to foreign keys introduce greater tonal variety than modulations to closely related keys.
2. F-sharp minor and A major are foreign keys.

True statements:
(1) _____ (2) _____ Both _____ Neither _____

True.

625. Change of mode makes the key of C-sharp minor readily available to the key of A minor. (True/False) _____

No.

626. The process of "diatonic" common chord modulation is presented in Chapter 4. In this type of modulation the common chord is a diatonic (unaltered) chord in each of the two keys involved. Now we shall extend this principle to include the use of chords which are altered in one (or both) of the keys.*

  Can altered chords be used as common chords in *diatonic* modulations? _____

_____

*Some writers classify such modulations as *chromatic.* We shall refer to them simply as common chord modulations.

---

(2).
(diatonic = altered)

627. The chart on the following page shows all of the possible relationships which the common chord may bear to the old and new keys.

	OLD KEY		NEW KEY
(1)	diatonic	=	diatonic
(2)	diatonic	=	altered
(3)	altered	=	diatonic
(4)	altered	=	altered

  Which of these possibilities is used in the modulation on the following page? _____

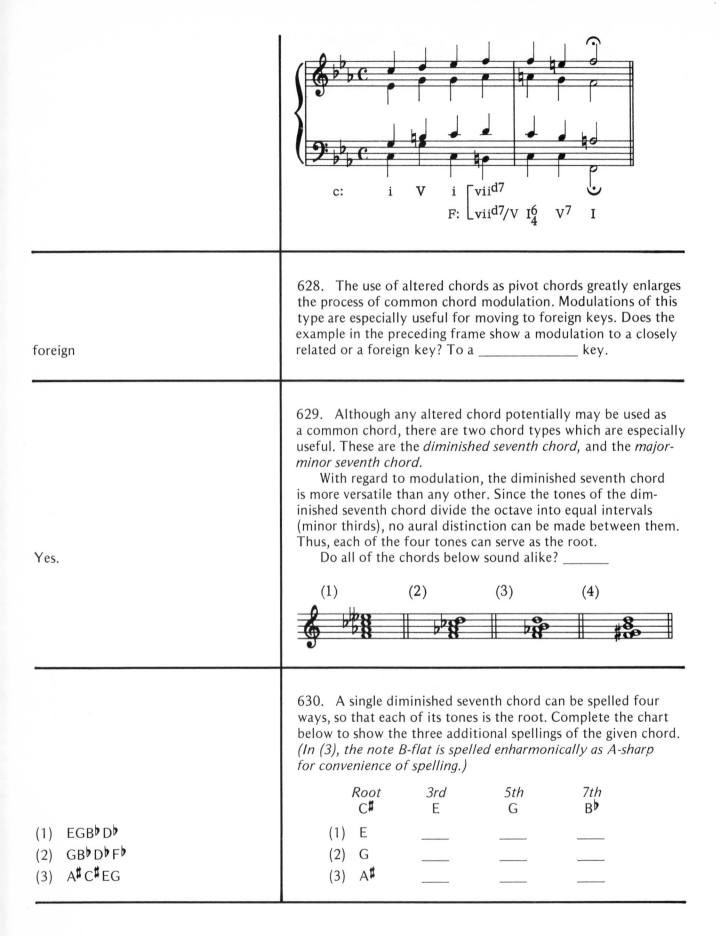

c: i   V   i   ⌈viiᵈ⁷
F: ⌊viiᵈ⁷/V I⁶₄   V⁷   I

---

628. The use of altered chords as pivot chords greatly enlarges the process of common chord modulation. Modulations of this type are especially useful for moving to foreign keys. Does the example in the preceding frame show a modulation to a closely related or a foreign key? To a _____ key.

foreign

---

629. Although any altered chord potentially may be used as a common chord, there are two chord types which are especially useful. These are the *diminished seventh chord,* and the *major-minor seventh chord.*

With regard to modulation, the diminished seventh chord is more versatile than any other. Since the tones of the diminished seventh chord divide the octave into equal intervals (minor thirds), no aural distinction can be made between them. Thus, each of the four tones can serve as the root.

Do all of the chords below sound alike? _____

Yes.

(1)   (2)   (3)   (4)

---

630. A single diminished seventh chord can be spelled four ways, so that each of its tones is the root. Complete the chart below to show the three additional spellings of the given chord. *(In (3), the note B-flat is spelled enharmonically as A-sharp for convenience of spelling.)*

	Root C♯	3rd E	5th G	7th B♭
(1)	E	___	___	___
(2)	G	___	___	___
(3)	A♯	___	___	___

(1) EGB♭D♭
(2) GB♭D♭F♭
(3) A♯C♯EG

631. Continue as in the preceding frame.

	Root D♯	3rd F♯	5th A	7th C
(1)	F♯	___	___	___
(2)	A	___	___	___
(3)	C	___	___	___

(1) F♯ACE♭

(2) ACE♭G♭

(3) CE♭G♭B♭♭

---

632. Because any of the four tones of a diminished seventh chord can be the root, a high degree of mobility results. Consider, for example, the fact that the chord F♯ACE♭ is the vii^{d7}/V in the key of C major, but is capable of performing the same harmonic function in three other major keys as well. *(Remember, too, that this chord could lead to the parallel minor in each case.*

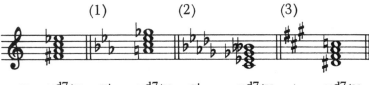

C: vii^{d7}/V   E♭: vii^{d7}/V   G♭:   vii^{d7}/V   A: vii^{d7}/V

The example above shows that a diminished seventh chord can be approached as a vii^{d7}/V in one key and left as the same type chord in another by merely respelling the chord.

(No response.)

---

633. In order to pursue the possibility presented in the preceding frame a bit further, we shall construct a modulation from the key of C-sharp minor to G major. First write the notes on the staff which produce the chords indicated by the chord symbols. *(No key signature is given, so you must write the proper accidentals.)*

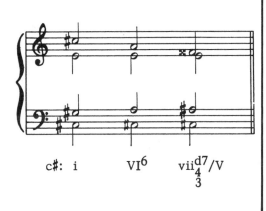

c♯: i   VI^6 vii$^{d7}_{4\atop3}$/V

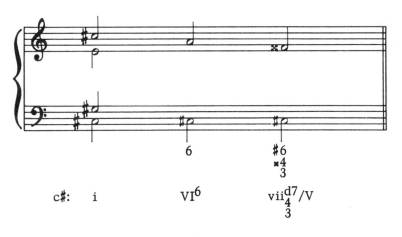

c♯:   i   VI^6 vii$^{d7}_{4\atop3}$/V

---

634. Now re-spell the last chord in the preceding frame as a vii^{d7}/V in the key of G major.

c : vii^{d7}/V is spelled F✗A♯C♯E

G: vii^{d7}/V is spelled _____

C♯EGB♭

---

635. Complete the alto and tenor voices in accordance with the chord symbols. *(Since no key signature is given, be sure to ascertain the exact pitches required, and write the appropriate accidentals.)*

G: vii^{d7}/V   I$^6_4$ V^7 I

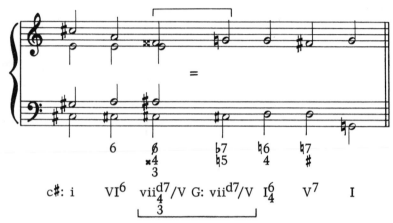

6   ⌀   ♭7   ♮6   ♮7
✗4   ♮5   4   ♯
3

c♯: i   VI^6 vii$^{d7}_{\substack{4\\3}}$/V G: vii^{d7}/V I$^6_4$ V^7 I

---

636. In actual music the pivot chord is usually not re-spelled.* In most cases, a single spelling is correct in only one of the two keys involved. Thus, a choice must be made between the possible spellings. That which is used should result in the simplest notation possible and cause the voices to lead smoothly into and out of the pivot chord.

Examine carefully the example below. It served as the basis for the chord progression presented in Frames 633-635.

Haydn, *Quartet*, Op. 74, No. 1

Andante grazioso

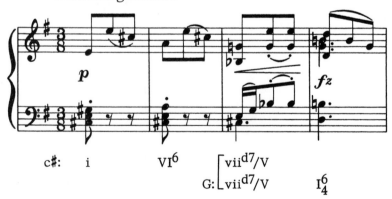

c♯:   i   VI^6 ⌈vii^{d7}/V
                    G:⌊vii^{d7}/V   I$^6_4$

V^7 I

G major.

Is the pivot chord as notated spelled correctly in the key of C-sharp minor or G major? _____

_____

*Enharmonic spellings will be encountered frequently throughout this chapter. The term "enharmonic" modulation is sometimes used to refer to any type of modulation in which there is an enharmonic change of one or more notes.

637. The multiplicity of roots inherent in the diminished seventh chord results in a wide choice of possible resolutions. The mobility of this chord is extended by its numerous uses in both major and minor keys. The example below shows that a diminished seventh chord occurs on every degree of the major scale as an altered chord of one kind or another.

(No response.)

638. The fact that a diminished seventh chord can appear on virtually every scale degree in both major and minor keys means that it may be both approached and left with ease. This, plus the possibility of regarding any one of the four tones as the root, results in a large number of possible uses.

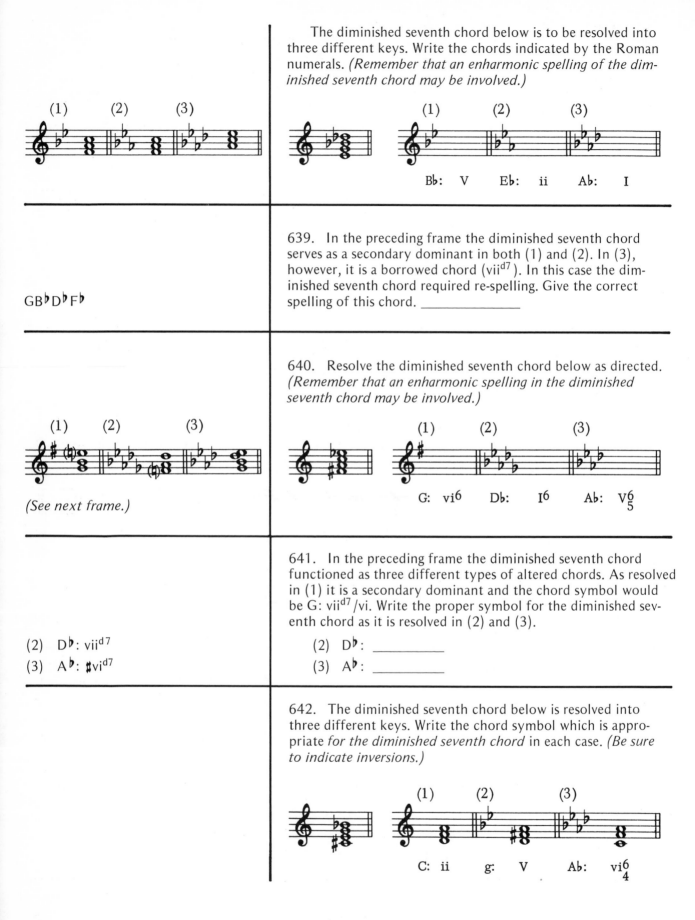

The diminished seventh chord below is to be resolved into three different keys. Write the chords indicated by the Roman numerals. *(Remember that an enharmonic spelling of the diminished seventh chord may be involved.)*

(1) (2) (3)

Bb: V   Eb: ii   Ab: I

GB♭D♭F♭

639. In the preceding frame the diminished seventh chord serves as a secondary dominant in both (1) and (2). In (3), however, it is a borrowed chord (vii^{d7}). In this case the diminished seventh chord required re-spelling. Give the correct spelling of this chord. _____

640. Resolve the diminished seventh chord below as directed. *(Remember that an enharmonic spelling in the diminished seventh chord may be involved.)*

(1) (2) (3)

G: vi^6 Db: I^6 Ab: V$^6_5$

(1) (2) (3)

(See next frame.)

641. In the preceding frame the diminished seventh chord functioned as three different types of altered chords. As resolved in (1) it is a secondary dominant and the chord symbol would be G: vii^{d7}/vi. Write the proper symbol for the diminished seventh chord as it is resolved in (2) and (3).

(2) D♭: _____

(3) A♭: _____

(2) D♭: vii^{d7}
(3) A♭: ♯vi^{d7}

642. The diminished seventh chord below is resolved into three different keys. Write the chord symbol which is appropriate *for the diminished seventh chord* in each case. *(Be sure to indicate inversions.)*

(1) (2) (3)

C: ii   g: V   Ab: vi$^6_4$

Chapter 9

(1) C: vii^{d7}/ii

(2) g: vii^{d7}/V

(3) A♭: vii$^{d7}_{4\atop2}$/vi

---

(1) C: _____

(2) g: _____

(3) A♭: _____

---

643. Continue as in the preceding frame.

f: V$^6_4$ A: vi^6 c: i$^6_4$

---

(1) f: vii$^{d7}_{4\atop2}$/V

(2) A; vii$^{d7}_{6\atop5}$/vi

(3) c: vii$^{d7}_{4\atop2}$

---

(1) f: _____

(2) A: _____

(3) c: _____

---

644. In each case below, the diminished seventh chord must be re-spelled in order for it to relate correctly to the chord to which it resolves. Supply the correct spelling in each case.

b♭:   VI$^6_4$ D: V^6 C: I^6

---

(1) F A♭ C♭ E♭♭

(2) G♯ B D F

(3) B D F A♭

---

(1) _____

(2) _____

(3) _____

---

645. Continue as in the preceding frame.

b: i^6 D♭: V$^6_4$ A♭: vi$^6_4$

---

(1) A♯ C♯ E G

(2) G B♭ D♭ F♭

(3) E G B♭ D♭

---

(1) _____

(2) _____

(3) _____

646. The example below shows a modulation from the key of C major to E-flat major.

Haydn, *Quartet*, Op. 54, No. 1

C: I   V⁺/IV   IV   IV⁺

ii$^6_5$ ⌐vii^{d7}/V
E♭: ⌐vii$^{d7}_{4}$/V   I$^6_4$ V⁷   I
        2

The diminished seventh chord which serves as a common chord is spelled correctly in the key of C major. Its correct spelling in the key of E-flat major would be _____.

ACE♭G♭

A: I   V6 ⌐vii$^{d7}_{4}$/ii
               2
        b: ⌐vii$^{d7}_{4}$
               2

i$^6_4$ vii$^{d7}_{4}$ i6 vii$^{d7}_{4}$/V   V
          3   2

647. In the example below, there is a modulation from the key of A major to B minor. The chord at the asterisk is the common chord. Supply the Roman numeral analysis.

Bach, Chorale: *Was mein Gott will, das g'scheh' allzeit*

A:

both

648. Although the use of altered chords as common chords is usually associated with modulations to foreign keys, the example in the preceding frame shows that modulations to closely related keys may be accomplished in this way too. The common chord in this example is spelled correctly in (the first/the second/both/neither) _____ key(s).

3.

649. A modulation from the key of E-flat major to D major is shown below. In this example diminished seventh chords occur four times. Each of these chords is numbered. Write the number of the chord which is used to modulate. _____

Beethoven, *Sonata*, Op. 13

---

650. Chord number three in the preceding frame is used to modulate from the key of E-flat major to D major. This chord is shown again in the example on the following page. Notice that it is spelled correctly in the new key (D major), but not in the old. The correct spelling of the chord (vii^d7^/ii) in E-flat major would be EGB♭D♭.

Complete the Roman numeral analysis.

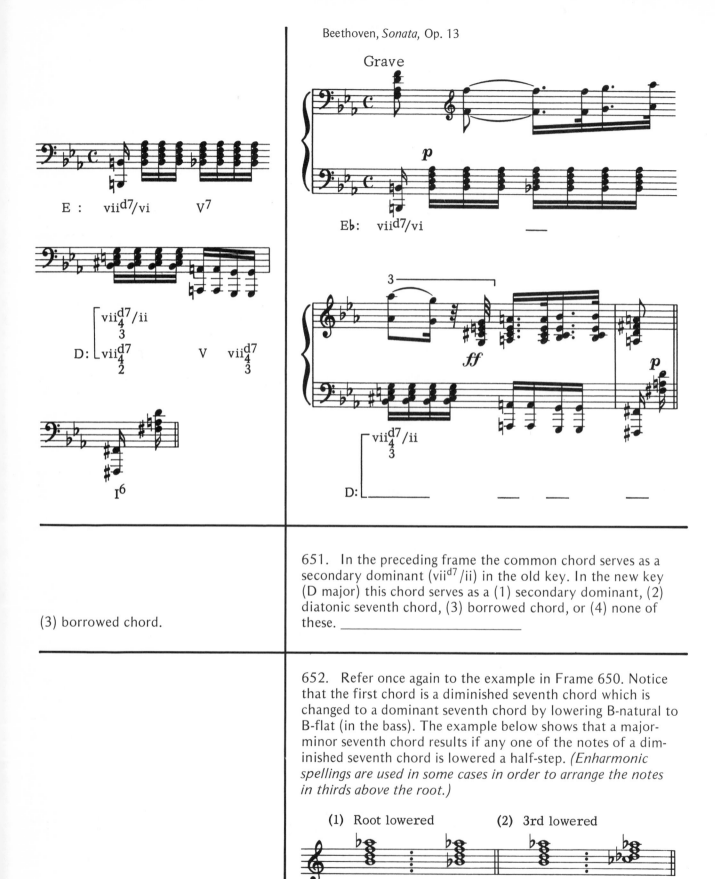

Beethoven, *Sonata*, Op. 13

(3) borrowed chord.

651. In the preceding frame the common chord serves as a secondary dominant (vii^{d7}/ii) in the old key. In the new key (D major) this chord serves as a (1) secondary dominant, (2) diatonic seventh chord, (3) borrowed chord, or (4) none of these. _____

652. Refer once again to the example in Frame 650. Notice that the first chord is a diminished seventh chord which is changed to a dominant seventh chord by lowering B-natural to B-flat (in the bass). The example below shows that a major-minor seventh chord results if any one of the notes of a diminished seventh chord is lowered a half-step. *(Enharmonic spellings are used in some cases in order to arrange the notes in thirds above the root.)*

(1) Root lowered   (2) 3rd lowered

(3) 5th lowered   **(4)** 7th lowered

If the second chord in each case above should be used as a dominant seventh (V^7), the major (or minor) key in which each functions is:

(1) E♭	(2) G♭
(3) A	(4) C

(1) _____   (2) _____

(3) _____   (4) _____

---

653. Convert the diminished seventh chords to dominant seventh chords by lowering one note a half-step as directed. *(Use enharmonic spellings when necessary in order that each chord consists of thirds above the root.)*

(1) Root lowered   **(2)** 3rd lowered

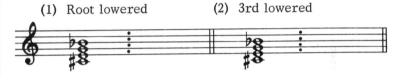

(3) 5th lowered   **(4)** 7th lowered

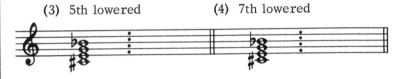

---

654. In the example below, a modulation from the key of G major to C-sharp minor is accomplished by lowering one of the tones of a diminished seventh chord a half-step to produce a dominant seventh chord.

Haydn, *Quartet*, Op. 74, No. 1

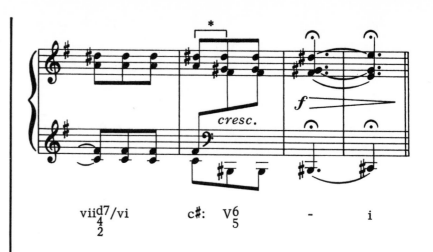

viid7/vi
  4
  2
          c#:   V6
                 5   -   i

The note C is re-spelled
B♯ (in the bass).

At the asterisk the fifth of the diminished seventh chord (A) is lowered a half-step to G-sharp, which becomes the root of the dominant seventh chord. What other change is made at this point to produce correct spelling? _____

_____

SUMMARY.

We have seen that diminished seventh chords are useful for modulating to both closely related and foreign keys. Inherent ambiguity of root, plus the large number of possible resolutions give them remarkable mobility. Like other symmetrical chords, the diminished seventh chord possesses a "neutral" quality, which facilitates both the approach to and departure from them.

Movement from one diminished seventh chord to another occurs frequently in nineteenth-century music. Such passages produce the effect of suspended tonality, and are often quite effective. But such passages should not appear too often, unless tonal ambiguity is desired for expressive purposes.

10   Modulation to Foreign Keys 2

Chords which may be resolved several ways serve especially well as common chords in modulations to foreign keys. Like the diminished seventh chord, the major-minor seventh chord not only possesses strong activity, but is capable of performing many harmonic functions. This chapter focuses on modulations by means of the major-minor seventh chord; it also deals with the Neapolitan sixth chord, sequence modulation, and pivot tone modulation.

655. The major-minor seventh chord may function in three ways: (1) as a diatonic seventh chord (V^7); (2) a secondary dominant; and (3) enharmonically as a German sixth chord. To demonstrate these possibilities the major-minor seventh chord on G is resolved three different ways in the example below:

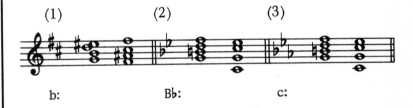

b: Bb: c:

Indicate the function of the major-minor seventh chord in each case.

(1) German sixth   (1) _____

(2) Secondary dominant (V^7/ii)   (2) _____

(3) Diatonic seventh (V^7)   (3) _____

656.   Resolve the major-minor seventh chord on D as directed, and supply the proper chord symbols.

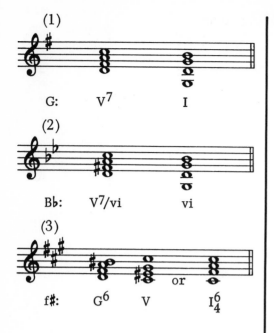

(1)

G: V⁷   I

(2)

B♭:   V⁷/vi   vi

(3)

f♯:   G⁶   V   I⁶₄   or

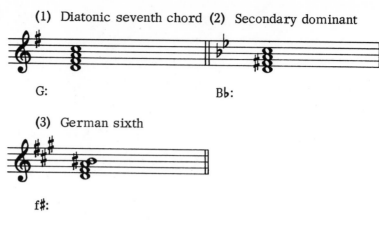

(1) Diatonic seventh chord (2) Secondary dominant

G: B♭:

(3) German sixth

f♯:

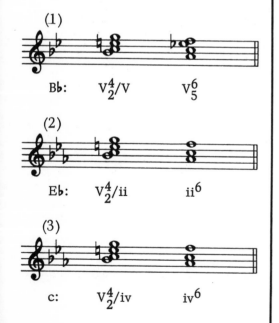

(1)

B♭:   V⁴₂/V   V⁶₅

(2)

E♭:   V⁴₂/ii   ii⁶

(3)

c: V⁴₂/iv   iv⁶

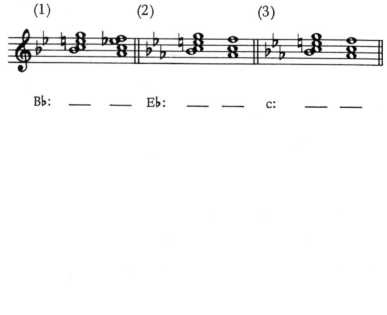

657.   The next few frames demonstrate the versatility of the major-minor seventh chord. Supply the Roman numeral analysis. *(Indicate inversions.)*

(1)   (2)   (3)

B♭: ___ ___   E♭: ___ ___   c: ___ ___

658. Continue as in the preceding frame.

(1)   (2)   (3)

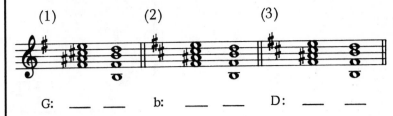

G: ___ ___   b: ___ ___   D: ___ ___

(1)

G: V⁷/iii   iii

(2)

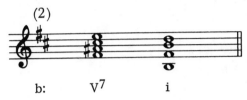

b: V⁷   i

(3)

D: V⁷/vi   vi

659. Continue as in the preceding frame.

(1)   (2)   (3)

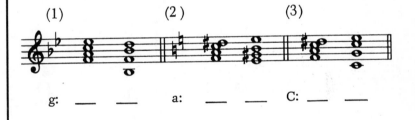

g: ___ ___   a: ___ ___   C: ___ ___

(1)

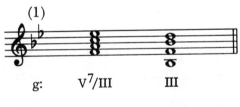

g: V⁷/III   III

(2)

a: G⁶   V

(3)

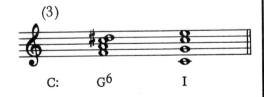

C: G⁶   I

660. The chord at the asterisk is spelled and resolved as a German sixth in the key of C major. Supply the chord symbol for this chord in the key of A-flat major. *(Watch for enharmonic spelling.)*

Beethoven, *Symphony No. 5*, Op. 67

Andante con moto

Ab: I – – V⁷ I – –

V⁷/IV

viiᵈ⁷/ii –

C: G⁶

I⁶₄ – V⁷ I

661. In the example on the following page, the pivot chord (at the asterisk) is re-spelled by the use of enharmonic equivalents (D♯=E♭, B=C♭). This results in correct spelling in both of the keys involved. Supply the chord symbol for this chord in the new key (E-flat major).

Chapter 10

Chopin, *Mazurka*, Op. 56, No. 1

Andante non tanto

Poco più mosso

(*f*)

rit.

p *leggiero*

B: V⁷ - - I ⌐ V⁷/IV

                Eb: ⌐___ I⁶₄

G⁶

---

enharmonic

662. Modulations which involve enharmonic spellings (such as in the preceding frame) are sometimes called _____ modulations.

Yes.

663. Is it correct to say that the keys of B major and E-flat major bear a chromatic mediant relation to one another? _____

---

664. The example below shows a modulation from the key of C minor to C-sharp minor. The chord at the asterisk is a pivot chord and is spelled correctly in the *new* key. Supply the chord symbols for this chord in both keys.

Beethoven, *Sonata*, Op. 90

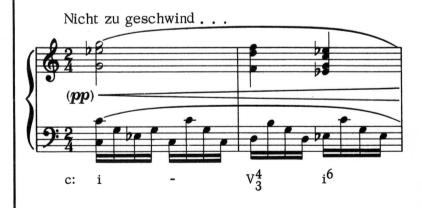

Nicht zu geschwind . . .

(*pp*)

c: i   -   V⁴₃   i⁶

c: ⌈G⁶
c♯: ⌊V⁷

ii°⁶   vii^{d7}/V   i⁶₄   c♯:⌈ ___

i   V⁴₃   i⁶

A♭CE♭F♯

665. In the preceding frame the chord at the asterisk is spelled correctly in the new key but not the old. Give the correct spelling of this chord in the key of C minor. _____

---

666. We have seen that diminished seventh chords and major-minor seventh chords often serve as pivot chords. Actually, any altered chord may be used in this way. In the example below, the French sixth is used to modulate from the key of A-flat minor to D-flat major.

Wagner, *Die Walküre,* Act II, Scene 4

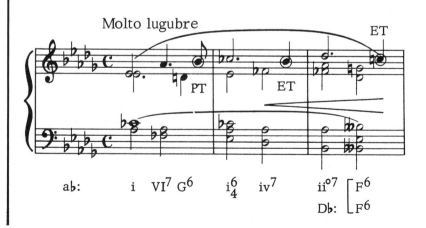

Molto lugubre

ab: i   VI⁷ G⁶   i⁶₄   iv⁷   ii°⁷ ⌈F⁶
                                      D♭: ⌊F⁶

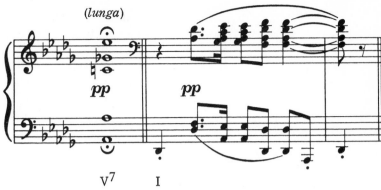

V^7 I

In the key of A-flat minor the French sixth is built on the lowered second scale degree. This chord is left as a French sixth built on the lowered _____ degree in D-flat major.

sixth

667. The Neapolitan sixth chord sometimes is used as a pivot chord. Complete the Roman numeral analysis.

Wagner, *Fünf Gedichte, "Schmerzen"*

Langsam und breit

schö-nen Au - gen roth, wenn im Mee-res-spie-gel

c: i^6_4 V^7 VI N^6

ba-dend dich er - reicht der frü-he Tod;

g: $\left[\begin{matrix} \text{VI} \\ \text{N} \end{matrix} \right.$ N^6 i^6_4 V^7

i

g: $\left[\text{VI} \right.$ —   —   —   —

668. In the example of the preceding frame, the pivot chord is spelled correctly in both keys. The chord at the asterisk below, however, is spelled correctly in the new key but not in the old. Supply the chord symbol for this chord in both keys. *(Be sure to take into account the enharmonic spelling.)*

Mozart, *Symphony No. 39*, K. 543

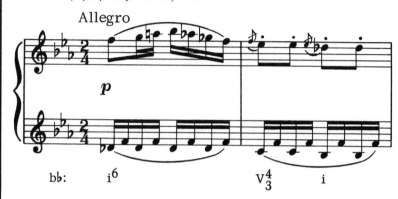

b♭:   i⁶   v$_3^4$ i

b♭: ⌐N⁶

F♯: ⌐IV⁶

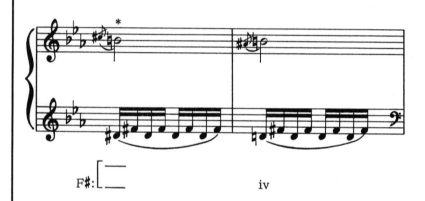

F♯: ⌐___ ___⌐   iv

V⁷

669. Several enharmonic spellings are involved in the example on the following page. The modulation is from B-flat minor to B major, but not all of the voices move into sharps at the same time. Complete the Roman numeral analysis.

Haydn, *Quartet,* Op. 76, No. 6

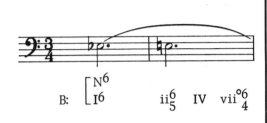

B: N6
    I6   ii6 5   IV   vii°6 4

I6 4 - V7 I

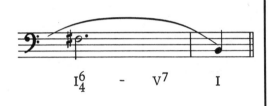

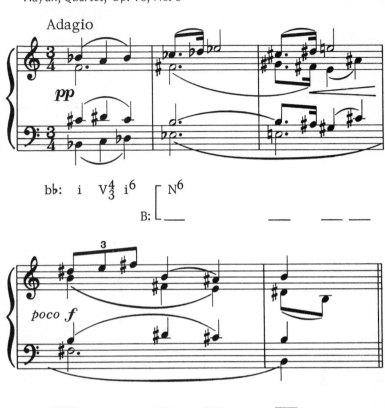

bb: i   V4 3   i6   N6

B:

670. Sequences may result in modulations to foreign keys.

Chopin, *Mazurka,* Op. 56, No. 1

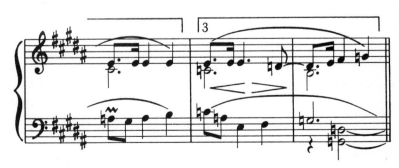

(1) B major

(2) A major

(3) G major

Play the example on the preceding page at the piano and identify each of the three keys involved in the sequence.

(1) _____

(2) _____

(3) _____

671. In the example below, modulations occur not only between the sequence units, but within them as well.

Franck, *Prélude, Aria et Final*

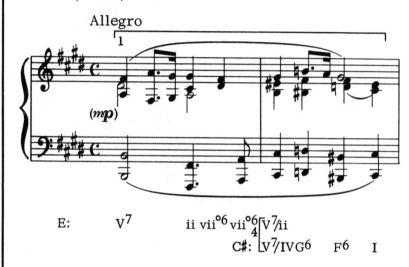

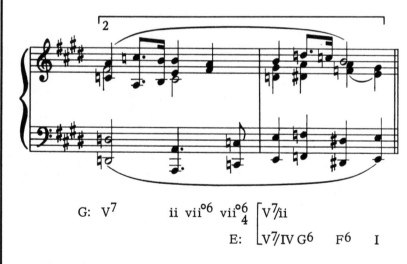

The sequence begins in the key of E major and modulates within the first unit to C-sharp major. The second unit begins in the key of G major and modulates to E major. If this pattern of key relationships were continued to complete a third sequence unit, the final key would be _____.

G major

672. Used excessively, sequences may result in "mechanical" effects. But they are useful in modulations involving foreign keys, for the repetition of a melodic, rhythmic, and harmonic pattern causes the ear to accept even the most remote tonal relationships.

No.

Do all sequences result in modulation? _____

---

673. A single tone sometimes serves to link one key with another. Such a tone is called a "pivot" tone.

Chopin, *Mazurka*, Op. 33, No. 3

third

The note C is the first scale degree in the old key and the _____ scale degree in the new key.

674. The example below shows a pivot tone modulation from the key of B minor to D major.

Mozart, *Fantasia in C Minor*, K. 475

b: i   V   —   —

D: I   —   V⁷   —   I

fifth
third

The note F-sharp is the _____ scale degree in the old key and the _____ scale degree in the new key.

675. The pivot tone performs the same function as a common chord; it provides a link between two keys. In the example below, the pivot tone is G-sharp (at the asterisk). An enharmonic change is involved here.

Schumann, *Die Nonne*, Op. 49, No. 3

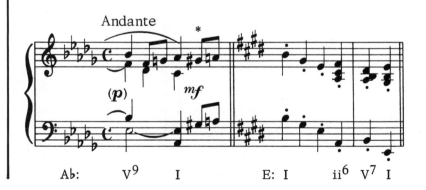

Ab: V⁹   I   E: I   ii⁶   v⁷   I

first	The note G-sharp is the third scale degree in the key of E major. It is the enharmonic equivalent of the _____ scale degree in A-flat major.

SUMMARY.

Chapters 9 and 10 have shown that modulations to foreign keys may extend the range of keys related to a particular tonal center as far as the system of equal temperament permits. Frequent modulation (especially to foreign keys) tends to undermine the authority of the principal tonality. The degree of stability desired in a composition is not only a matter of style; it varies according to formal and expressive requirements. Fluctuations in tonal stability help elicit a variety of emotional responses. Insistence upon the tonal resources of a single key provides the maximum degree of tonal stability, whereas liberal use of altered chords and frequent modulations to foreign keys produces tonal instability.

Chapter 9 explored the use of the diminished seventh chord to modulate to foreign keys. The techniques presented in Chapter 10 are listed below:

1. The *major-minor seventh chord* (including the German sixth chord as an enharmonic equivalent) used as a common chord (either diatonic or altered in one or both of the keys).

2. The *French sixth chord* used as a common chord.

3. The *Neapolitan sixth chord* used as a common chord.

4. The modulating sequence.

5. Modulation by means of a pivot tone.

11 Ninth, Eleventh, and Thirteenth Chords

The interval of a third is the basic unit for building chords in tonal music. Two superimposed thirds produce a triad, three a seventh chord. Continuing further, chords of four, five, and six thirds form harmonic structures called ninth, eleventh, and thirteenth chords after the interval which occurs between the root and the highest note. Consisting of as many as seven tones, these chords are fairly dissonant, and are used only when colorful effects are desired. Used sparingly by earlier composers, ninth, eleventh, and thirteenth chords occur more frequently toward the end of the nineteenth century. They are especially characteristic of impressionistic music.

676. Chords of more than four tones can be produced by superimposing additional thirds above the seventh of seventh chords. These are knows as NINTH, ELEVENTH, and THIRTEENTH CHORDS.

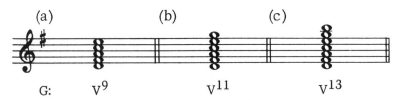

If an additional third were to be added above the thirteenth chord, a fifteenth would result. Since the fifteenth merely duplicates the root two octaves higher, the thirteenth chord is the limit of tertian extention possible unless chromatic notes are used.

The thirteenth chord consists of _____ notes.

seven

677. Ninth, eleventh, and thirteenth chords may occur on any scale degree, but the majority are dominant chords. This results from the desire evidenced by many composers to increase the activity of dominant harmony. Extended and altered dominant sonorities were exploited chiefly by late nineteenth-century composers, but ninth, eleventh, and thirteenth chords are part of the harmonic vocabulary of earlier composers as the examples which follow will show.

(No response.)

The chord in example (a) of the preceding frame is called a dominant ninth chord; chord (b) is called a dominant eleventh chord.

---

678. Write the chord symbol for each chord.

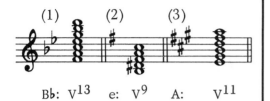

Bb: V^{13} e: V^{9} A: V^{11}

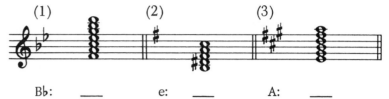

Bb: ___   e: ___   A: ___

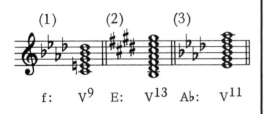

f: V^{9} E: V^{13} Ab: V^{11}

679. Continue as in the preceding frame.

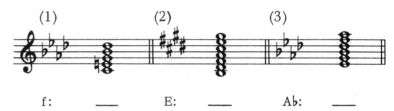

f: ___   E: ___   Ab: ___

(No response.)

680. Ninth, eleventh, and thirteenth chords pose two special problems which will concern us throughout this chapter. First, they rarely appear as complete chords. Since most music is based on a texture of three, four, or five separate parts, with four being the most prevalent, one or more tones are usually omitted. The second problem results from the manner in which the higher chord members are introduced into the musical texture. Since these tones often appear as nonharmonic devices, it is sometimes difficult to decide whether they should be interpreted as members of the harmony or as incidental melodic occurrences.

---

681. Now we shall direct our attention to ninth chords. The most frequently used ninth chords are shown below:

(a) Major key   **(b)** Minor key

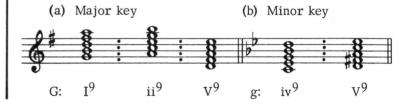

G: I^{9} ii^{9} V^{9} g: iv^{9} V^{9}

Ninth, Eleventh, and Thirteenth Chords

243

No. *(See next frame.)*	The dominant ninth chord is used more frequently than any other, so we shall start with this chord. In the preceding example, the dominant ninth chord (V^9) is shown in both a major and minor key. Do these chords sound the same in each case? _____

minor	682. The two forms of the dominant ninth are identified according to the type of interval between the root and ninth of the chord. The interval in (a) below is a major ninth whereas the interval in (b) is a _____ ninth.
	
	        (a) (b)
	
	    G: V^9 g: V^9

major	683. The chord in (a) of the preceding frame is commonly referred to as the "major ninth chord." It consists of a major-minor seventh chord plus a _____ ninth above the root.
major-minor	684. The chord in (b) of Frame 682 is called a "minor ninth chord." This term derives from the interval of a minor ninth which appears above the root. The sonority also includes a _____-_____ seventh chord.
major-minor-minor	685. The terms "major ninth chord" and "minor ninth chord" refer to *dominant* ninths. Thus the seventh chord to which the ninth is added is assumed to be major-minor in quality. When it is necessary to refer accurately to the various qualities of ninth chords, one may extend the system used for seventh chords. The major ninth, for example, could be termed a "major-minor-major ninth chord." *(The quality of the ninth is added to the term which designates the quality of the seventh chord.)* The chord in example (b) of Frame 682 is commonly called a "minor ninth chord." Its more specific term is _____-_____-_____ ninth.

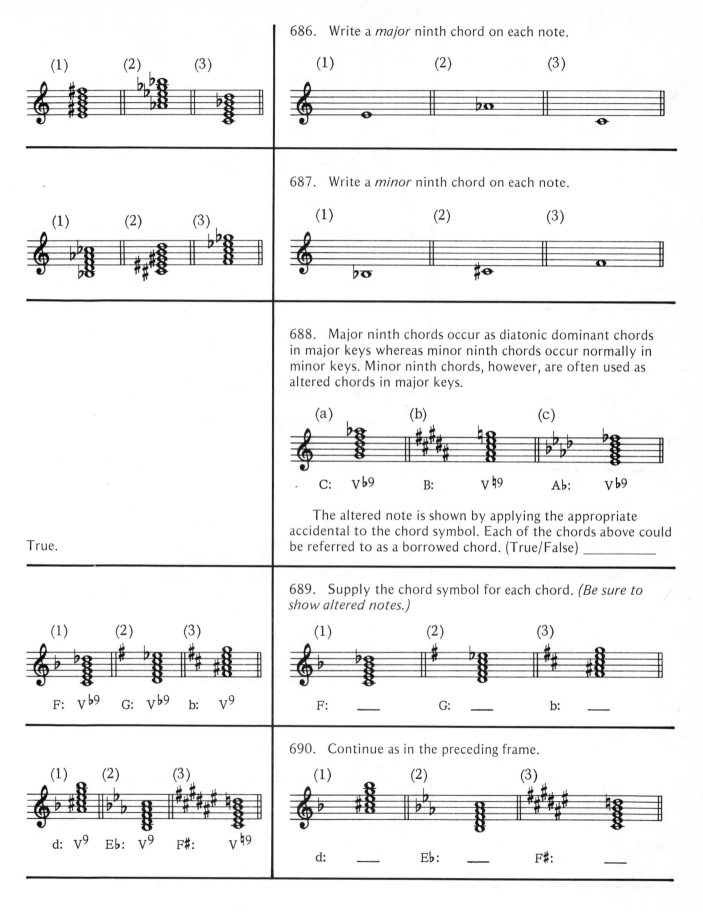

686. Write a *major* ninth chord on each note.

687. Write a *minor* ninth chord on each note.

688. Major ninth chords occur as diatonic dominant chords in major keys whereas minor ninth chords occur normally in minor keys. Minor ninth chords, however, are often used as altered chords in major keys.

C: V♭9   B: V♮9   A♭: V♭9

The altered note is shown by applying the appropriate accidental to the chord symbol. Each of the chords above could be referred to as a borrowed chord. (True/False) _____

True.

689. Supply the chord symbol for each chord. *(Be sure to show altered notes.)*

F: V♭9   G: V♭9   b: V9

F: ___   G: ___   b: ___

690. Continue as in the preceding frame.

d: V9   E♭: V9   F♯: V♮9

d: ___   E♭: ___   F♯: ___

Ninth, Eleventh, and Thirteenth Chords

No.
(In (c) the 7th is omitted; in (d) the third is omitted.)

691. A ninth chord contains five tones. Obviously one of these tones must be omitted in four-part writing. *Usually the fifth is omitted.*

Check the doubling in each chord below. Is the fifth omitted in each case? _____

    (a)   (b)   (c)   (d)

C: V⁹   D: V⁹   e: V⁹   F: V♭⁹

(c) and (d).

692. Although the fifth is the chord member which is usually omitted when a ninth chord is sounded by four voices, a satisfactory sonority can be produced by omitting either the third or seventh. The root and ninth, of course, must be present.

Which of the chords in the preceding frame are minor ninth chords? _____

(No response.)

693. Ninth chords are usually in root position and the ninth is at least a ninth above the root (often in the highest voice). The effect of a chord built in thirds may be lost if the higher chord members are set too close to the root.

        (a)   (b)

The effect in (a) is of a dominant seventh chord with an added second. In (b) the tones of the ninth chord are placed as close together as possible with the seventh in the lowest voice. Rather than sounding like a chord built in thirds, this arrangement produces the effect of a "tone cluster."

The ninth of a ninth chord is usually more than an octave above the bass.

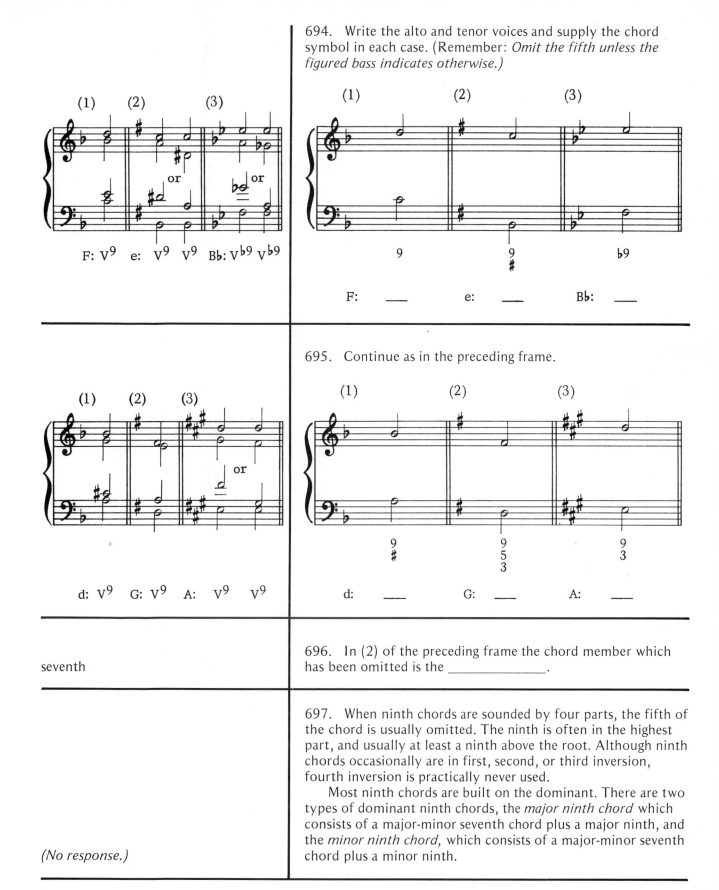

694. Write the alto and tenor voices and supply the chord symbol in each case. (Remember: *Omit the fifth unless the figured bass indicates otherwise.*)

seventh

(No response.)

695. Continue as in the preceding frame.

696. In (2) of the preceding frame the chord member which has been omitted is the _____.

697. When ninth chords are sounded by four parts, the fifth of the chord is usually omitted. The ninth is often in the highest part, and usually at least a ninth above the root. Although ninth chords occasionally are in first, second, or third inversion, fourth inversion is practically never used.

Most ninth chords are built on the dominant. There are two types of dominant ninth chords, the *major ninth chord* which consists of a major-minor seventh chord plus a major ninth, and the *minor ninth chord,* which consists of a major-minor seventh chord plus a minor ninth.

698.   The ninth of a ninth chord is a dissonant element. It often appears as a nonharmonic tone as at the asterisk in the example below:

Beethoven, *Symphony No. 6*, Op. 68

F: V⁹   (I)

The nonharmonic function of the ninth (D) is obvious. This passage shows that like the seventh, the ninth tends to resolve downward by step. What type of nonharmonic tone is the ninth in this example? _____

Appoggiatura.

---

699.   The ninth at the asterisk below has a somewhat higher status than does the one in the preceding frame. This is because it occurs on a stronger portion of the beat and is of relatively longer duration. Still, the note G is best analyzed as an appoggiatura, rather than a chord member.

Chopin, *Mazurka*, Op. 7, No. 1

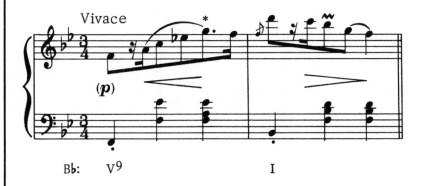

B♭:   V⁹   I

If analyzed as a ninth chord, the dominant ninth above is a (major/minor) _____ ninth.

major

F: V⁹ IV⁶ ii V⁹ V⁷

---

700. Supply the Roman numeral analysis for the example below:

Wagner, *Die Walküre*, Act I, Scene 1

(Lento)

F: ___ ___ ___ ___ ___

---

701. Supply the Roman numeral analysis for the example below. *(Analyze all of the notes in the second measure as constituting a single chord even though they do not sound simultaneously.)*

Beethoven, *Quartet*, Op. 135

Grave, ma non troppo tratto

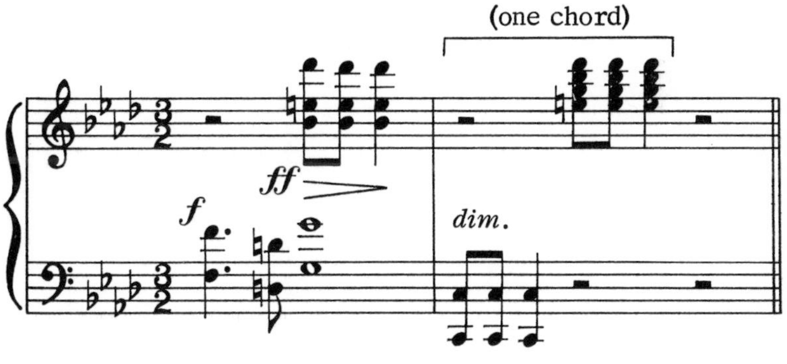

(one chord)

f: ___ ___

---

f: viid7 ⁶₅ V⁹

---

minor

---

702. The dominant ninth chord in the preceding frame is a (major/minor) _____ ninth.

703. The ninth of a ninth chord is not always resolved. In the example below there is no doubt that the ninth (at the asterisk) is an integral part of the chord. Although brief, it appears in a strong metrical position. Supply the Roman numeral analysis.

Beethoven, *Piano Concerto No. 3*, Op. 37

c: V⁹   i⁶

V   i   V

704. When the ninth is not resolved, it usually appears as part of an arpeggio.

Beethoven, *Quartet*, Op. 18, No. 1

Adagio affettuoso ed appassionato

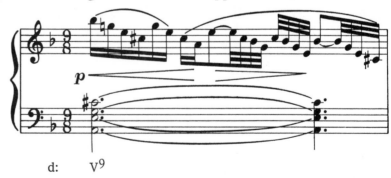

d: V⁹

i

The dominant ninth chord above is a (major/minor) _____ ninth.

minor

---

705. Although the majority of ninth chords are dominant chords, they may be built on other scale degrees as well. They often appear in sequence patterns such as in the example below:

Mozart, *Sonata*, for violin and piano, K. 380

No.

Are all of the ninth chords in the preceding example the same quality? _____

Ab: I

IV⁹ ii⁶ ii   I⁶₄ V

706. Supply the Roman numeral analysis for the example below. *(Analyze the chord at the asterisk as a ninth chord.)*

Beethoven, *Sonata* for violin and piano, Op. 30, No. 2

Adagio cantabile

Ab: ___   ___ ___ ___ ___

---

suspensions

707. The chord at the asterisk in the preceding frame is analyzed as a subdominant ninth chord. This chord could be analyzed as a supertonic triad in first inversion by regarding the two upper notes as nonharmonic tones. Specifically, they would be _____.

---

708. Supply the Roman numeral analysis for the example below:

Grieg, *Wedding Day at Troldhaugen*, Op. 65, No. 6

Tempo di Marcia un poco vivo

D: ___   ___

D: IV   ii⁹

709.   The major ninth chord appears on the tonic as an altered chord in the example below:

Strauss, *Morgen,* Op. 27, No. 4

The ninth chord resolves to a chromatic mediant seventh chord (F♯A♯C♯E). This is an example of (functional/non-functional) _____ harmony.

nonfunctional

710.   Although quite rare, ninth chords may be used in various inversions. To avoid undue complications chord symbols need not show inversions. If it is necessary to do so, the intervals which actually appear above the bass may be included as part of the chord symbol.

In the example on the following page, the chord at the asterisk is a ninth chord. Which chord member is in the lowest part? The _____.

seventh

Haydn, *Piano Sonata,* in D major

Largo e sostenuto

(*f*)

F: ii$^6_5$ V^9 I^6 ii^6 I$^6_4$ V^7 I

711. Supply the Roman numeral analysis for the example below. *(The chords at the asterisks need not be analyzed; they serve purely a nonharmonic function.)*

Schumann, *Scenes from Childhood,* Op. 15, No. 2

Allegro giocoso

mf

D: —   —   —   —   —

D: I   V$^4_3$ -   V^9

I^6

---

third

712. Since the ninth chord in the preceding frame has the seventh in the lowest part, it is in _____ inversion.

---

third

713. In the ninth chord on the following page, the chord member which is in the bass is the _____.

Dvořák, *Quartet*, Op. 105

Lento e molto cantabile

F: I   V⁹

---

714. Ninth chords may be used as secondary dominants. Complete the Roman numeral analysis for the example below:

Tchaikovsky, *Nutcracker Suite*, "Overture"

Allegro giusto

B♭:   I   IV⁶₄   I   V⁴₂/V vii°7 I V⁴₂/IV

IV⁶ I ii⁶ IV V⁹/V V

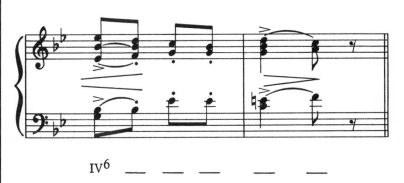

IV⁶   __ __ __ __ __

---

715. The ninth chord in the example below appears in arpeggiated form. Take this into account in writing the Roman numeral analysis.

Bach, *Well-Tempered Clavier*, Vol. I, Prelude XII

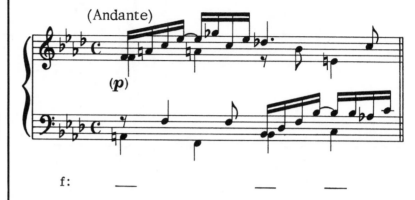

f: V^9/iv   iv V^7

716. The analyzed portion of the example below shows a secondary dominant (V/ii), which becomes a ninth chord by the gradual addition of tones.

Schumann, *Album for the Young*, Op. 68, No. 15

E: V/ii

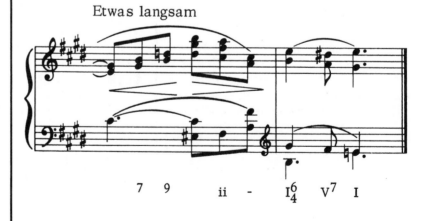

7   9   ii - I^6_4 V^7 I

(No response.)

717. Complete the Roman numeral analysis.

Fauré, *Après un Rêve*, Op. 7, No. 1

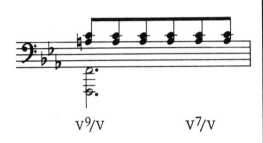

V^9/V V^7/V

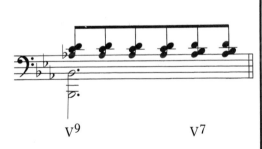

V^9 V^7

suspensions

718. The ninth chords at the asterisks in the preceding frame could be eliminated from the analysis by regarding the ninths as nonharmonic tones. What type of nonharmonic tone is employed? Both are _____.

Ninth, Eleventh, and Thirteenth Chords   257

719. Ninth chords frequently are the result of nonharmonic tones; but if the ninth is sufficiently prolonged or made prominent through rhythmic accentuation, the effect of an actual ninth chord may be strong enough to warrant the acceptance of the tone as an integral member of the chord.

Referring again to the example in Frame 717, do you think the ninths in this case are best analyzed as nonharmonic tones or as members of actual ninth chords? _____

(You are entitled to your opinion.)

True.

720. The majority of ninth chords are dominant ninths. (True/False) _____

False.

721. There is only one type of dominant ninth chord. (True/False) _____

---

1. Major ninth chord
2. Minor ninth chord

722. Name the two types of dominant ninth chords.

1. _____
2. _____

False.
(The minor ninth chord may occur in major as a borrowed chord.)

723. Minor ninth chords may be used only in minor keys. (True/False) _____

---

724. An ELEVENTH CHORD is written by superimposing another third on top of a ninth chord.

G: V^{11}

The chord above is called a *dominant eleventh chord*. Complete eleventh chords consist of _____ tones.

six

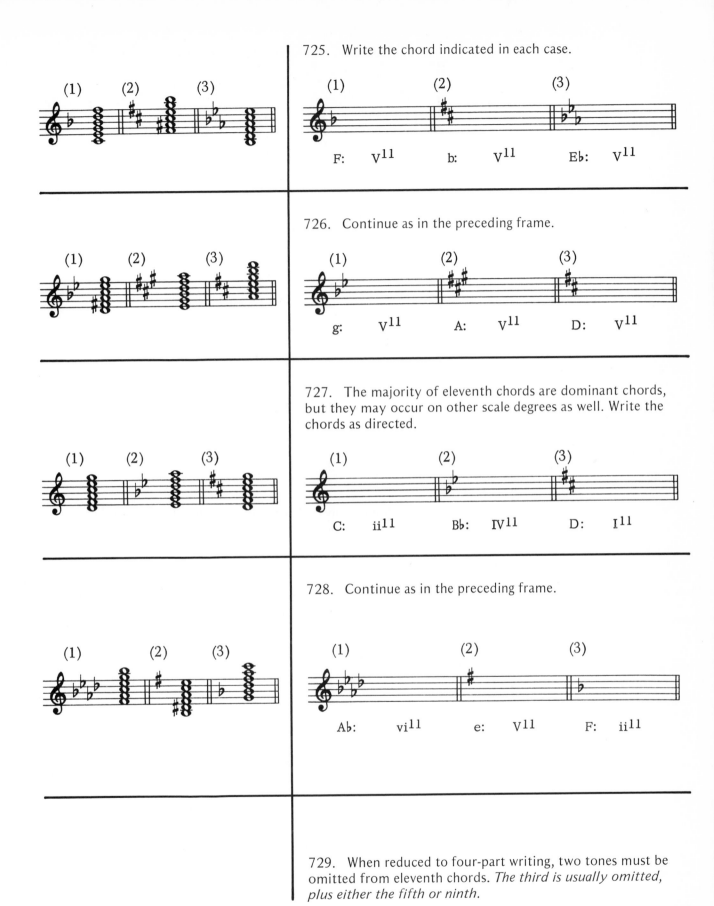

725. Write the chord indicated in each case.

(1)   (2)   (3)

F: V¹¹   b: V¹¹   Eb: V¹¹

726. Continue as in the preceding frame.

(1)   (2)   (3)

g: V¹¹   A: V¹¹   D: V¹¹

727. The majority of eleventh chords are dominant chords, but they may occur on other scale degrees as well. Write the chords as directed.

(1)   (2)   (3)

C: ii¹¹   Bb: IV¹¹   D: I¹¹

728. Continue as in the preceding frame.

(1)   (2)   (3)

Ab: vi¹¹   e: V¹¹   F: ii¹¹

729. When reduced to four-part writing, two tones must be omitted from eleventh chords. *The third is usually omitted, plus either the fifth or ninth.*

Ninth, Eleventh, and Thirteenth Chords   259

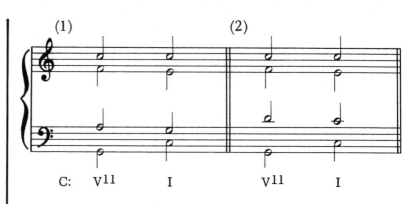

C: V¹¹   I   V¹¹   I

Name the chord members which are omitted from each of the eleventh chords above.

(1) _____ and _____.

(2) _____ and _____.

(1) Third (and) fifth

(2) Third (and) ninth

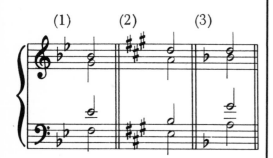

730. Write each chord according to the figured bass symbols.

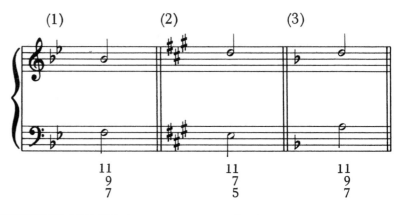

$$\begin{matrix}11\\9\\7\end{matrix} \qquad \begin{matrix}11\\7\\5\end{matrix} \qquad \begin{matrix}11\\9\\7\end{matrix}$$

731. Composers of the Classical and early Romantic eras used eleventh chords largely in a nonharmonic fashion.

Mendelssohn, *Songs Without Words,* Op. 53, No. 2

Allegro non troppo

p

ab: V¹¹   -   V⁷   i

suspension	In the dominant eleventh chord (at the asterisk) the ninth (F♭) appears as a neighboring tone, and the eleventh (A♭) can be analyzed as a _____.
third	732. What chord member has been omitted from the dominant eleventh in the preceding frame? The _____.
Active. *(Activity is relative, of course, but in terms of traditional music, this is an active sonority.)*	733. Notice in the example below that the tonic eleventh chord contains not only the tones of the tonic triad, but also the dominant seventh chord. KEY OF A MAJOR While all ninth, eleventh, and thirteenth chords may be approached as resulting from combinations of two or more triads or seventh chords, the effect of a "polychord"* is strongest in the case of the tonic eleventh. Would you expect a sonority such as this to be active or inactive? _____ _____ *A polychord consists of two or more triads or seventh chords sounded simultaneously.
True.	734. If you will play the tonic eleventh below at the piano, you will find that the tones which are the seventh, ninth, and eleventh tend to be attracted to the root and third of the tonic triad as indicated by the arrows. The upper three tones of a tonic eleventh chord may be regarded as nonharmonic tones. (True/False) _____

735. The example below shows a chord which can be analyzed as a tonic eleventh chord, but which actually is the result of a combination of the tonic triad and the dominant seventh chord.

Beethoven, *Sonata*, Op. 2, No. 2

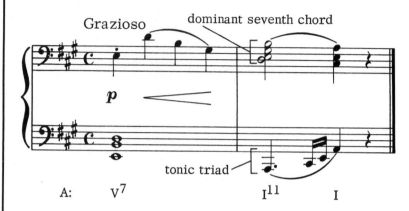

Cadence effects such as this occur fairly often in traditional music. While these sonorities are undoubtedly the result of nonharmonic factors (the dominant seventh chord can be called an appoggiatura chord), they can also be related to expanded tertian sonorities such as eleventh chords, and provide a logical steppingstone to the use of polychords by later composers.

The dominant seventh chord superimposed on a tonic triad contains the tones of a tonic eleventh. The term which refers to a sonority consisting of two different chords sounding simultaneously is _____.

polychord

---

736. The first chord in the example below is an eleventh chord with the third and ninth omitted. Since this is the beginning of the composition, there can be no question as to the harmonic status of the eleventh. No nonharmonic interpretation is valid here. Analyze with Roman numerals.

Schumann, *Noveleten*, Op. 21

Munter, nicht zu rasch

D: ___   ___   ___   ___

D: V^{11} I V^7/V V

737. In contrast to earlier practice, composers of the late nineteenth century tended to use eleventh chords more as integral harmonic units for the sake of their color. Supply the Roman numeral analysis for the example below:

Wolf, *Goethe Lieder,* No. 45

The 3rd,
and 5th

738. Which chord members have been omitted from the dominant eleventh chords in the previous example? _____ _____

739. Seventh, ninth, and eleventh chords are used in a non-functional manner in the example below:

Debussy, *Pelléas et Mélisande,* Act II, Scene 1

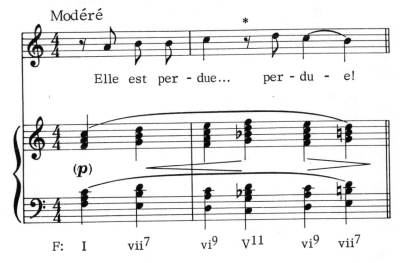

Ninth, Eleventh, and Thirteenth Chords

No.
(The 3rd is missing.)

Is the chord at the asterisk a complete dominant eleventh chord? _____

True.

740.   The style of writing shown in the preceding frame is characteristic of impressionist composers. Chords are often used for their color effect, and the concept of active and inactive tones is broadened so that ninth, eleventh, and thirteenth chords perform as relatively consonant sonorities. Further, roots progress more freely (with a higher incidence of seconds) than in music which is more strongly governed by traditional harmonic principles.
   All chords in the preceding frame are in root position. (True/False) _____

Yes.
(Roots progress entirely by seconds—from F down to C, then back up to E. This symmetrical pattern is an expressive factor.)

741.   Another feature of the example in Frame 739 warrants further comment. Notice that each chord from the first to the fourth is progressively more complex. The first is a triad, the second a seventh chord, the third a ninth chord, and the fourth (at the asterisk) an eleventh chord. From this point the sequence is reversed. Since this subtle gradation of tension coincides with the contour of the melody and is reinforced by the dynamic indications, it is obvious that the composer used the varying degrees of tension possessed by these chords to help accomplish his expressive purpose.
   Gradations of tension, produced not only by harmony, but through rhythm, dynamics, melody, and timbre as well, lie at the root of musical expression. Does the progression of roots in Frame 739 contribute to the tension pattern of the phrase? _____

True.

742.   The third is usually omitted from eleventh chords. (True/False) _____

False.
(The dominant eleventh is the most common.)

---

(2) √
(The first statement is false because TWO tones must be omitted.)

---

seven

5th, 9th, (and) 11th

---

743. Eleventh chords occur with approximately equal frequency on all scale degrees. (True/False) _____

---

744. Check (√) the correct option:

1. An eleventh chord may be set into four parts if one of the tones (usually the third) is omitted.
2. In music prior to the nineteenth century most eleventh chords are the result of nonharmonic tones.

True statements:
(1) _____   (2) _____   Both _____   Neither _____

---

745. A chord consisting of six superimposed thirds is called a THIRTEENTH CHORD.

F: V^{13}

Limited to diatonic tones further extension in thirds beyond the thirteenth is impossible because additional tones merely duplicate lower members of the chord.

A complete thirteenth chord consists of _____ tones.

---

746. We shall concentrate on the dominant thirteenth chord as all others are extremely rare. When set into four parts, three chord members must be omitted. There are several acceptable possibilities, but generally *the third and eleventh are not present at the same time.* In other words, the third is omitted if the eleventh is present, but is included if the eleventh is omitted.

The example on the following page shows a dominant thirteenth chord and its resolution to a tonic triad. Which chord members are omitted from the thirteenth chord? The _____, _____, and _____.

F: V¹³   I

3rd, 5th, (and) 9th

747.   Which chord members are omitted from the thirteenth chord below? The _____, _____, and _____.

F: V¹³   I

---

748.   Write the alto and tenor voices in accordance with the figured bass symbols. Supply, also, the Roman numeral analysis.

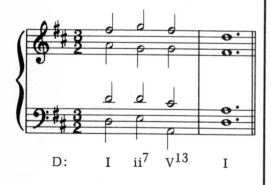

D: I   ii⁷   V¹³   I

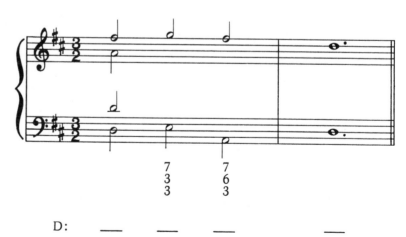

$$\begin{matrix} 7 & & 7 \\ 3 & & 6 \\ 3 & & 3 \end{matrix}$$

D: ___   ___   ___   ___

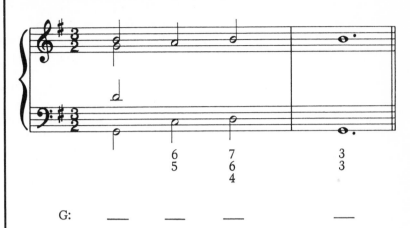

749. Continue as in the preceding frame.

G: I   ii$^6_5$ V^{13} I

G: —   —   —   —

750. The thirteenth often is the result of a nonharmonic tone. A typical example is shown below. The escape tone (C) is the thirteenth over the dominant seventh chord. Supply the Roman numeral analysis.

Chopin, *Prelude*, Op. 28, No. 2

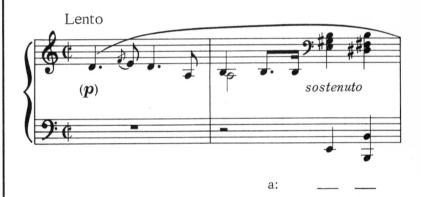

a: —   —

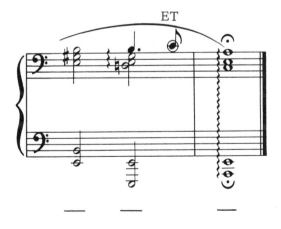

a: V V/V V V^7 i

Ninth, Eleventh, and Thirteenth Chords

751. In the preceding frame the thirteenth is merely suggested by the escape tone. While still nonharmonic, the thirteenth (C) at the asterisk in the example below is a bit closer to achieving harmonic status. This is due to its longer duration, and being placed in a relatively strong rhythmic position.

Chopin, *Prelude,* Op. 28, No. 20

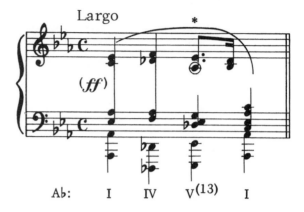

The nonharmonic tone used to produce the effect of a dominant thirteenth above is called an accented _____ tone.

passing

---

752. The note which is circled in the example below could be analyzed as a free tone or as an eleventh. Likewise, the note C (at the asterisk) may be regarded as a thirteenth, or as a(n) _____.

escape tone

Chopin, *Valse Brillante,* Op. 34, No. 2

---

753. The thirteenth chord at the asterisk on the following page is not the result of a nonharmonic tone; it has complete harmonic status. Take into account the pedal tones (G and D) as indicated when writing the Roman numeral analysis.

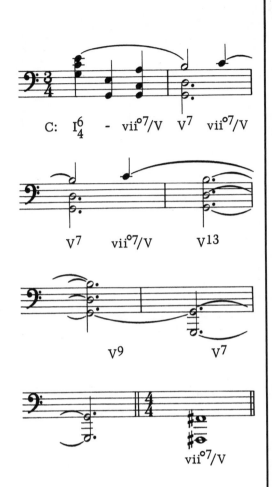

C: I$^6_4$ - vii°7/V   V^7 vii°7/V

V^7 vii°7/V   V^{13}

V^9 V^7

vii°7/V

Wagner, *Die Meistersinger*, Act III, Scene 5

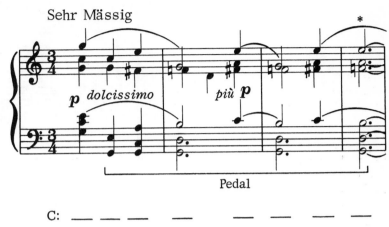

Sehr Mässig

p dolcissimo   *più* *p*

Pedal

C: _ _ _ _ _ _ _ _ _

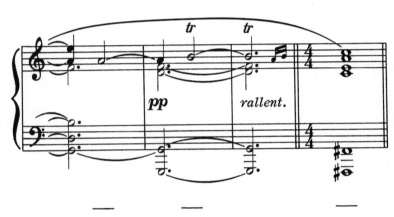

tr   *tr*

pp   *rallent.*

___   ___   ___

754. Dominant thirteenth chords are used prominently in the example below.

Ravel, *Valses noble et sentimentales*, No. 1

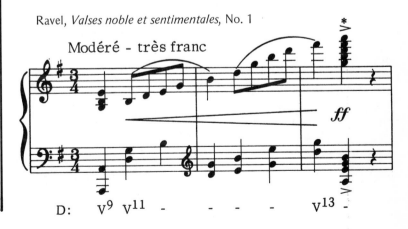

Modéré - très franc

ff

D: V^9 V^{11} - - - - - V^{13} -

Ninth, Eleventh, and Thirteenth Chords

269

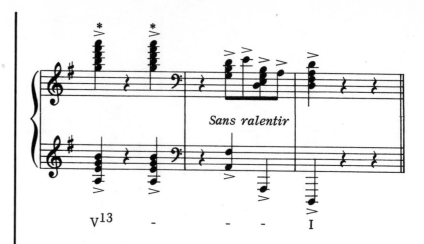

$$\text{V}^{13} \quad - \quad - \quad - \quad \text{I}$$

Are any triad tones omitted from the thirteenth chords at the asterisks? _____

Yes.
(The 3rd is not present.)

SUMMARY.

Ninth, eleventh, and thirteenth chords are used sparingly except in late nineteenth-century music. Impressionist composers, in particular, made extensive use of these chords to achieve the shimmering harmonic effects which are characteristic of their music.

Extensive use of these chords tends to produce a "diffuse" harmonic idiom. The complete thirteenth chord, for example, contains all seven tones of a diatonic scale. Ambiguity of root and even tonal center often result when these chords are used extensively. Spacing and doubling is of crucial importance, and delicate decisions must be made as to which tones should be omitted in order to produce the desired effect. The judgment of the ear must be relied on, since principles and rules are not adequate to control all of the variable factors present in this kind of writing.

We are dealing here with material that stands at the boundary between functional harmonic practices and more modern techniques. It is but one short step to techniques such as pandiatonicism in which the tones of the diatonic scale lose their functional values, and atonality in which the stabilizing and referential influence of the key center is rejected entirely.

Appendix A
Glossary of Altered Chords

Most of the altered chords which occur in traditional music are included in this list. The usual resolutions are given for each chord. These resolutions should not be regarded as definitive; there are many other possibilities which may occur.

Chord Types	Symbols	Resolutions
Secondary dominants	V/x V^7/x vii^o vii^{o7} vii^{d7}	Root down a P5 Root up a m2
Borrowed chords	ii^o ii^{o7} $\flat III$ $\flat III^+$ iv $\flat VI$ vii^{d7} I (in minor)	V $\flat VI$ I V IV iv ii^o I Various
Augmented sixth chords	It^6 G^6 F^6 (on 6) (on 2) (on 4)	V I I I^6
Neapolitan sixth chord	N^6 (N N_4^6)	V I_4^6
Altered dominants	V^+ V^{+7} $V^{\flat 5}$ $V_{\flat 5}^7$	I I

Chord Types	Symbols	Resolutions
Diminished seventh chords on raised 2nd and 6th scale degrees	$\sharp$ii^{d7} $\sharp$vi^{d7}	I^6 V^6 V$^6_5$
Chromatic mediants	II $\flat$II $\flat$ii III $\flat$III $\flat$iii VI $\flat$VI $\flat$vi	IV I V I IV

Appendix B
Supplementary Assignments

The material supplied here is intended to be both useful in itself and suggestive of other supplementary work designed by instructors to serve their student's particular needs.

Chapter 1. *Introduction to seventh chords: the dominant seventh*

ASSIGNMENT 1

1. Indicate the quality of each chord. Use symbols such as Mm^7, m^7, etc.

2. Write chords as indicated.

(Given note is the root)

        dm^7 AM^7 mM^7 d^7 Mm^7

3. Supply the chord symbol for each chord. *(Indicate inversions.)*

    F: ____   D: ____   f#: ____   c: ____   B♭: ____

    g: ____   A: ____   d: ____   E: ____   f: ____

4. Write chords as indicated.

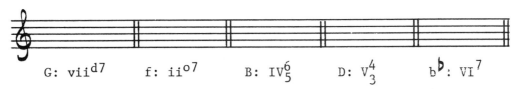

    G: vii^{d7} f: ii^{o7} B: IV^6_5 D: V^4_3 b♭: VI^7

ASSIGNMENT 2

1. Write the second chord in each case so that *all* active tones are resolved in the direction of their activity.

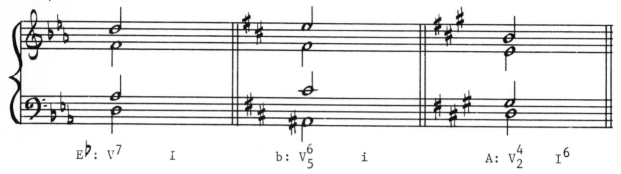

2. Supply the chord symbols for the six chords in the example below:

Kuhlau: *Sonatina*

Chapter 2. *Nondominant seventh chords*

ASSIGNMENT 3

1. Supply the Roman numeral analysis.

Chopin: *Scherzo*, Op. 39

2. Write soprano, alto, tenor, and bass voices to conform to the chord symbols.

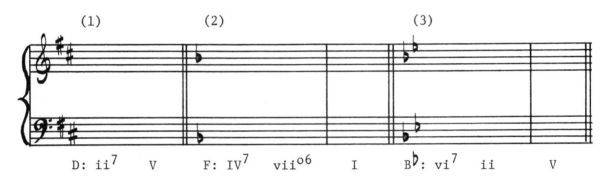

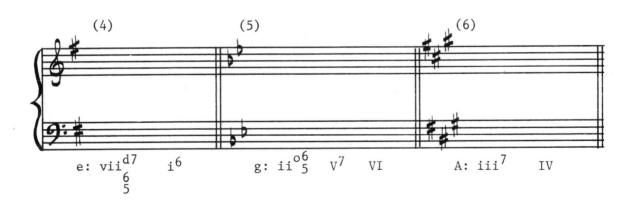

ASSIGNMENT 4

1. Compose two-phrase periods for piano based on the harmonic schemes below. You may consult Appendix A: *Piano Styles* in Part 1 of this course. For this assignment styles 19-20 are recommended.

   a. Major key of your choice.

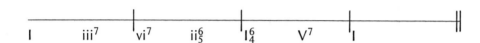

   b. Minor key of your choice.

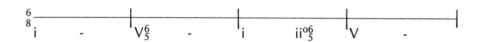

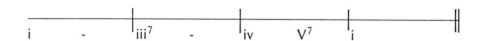

Appendix B

Chapter 3. *Altered nonharmonic tones and secondary dominants*

ASSIGNMENT 5

1. Seven nonharmonic tones are identified in the example below. Complete the analysis by supplying the information requested.

Haydn: *Quartet,* Op. 76, No. 4 ("The Sunrise")

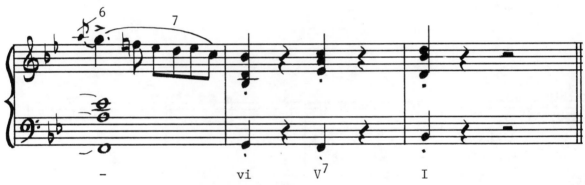

	Type of Nonharmonic Tone	Diatonic	Altered
1.	_____	_____	_____
2.	_____	_____	_____
3.	_____	_____	_____
4.	_____	_____	_____
5.	_____	_____	_____
6.	_____	_____	_____
7.	_____	_____	_____

ASSIGNMENT 6

1. Label each altered nonharmonic tone as to type (use abbreviations P.T., App., etc.). *Refer to the harmonic analysis.*

Schumann: *Carnival* ("Eusebius")

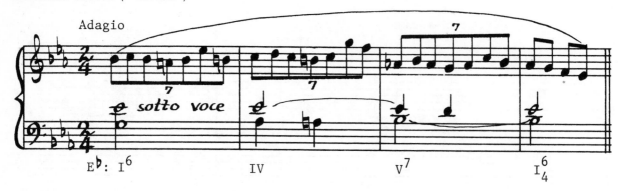

2. Supply the harmonic analysis and label each *altered* nonharmonic tone as to type.

Schumann: *Carnival* ("Valse noble")

ASSIGNMENT 7

1. The chords below are various types of secondary dominants. Write the proper chord symbol for each.

a: _____   B♭: _____   G: _____   E♭: _____   e: _____

2. Write chords as indicated by the chord symbols.

C: vii°⁷/V   F: vii°/ii   g: vii^{d7}/VI   b: V⁷/iv   A: V⁷/iii

3. Write the chord to which each of the secondary dominants below normally resolves. Also, supply the proper chord symbol for each chord.

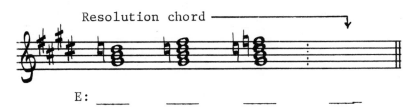

E: _____   _____   _____   _____

4. Proceed as in 3 above.

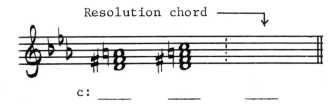

c: _____   _____   _____

ASSIGNMENT 8

1. Analyze with Roman numerals.

Beethoven: *Sonata,* Op. 49, No. 1

Rondo

Allegro

G:

2. Analyze with Roman numerals. This example contains several types of secondary dominants. Take care to indicate precisely the quality of each.

Schumann: *Nachtstucke,* Op. 23, No. 2

Markirt und lebhaft

F: ___

ASSIGNMENT 9

Compose a small composition (at least four phrases long) which exploits both altered nonharmonic tones and secondary dominants.

Suggested working method:

1. For each phrase construct a simple harmonic background consisting of diatonic chords as below:

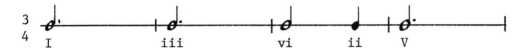

2. Embellish some chords with secondary dominants.

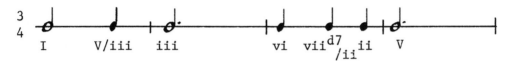

3. Write a melody which conforms to the harmonic background.

4. Supply an appropriate accompaniment configuration.

5. Complete your composition paying particular attention to these points:

   a. Refine the doubling and voice leading.

   b. Provide complete and correct notation, including tempo, dynamic, and phrasing indications.

   c. Make a final copy (preferably in ink) suitable for performance.

Chapter 4. *Modulation to closely related keys*

ASSIGNMENT 10

1. The signatures of closely related keys differ by not more than _____ accidental(s).

2. List the keys which are closely related to A major.

   _____

   _____

3. List the keys which are closely related to B-flat minor.

   _____

   _____

4. Which keys are closely related to E major? _____

    (1) f♯   (2) d♯   (3) b   (4) A   (5) g♯

5. Which keys are NOT closely related to F minor? _____

    (1) c   (2) g   (3) D♭   (4) a♭   (5) E♭

6. The keys of D major and D minor are called _____ keys.

7. The example below shows a modulation from E-flat major to B-flat major. Supply the harmonic analysis.

   Bach, *Chorale:* "Wachet auf, ruft uns die Stimme"

ASSIGNMENT 11

1. What type of modulation is illustrated in Question 7 in Assignment 10? _____

2. Supply the harmonic analysis for the example below:

Beethoven: *Sonata,* Op. 2, No. 1

f:

3. What type of modulation is illustrated in the previous example? _____

4. A modulation in which the common chord has little functional value in one or both of the keys involved is often called a _____ modulation.

ASSIGNMENT 12

Supply a four-voice harmonization in chorale style for each of the melodies below. Modulate as directed.

(1)   (G to D)

(2)   (C to a)

(3)   (A♭ to b♭)

Chapter 5. *Borrowed chords*

ASSIGNMENT 13

1. Which are borrowed chords? _____

D:

2. Which chord agrees with the chord symbol? _____

3. Which chord symbol is correct? _____

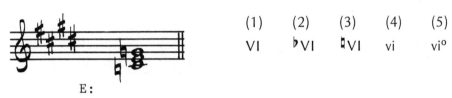

E:

	(1)	(2)	(3)	(4)	(5)
	VI	♭VI	♮VI	vi	vi°

4. Which chord symbol is correct? _____

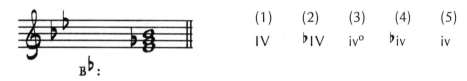

B♭:

	(1)	(2)	(3)	(4)	(5)
	IV	♭IV	iv°	♭iv	iv

5. List (by chord symbol) the more common borrowed chords in major and minor keys.

Major: _____

Minor: _____

ASSIGNMENT 14

1. Supply the harmonic analysis for the examples below:

Chopin: *Mazurka,* Op. 7, No. 4

A♭: _____

Beethoven: *Sonata,* Op. 31, No. 1

G: _____

Chapter 6. *Augmented sixth chords*

ASSIGNMENT 15

1. Add the three upper voices.

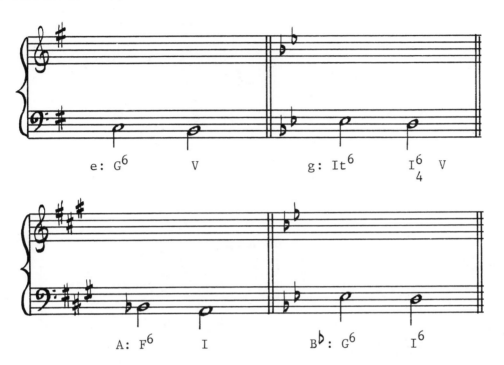

e: G⁶   V   g: It⁶   I⁶₄ V

A: F⁶   I   B♭: G⁶   I⁶

2. Which figured bass symbol represents a French sixth chord? _____

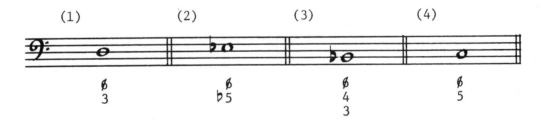

3. Which chord is a "doubly augmented six-four-three" chord? _____

ASSIGNMENT 16

1. Supply the chord symbols, and identify each nonharmonic tone.

   Chopin: *Mazurka*

   c: ___ — ___ —

2. Supply the chord symbols.

   Beethoven:*Sonata,* Op. 78

   F♯: ___

3. Supply the chord symbols.

   Chopin: *Nocturne,* Op. 48, No. 2

   A: ___ ___ ___ ___

4. Compose a single phrase which contains an augmented sixth chord. Choose your own key and time signature; take care to notate completely.

Chapter 7. *The Neapolitan sixth, altered dominants, and diminished seventh chords*

ASSIGNMENT 17

1. Which chord is a Neapolitan sixth chord? _____

2. Which is the best resolution of the Neapolitan sixth chord? _____

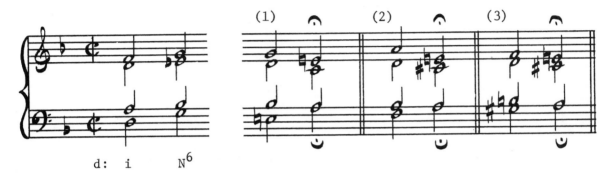

3. Supply the harmonic analysis.

   Schumann: *Waltz*

ASSIGNMENT 18

1. Which is the best resolution of the V^{+7} chord? _____

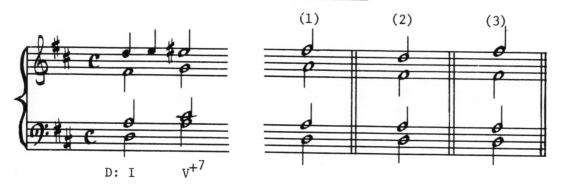

D: I   V^{+7}

2. Which is the best resolution of the V$\flat^7_5$ chord? _____

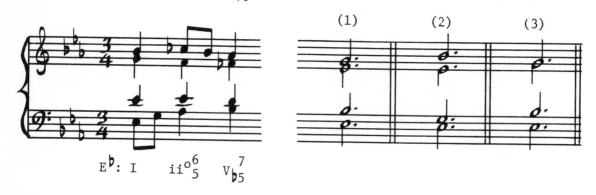

E$\flat$: I   ii°$^6_5$ V$\flat^7_5$

3. Write the alto and tenor voices, and analyze with Roman numerals.

B$\flat$: ___ ___ ___ ___ ___ ___

ASSIGNMENT 19

1. Supply the harmonic analysis for the example below:

Chopin: *Nocturne,* Op. 32, No. 2

2. Compose a single phrase which contains either a ♯ii^{d7} or a ♯vi^{d7} chord. Choose your own key and time signature; take care to notate completely.

ASSIGNMENT 20

1. List (by number) the chords which have a *mediant* relation to the D major triad. _____

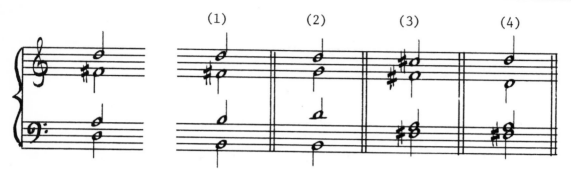

2. List (by number) the chords which have a *chromatic mediant* relation to the E-flat major triad.
    _____

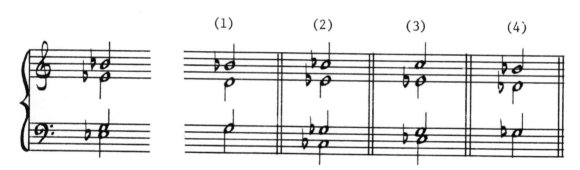

3. Identify each chord as one of the following types of altered chords. *(List by number.)*

    1. Augmented sixth
    2. Borrowed chord
    3. Chromatic mediant
    4. Neapolitan sixth

ASSIGNMENT 21

1. Supply chord symbols for the example below:

Franck: *Chorale*

2. Compose a single phrase which contains several chromatic mediants. Choose your own key and time signature; take care to notate completely.

ASSIGNMENT 22

1. Which keys are *foreign* to the key of E major? _____

       (1) f♯   (2) d♯   (3) B   (4) C♯   (5) e

2. The single diminished seventh chord below may appear in any of the keys indicated. Supply the correct chord symbol for each key.

                                              g: _____

                                              c: _____

                                              F: _____

                                            E♭ :   _____

                                            B♭ :   _____

                                            A♭ :   _____

3. The diminished seventh chord in the preceding question could also be analyzed as ♯ii^{d7} in the key of E-flat. Through the device of enharmonic change, the same chord could be used as the ♯ii^{d7} in three other keys. Name these keys.

    1. _____

    2. _____

    3. _____

4. Explain the reasons why the diminished seventh chord is capable of so many different resolutions.

_____

_____

_____

_____

_____

_____

_____

_____

ASSIGNMENT 23

1. Supply the missing chord symbol.

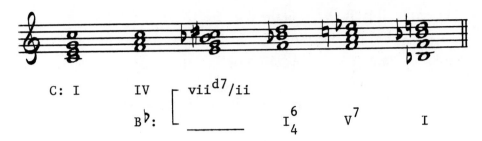

    C: I   IV   ⌐ vii^d7/ii

        B♭: ⌐   I^6_4   V^7   I

2. Supply the missing chord symbol.

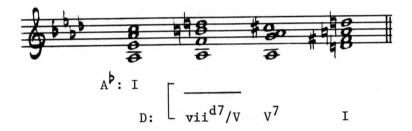

    A♭: I   ⌐ _____
        D: ⌐ vii^d7/V   V^7   I

3. Compose three single-phrase examples which modulate by means of the devices below:

    1. The common chord is vii^d7/V in the new key.

    2. The common chord is vii^d7/ii in the new key.

    3. The common chord is vii^d7/vi in the new key.

ASSIGNMENT 24

1. The chord AC#EG is V^7 in D major; it is also V^7/vi in the key of _____.

2. The chord B♭DFA♭ is V^7/ii in D-flat major; it is also_____ in the key of A-flat minor.

3. Which augmented sixth chord sounds the same as a major-minor seventh chord? _____

4. The example below contains a modulation from C minor to C-sharp minor. Supply the harmonic analysis. Because the common chord is spelled correctly in only one of the two keys, be alert for enharmonic equivalents.

Beethoven: *Sonata,* Op. 90

c:

Appendix B

ASSIGNMENT 25

1. The modulation in the example below is from F major to E major. Supply the harmonic analysis.

J. Strauss: "Artist's Life Waltzes," Op. 316

F:

2. The chord below is analyzed in the key of C major. Show with chord symbols additional functions of the same chord. *(Indicate the key in each case. Also, do not overlook enharmonic spellings.)*

C: V^7

_____   _____

_____   _____   _____

_____   _____   _____

ASSIGNMENT 26

Compose three single-phrase examples which modulate according to the conditions stated.

1. C: 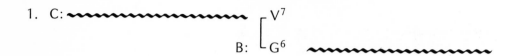 $\begin{bmatrix} \text{V}^7 \\ \text{G}^6 \end{bmatrix}$ B:

2. c#: 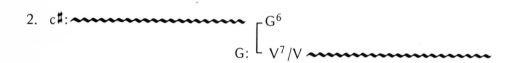 $\begin{bmatrix} \text{G}^6 \\ \text{V}^7/\text{V} \end{bmatrix}$ G:

3. D: 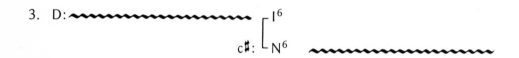 $\begin{bmatrix} \text{I}^6 \\ \text{N}^6 \end{bmatrix}$ c#:

Appendix B

Chapter 11. *Ninth, eleventh, and thirteenth chords*

ASSIGNMENT 27

1. Write the chord symbol for each chord.

        g: ___   A: ___   E♭: ___   f: ___

2. Write a *major* ninth chord on each note.

3. Write a *minor* ninth chord on each note.

4. Spell the chords as indicated.

    1. A♭: ii^9 _____   4. e♭: iv^9 _____

    2. f♯: V^9 _____   5. D♭: iii^9 _____

    3. E: I^9 _____   6. B: vi^9 _____

ASSIGNMENT 28

Provide the harmonic analysis for the examples below:

Chopin: *Fantasie*

Grieg: *Wedding Day at Troldhaugen,* Op. 65, No. 6

ASSIGNMENT 29

Provide the harmonic analysis for the examples below:

J. Strauss: "Artist's Life Waltzes," Op. 316

Chopin: *Polonaise-Fantasie,* Op. 61

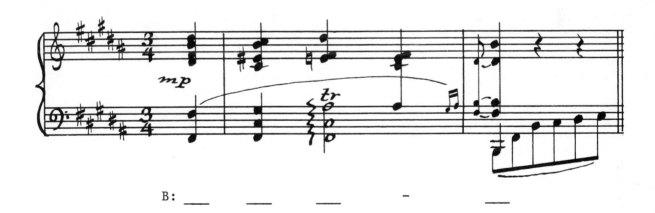

Index of Musical Examples

(Numbers refer to frames.)

Chopin, Frédéric
   Ballade, Op. 52, 366
   Etude, Op. 10, No. 1, 110
   Grande Valse Brillante, Op. 18, 542
   Mazurka, Op. 7, No. 1, 699
   Mazurka, Op. 33, No. 3, 153, 209, 673
   Mazurka, Op. 56, No. 1, 661, 670
   Mazurka, Op. 67, No. 3, 203
   Nocturne, 438
   Nocturne, Op. 27, No. 1, 527
   Prelude, Op. 28, No. 2, 750
   Prelude, Op. 28, No. 4, 460
   Prelude, Op. 28, No. 7, 188
   Prelude, Op. 28, No. 9, 605
   Prelude, Op. 28, No. 20, 502, 751
   Prelude, Op. 28, No. 22, 107
   Valse, Op. 64, No. 1, 155
   Valse Brillante, Op. 34, No. 2, 458, 486, 752

Debussy, Claude
   Pelléas et Mélisande, Act II, Scene 1, 739
Dvořák, Antonin
   Quartet, Op. 105, 713
   Symphony No. 9, "From the New World," Op. 95, 464

Fauré, Gabriel-Urbain
   Après un Rêve, Op. 7, No. 1, 717
   Au bord de l'Eau, Op. 8, No. 1, 478
Franck, César
   Chorale No. 1, 606
   Prélude, Aria et Final, 671
   Symphony in D Minor, 463, 465

Gounod, Charles-François
   Faust, "Introduction," 485
Grieg, Edvard
   First Meeting, 484
   Hoffnung, 483
   Wedding Day at Troldhaugen, Op. 65, No. 6, 708

Haydn, Josef
   Piano Sonata No. 7, in D major, 259, 710
   Quartet, Op. 54, No. 1, 646
   Quartet, Op. 64, No. 5, 446
   Quartet, Op. 74, No. 1, 636, 654
   Quartet, Op. 76, No. 4, 87
   Quartet, Op. 76, No. 6, 669

Kuhlau, Friedrich
   Sonatina, Op. 88, No. 3, 135

Liszt, Franz
   Du bist wie eine Blume, 154
   Sonetto 47 del Petrarca, 582

Mendelssohn, Felix
   Andante con Variazione, Op. 82, 99

Songs Without Words, Op. 53, No. 2, 731
Mozart, Wolfgang Amadeus
   Fantasia in C Minor, K. 475, 82, 197, 674
   Mass in C Major, K. 317, 377
   Quartet, K. 458, 127
   Quartet, K. 465, 104
   Quintet, K. 515, 507
   Sonata, K. 284, 221, 280, 440
   Sonata, K. 330, 360
   Sonata, K. 331, 253
   Sonata, K. 332, 134
   Sonata, K. 333, 130
   Sonata, K. 533, 621
   Sonata, K. 545, 541
   Sonata, K. 576, 369
   Sonata, for violin and piano, K. 380, 705
   Symphony No. 39, K. 543, 668
   Symphony No. 40, K. 550, 451
   Symphony No. 41, K. 551, 72

Nielsen, Carl
   Sinfonia Espansiva, Op. 27, 379

Puccini, Giacomo
   La Bohème, Act IV, 124

Ravel, Maurice
   Valse noble et sentimentales, No. 1, 754
Rossini, Gioacchino
   William Tell, "Overture," 539

Scarlatti, Domenico
   Sonata, in G minor, 312
Schubert, Franz
   Doppelgänger, Der, 441
   Erlkönig, Op. 1, 193, 498, 519
   Mass in G Major, "Sanctus," 439, 499
   Quintet, Op. 163, 545
   Symphony No. 5, in B-flat major, 361
   Symphony No. 8, in B minor, 190
   Waltz, Op. 9a, No. 13, 100
   Waltz, Op. 27, No. 12, 331
   Wirtshaus, Das, 359
Schumann, Robert
   Album for the Young, Op. 68:
     No. 15, 716
     No. 31, 191
   Dichterliebe, Op. 48:
     No. 7, 552
     No. 12, 442
   Die Nonne, Op. 49, No. 3, 675
   Noveleten, Op. 21, 736
   Papillons, Op. 2, 86, 452, 538
   Scenes from Childhood, Op. 15, No. 2, 711
Sibelius, Jean
   Finlandia, Op. 26, 479

Subject Index

(Numbers refer to frames.)

Active tones, 70-72, 511, 515
Altered chords, 158-160 (*see also* separate entries, e.g., Secondary dominants, Borrowed chords, etc.)
Altered dominant seventh chords, 476, 477
Altered dominants, 510-533
  inversion, 513
  lowered fifth, 522-528, 531-532
    chord symbols, 523
  raised fifth, 528-529
  resolution, 521
  used as secondary dominants, 520
Altered nonharmonic tones, 143-157
Altered tones, 146, 151-152, 157, 224, 344, 511
Appoggiatura (*see* Nonharmonic tones, appoggiatura)
Appoggiatura chord, 735
Arpeggiation, 704, 715
Augmented-minor seventh chord, 510
Augmented sixth chords, 387-485
  chord symbols, 422-424
  doubly augmentes six-four-three, 444-448, 463
  figured bass symbols, 410, 420
  French sixth, 388, 412-424, 431-432, 450, 471, 477, 524-525, 666
  German sixth, 388, 403-411, 420-424, 431-432, 438-448, 450, 457-465, 655, 660
  inversion, 457-465
  Italian sixth, 388, 392-401, 420-426, 430-432, 439, 467
    doubling, 392, 397
  location, 426, 466, 475-484
  resolution, 431-442, 466, 476, 478, 484
  sounding root, 430
Augmented triad, 173, 510, 572
Authentic cadence, 215-216

Borrowed chords, 340-386, 472, 504-505, 577, 651, 688

Cadences, 228 (*see also* separate entries, e.g., Authentic cadence, Plagal cadence, etc.)
Change of mode, 249, 377-379, 618-625
Chord symbols, 343-344
  accidental, 343-344

altered dominants, 510
chromatic mediants, 582-587
Neapolitan sixth chord, 488
secondary dominants, 164-167, 180, 184
seventh chords, 27-48
Chromatic half-step, 316
Chromatic mediant relation, 566-575, 605, 663
Chromatic mediants, 566-609
  chord symbols, 582-587
Chromatic modulation, 321-336
Chromaticism, 602-603
Circle, 35, 60
Closely related keys, 229-252, 283, 296, 620
Color harmony (*see* Nonfunctional harmony)
Common chord, 272-277, 281-306, 314, 323-324, 335-336, 636
Common chord modulation, 267-317, 333-335
Cross relation (*see* False relation)

Debussy, Claude, 575
Deceptive cadence, 198
Diatonic half-step, 316
Diatonic modulation, 317-318
Diatonic triad, 306
Diminished-minor seventh chord, 11-12, 25, 37-41, 168-169
Diminished seventh chord, 15, 17, 26-27, 35-38, 58-60, 168, 534-561, 629-654
  enharmonic spellings, 630, 636-640, 644-646, 650
  on raised second scale degree, 534-547
    chord symbols, 540, 544
    enharmonic spellings, 543-547
    inversion, 539-545
    resolution, 534, 547, 558
  on raised sixth scale degree, 534, 548-561
    enharmonic spelling, 556
    inversion, 555
    resolution, 534, 548, 558
Diminished triad, 173, 572
Distant keys (*see* Foreign keys)
Dominant function, 528, 534

Dominant ninth chords (*see* Ninth chords, dominant)
Dominant seventh chord, 66-92
    dissonant elements, 67
    first inversion, 82-85
    resolution, 66-80
    second inversion, 86-89
    third inversion, 90-92
Dominant triad, 562, 588-589
Doubly augmented six-four-three chord (*see* Augmented
    sixth chords, doubly augmented six-four-three)

Eleventh chords, 676-680, 724-744
    dominant, 724-726, 731
    doubling, 680, 729
    resolution, 734
    tonic, 733-735
Enharmonic spelling, 595, 661-662, 668-669, 675
Escape tone (*see* Nonharmonic tones, escape tone)
Extended tertian sonorities, 676, 735 (*see also* separate
    entries, e.g., Ninth chords, etc.)

False relation, 155, 602-605
    simultaneous, 155
Foreign keys, 610-624, 628
Foreign tones (*see* Altered tones)
Free tone (*see* Nonharmonic tones, free tone)
French sixth chord (*see* Augmented sixth chords, French
    sixth)

German sixth chord (*see* Augmented sixth chords, German
    sixth)

Half cadence, 215-216
Harmonic tension, 528, 741
Harmonization, 139-142

Inactive tones, 70-71
Intervals
    augmented sixth, 387-389, 404, 424, 431-433, 457,
        471, 476
    diminished fourth, 595
    diminished third, 424, 431, 457, 469, 496
    doubly-augmented fourth, 444
    enharmonic, 404
    fifteenth, 676
Irregular doubling, 72, 76-77, 511
Italian sixth chord (*see* Augmented sixth chords, Italian
    sixth)

Key center, 590
Keynote, 82

Leading tone seventh chord, 35-38, 126-130
Liszt, Franz, 575

Major-minor seventh chord, 9-10, 16, 67, 398-399, 404,
    461, 464, 629, 652-665
Major seventh chord, 16-17
Mediant relation, 562, 565-566 (*see also* Chromatic
    mediant relation)
Mediant seventh chord, 109-111
Mediant triad, 562, 565, 567, 572
Melodic activity, 157
Melodic movement
    chromatic, 315-316, 318-321, 324, 445-446
    diatonic, 314-318, 321
Minor seventh chord, 13-14, 16-18, 24
Modal mixture, 341, 356 (*see also* Borrowed chords)
Modulating sequence, 260-264, 670-672
Modulation, 163-165, 218-228, 378
    chromatic, 626
    common chord, 626-651
    contribution to form, 219
    diatonic, 626-627
    enharmonic, 636, 662
    phrase, 253-266, 332-334
    pivot tone, 673-675
    sequence, 670-672
    to foreign keys, 613-675
    transient, 228

Neapolitan sixth chord, 486-509, 667-669
    chord symbol, 488
    doubling, 500
    harmonic function, 509
    resolution, 495-502
    root position, 502-504, 506
    second inversion, 507
Neighboring tone (*see* Nonharmonic tones, neighboring
    tone)
Ninth chords, 676-723
    dominant, 681-682, 697
    doubling, 680, 691-692, 697
    inversion, 697, 710-713
    major ninth, 682-683, 685-686, 688, 697, 709
    minor ninth, 682, 684-685, 687-688, 697
    resolution, 698, 703
    secondary dominant, 714
Nondominant harmony, 98
Nonfunctional harmony, 575, 591, 709, 739-740
Nonharmonic tones, 98-100
    altered, 195
    appoggiatura, 698-699, 752
    double, 156
    escape tone, 750
    free tone, 752
    neighboring tone, 143, 155
    passing tone, 145, 751